MICROPOLITICS

Dedicated to
Dr Edwin J. Feulner Jr.

MICROPOLITICS

Dr Madsen Pirie
President
Adam Smith Institute
London

Wildwood House

Published by
Wildwood House Limited
Gower House
Croft Road
Aldershot
Hants GU11 3HR
England

HB
846.8
P57
1988

Distributed in the United States by
Gower Publishing Company
Old Post Road
Brookfield
Vermont 05036
USA

British Library Cataloguing in Publication Data
Pirie, Madsen, 1940–
Micropolitics : the creation of successful
policy
1. Politics
I. Title
320

ISBN   0 7045 3103 8
       0 7045 0571 1 (pbk)

Linotron setting by Columns of Reading
Printed and bound in Great Britain by
Biddles Limited, Guildford & King's Lynn

Contents

PART V   SUMMATION

Acknowledgements

I wish to thank Robbie Gibb and Barnaby Towns for their help in preparing the typescript of this work, and I thank Dr Eamonn Butler and others for their help and encouragement.

PART I
THE ROLE OF IDEAS

1 Ideas and Events

The most difficult explanations to find are the ones no-one is looking for. The way in which ideas come to exert an influence on events comes into this class. People have supposed that there is nothing to explain, that events simply follow the ideas which suggest them.

In its very simplest form, this account has the political thinker producing the idea which the legislators then implement. This is obviously wrong. Many ideas are put forward, some of them conflicting with each other. Some attract attention at the time, others pass without notice. Some are put into effect, others are rejected. In democratic societies there is often a conflict of ideologies, with each putting forward ideas derived from opposing views about the way in which society should be organized. Clearly any explanation must take account of the fact that some ideas are implemented rather than others.

The simplest model may be modified to bring in the time factor. In the amended version, ideas are put forward. Then, over a period of time, the merits of some of them emerge and begin to influence the political process. This account allows for a 'drift of ideas' in which those deriving from a certain paradigm hold sway for a period, then are perhaps superseded by others. It might be the collectivist viewpoint whose ideas are in vogue at one time, and individualism at another. There may be periods in between the transition when the fashion swings towards a mixed economy.

This explanation is not obviously wrong, like the simple version, and does afford at first glance a means of interpreting political change. The thinkers put forward their ideas, and some are eventually adopted. As the practical experience of them deepens, people look for improvement and turn to the ideas which derive from an alternative paradigm. These hold sway in turn until they are eventually supplanted. We have what appears to be a plausible account of how *laissez-faire* interludes, for example, can alternate with periods of 'social conscience.'

Even the model with the time factor included is incomplete unless it supplies a mechanism to account for the 'emergence' of ideas. Granted that the scholars are at work producing the ideas, we need to be told how it is that some of them eventually attract the attention of policy-makers. Scholars usually work in the public domain; that is, they publish books or papers, or deliver lectures. We can take it that their ideas are normally available to interested parties.

Only rarely do we encounter a Gregor Mendel, whose work was unknown until after his death. Even more rarely in the field of social studies do we meet with a Giambattista Vico, whose pioneering work was insufficiently circulated to be influential either in its day or in the century which followed it. Scholars usually make their work available, especially if they are anxious to influence events.

This leaves us with the problem of tracing the ideas from their first publication to the point at which they are acted upon by legislators. How do they emerge? It would be naive to suppose that political leaders spend a great deal of time ploughing earnestly through scholarly publications to keep abreast of the output of ideas; so we have to look to some intermediate agency which brings the one to the attention of the other.

There are at least two possibilities, not mutually exclusive. One is that there is a body of persons who read and write about political ideas, and have contact both with the academic work of the scholars, and with the world of practical politics. They could be party activists, informed commentators, popular writers or lobbyists. All that is required of them in this respect is that they keep abreast of theoretical developments in politics and economics, and that they are in a position to influence those at work in active legislation.

A second possibility – although there may be many others – is that the ideas come to be of influence through a generational change. A significant proportion of our governing classes have undergone higher education. It could be during this process that they were exposed to the new ideas, either from the scholars themselves, or by the studying requirements of university and college courses. The process of immersion in an academic environment could suffice to make them aware of the new thinking, and influence them when young to such an extent as to influence their actions when they later rise to prominence. This version has the attraction of explaining why some political ideas seem to take a generation before they are applied in practice.

We still have to explain why it is that some ideas are taken up rather than others. Again, the simple answer is to suppose that their merits emerge in the process of academic discussion and critique. Both Milton and John Stuart Mill espoused the view that in a fair and open contest, truth would emerge triumphant. Both, indeed, regarded this as one good reason to advocate a high level of freedom of speech and discussion.

It would be pleasant if the real world took on the roseate aspect of this theoretical vision. Alas it does not.

In our world truth is often silenced by force. Galileo is made to recant; heretical books are consigned to the flames, sometimes accompanied by their hapless authors. The more velvet-gloved force of modern times gives academic preferment to those who toe the line, and denies it to others. Opinionated academics in positions of power advance supporters and sycophants, and try to deny a hearing to those who would challenge the work on which a lifetime's career has been built.

Still it is possible to argue that the base motives of men can only hold back the truth for a time. After all, was not Galileo vindicated? Does not Bruno hold more influence in today's world than the Inquisition which burned him? Similarly it could be argued that the outcast scholar will come through eventually if the ideas are sound. Rehabilitation and fame will come, even if posthumously. This is comforting to outcast scholars, but there is a strong element of hindsight to the argument.

It is true that some ideas did win through: these are the ones we know about. It is quite possible that other, true ideas did not: these are the ones we do not know about. We cannot say how many scholars failed to gain the position needed to develop and advance their ideas, or how many discontinued promising lines of research in order to be eligible for more temporal rewards. We do know of some ruined by poverty or driven to suicide. We know of many cases in which powerful men were able to swing influence behind inferior ideas by success-fully squeezing out better ones.

The argument that the truth wins through eventually commits the Whig fallacy of history by assuming that the function of the past was to lead up to the present. We see what did happen, we do not see what might have happened in its place. The ideas which won through are the ones which now hold sway; we cannot call this 'truth.'

If the truth of an idea does not bring about its acceptance, then some other means must be sought. If the idea's merits do not by themselves draw attention to it, perhaps advocacy fills the gap. Once the idea is in the public domain, there will be those who are attracted by the force of its arguments, and who recognize in it some basic truths. These advocates adopt the idea and publish papers in turn exploring its merits and perhaps developing it further than the originator took it.

In this way the idea has more support than its one source can give it. Those who take it up form a community of interest. They work together to put it forward, and make it less likely by their several efforts that the idea can be ignored. They may be outcasts themselves initially, working in a hostile intellectual climate to put across ideas of whose merits they are persuaded, and which they are convinced will one day win through. The advocates thus link their own careers with that of the originator and carve a pathway which diverges from the prevailing wisdom of the day. They constitute a kind of intellectual pressure group to keep reminding people of the idea until it wins wider acceptance.

Some of these advocates might be one-time students of the master; now they count themselves as disciples. Some might have encountered the idea through published work; others by word of mouth. Often they appear to the intellectual mainstream as dedicated bands of zealots, trying to talk to the academic and intellectual community in general, but talking much more often to each other. They hope that by their efforts the idea will spread until eventually it will be widely enough accepted to form the basis for action. That time, when it comes, will justify the years of struggling to be heard against a received wisdom which opposed them.

This picture of the way in which ideas influence events is now strikingly similar to Thomas Kuhn's account of the way in which scientific revolutions are brought about. The prevailing paradigm rules, and the only work which gains recognition is that which is done within the context of that paradigm. The ideas are explored, extended and developed. They are never subject to frontal challenge because such work gains no recognition, no credit, and no reward for its perpetrator. Eventually, says Kuhn, the paradigm is taken as far as it can go. Its inconsistencies and inadequacies begin to accumulate to the point at which more and more people are convinced of the need to replace it by a major shift in thinking. This brings on the truly creative period while the paradigm is in flux. A new model comes forward, usually from the next generation of scholars because their careers have not been inextricably bound up with the old one. As it wins acceptance, so work takes place to develop it and to extend it, and it settles into a new status quo. Scholars who first advocated it at an unfashionable time are now rehabilitated and given credit as trail-blazers.

If instead of scientific revolutions, we substitute the major changes which take place in political ideas, the Kuhn pattern is seen to be very close to the model considered so far. It could explain, at least at the theoretical level, how political ideas come to change. There would still remain the need for the group to act as a bridge between the theoretical realm of ideas and the world of practical politics. Given such a group, however, we would be able to explain how ideas at an intellectual level can eventually come to be accepted at the level where decisions are made and events are influenced.

The Kuhn model is particularly instructive because it operates on the level of psychology. It was proposed by Kuhn as a means of accounting for the growth of scientific knowledge; but instead of dealing with ideas themselves, it deals with the way in which people react to those ideas. Popper and Lakatos have criticized the account to good effect on the grounds that the acceptability of a theory, or the ways it might be used to make or thwart careers, tells us nothing about its content. The question is not whether the idea wins favour, but whether it passes the criteria we require for scientific knowledge.

Even if it can be faulted as an explanation of the growth of scientific knowledge, however, the Kuhn account does tell us a great deal about scientific fashion. It presents a very plausible explanation of the way in which theories come into vogue and inspire subsequent research. There is a good case for suggesting that this is comparable with the way in which political ideas fall into or out of favour. When they win acceptance, they stimulate research and attract notice for their adherents. When they are in the wilderness of opposition to prevailing consensus, neither they nor their adherents enjoy such attention.

A major point of departure from the Kuhn model is that Kuhn deals only with the way in which ideas come to dominate the academic community. His concern is with scientific revolutions, and he has little to say, therefore, about how ideas become popular, or how they come to influence events. Even if we accept his model for the victory of ideas in the intellectual world, we still have to account for their acceptability in society, and the way in which they come to alter what is done.

The intermediate groups of acolytes and advocates could provide a bridge between the two worlds. For every great original scholar, there might be dozens or even hundreds of derivative thinkers who explore the ramifications of the original insight, contributing their studies and critiques to the total. These are often college and university lecturers and professors. After them come the students they influence, some of whom become writers, journalists or opinion leaders of some variety.

Sometimes they band together in societies or institutes with the avowed purpose of securing wider recognition for the ideas which unite them, and to seek for those ideas an impact upon public policy. Writing and lecturing at a more popular level, their work can attract the attention of a wider audience, and perhaps merit coverage in the media to spread interest in the ideas ever more widely. This is the group which F.A. Hayek refers to as the 'secondhand dealers in ideas.' They perceive their task to be one of acting as salesmen for the original insights and ideas, taking them and explaining them at the level where they can be effective. This might be in front of decision-makers and legislators; it might be before the informed and educated public at large, in order to bring about pressure for their adoption.

All of the elements are now in place for the familiar picture of what is often called 'winning the battle of ideas'. The stage is set for a familiar scenario to unfold.

First comes the scholar. Going against the conventional political or economic wisdom of the day, he (or she) marks out an original position which suggests that the prevailing view is either mistaken or misconceived. A major work or series of works points to a radically new approach involving the overthrow of the existing paradigm. Shocked incredulity greets the exercise. The academic community either dismisses the work as absurdly out-of-date (always an excellent defence against new ideas), or resorts to the more traditional and more effective academic weapon of silence. The work is not reviewed, not cited, not taken seriously. The scholar is ostracized. He finds it difficult to have papers published or to give prominent lectures. The expected chair fails to appear; grants are hard to come by. Worst of all, his students find it difficult to gain appointments. The years in the wilderness have begun.

Lonely as this academic isolation is, the scholar is not totally alone. A handful of junior colleagues recognize the merit of the work and begin to write papers which circulate at first only in minor journals. The number of students who have been influenced by them builds up over the years. The group is still a minority, but a cohesive and loyal one.

Then come the popularizers. Some of them former students, some influenced by what they have read or been told, they work over the years in the cause they believe is correct. They influence a rising generation of lecturers and students. They reach out to the informed public with monographs, pamphlets and magazine articles. Some of those they influence enter the political world, where they are regarded as a small and eccentric minority working for some half understood and almost universally discredited idea.

Patiently, the lonely group labours on over the years, drawing comfort from each new convert, and never failing to point out the inadequacies and failings of the assumptions they are fighting. The familiar scenario calls for a happy ending. The existing political ideas reach crisis point as their failings are revealed by events. The systematic work has meanwhile paid off. A rising generation of new scholars accept the alternative paradigm. The ideas become respectable. Research workers rush to print with theses and studies derived from them.

Meanwhile the work of the popularizers has gone so far that the ideas have now trickled down to the informed and educated layman. Just at the time they become academically respectable, there is popular interest in the new alternative ideas. There is a demand for something to replace the system which is visibly failing. The combination of popular pressure and academic respectability now enables legislators to move in. Inspired by the new ideas they act to implement them.

The scholar, if this has happened in his lifetime, finds himself a celebrity. The lecture tours begin and the book offers flood in at last. The early supporters now break through the promotion barrier and gain the rewards for those wilderness years. An idea has succeeded in changing events. Meanwhile, of course, a lonely scholar is about to be ostracized for putting forward a radical new paradigm. . . .

The scenario is not only a familiar one; it is also a comforting one. Scholars who fail to gain recognition for their work can take solace from the thought that one day their turn will come. Even if it comes too late for them personally, they can hope for the posthumous triumph of their ideas. Latterday Marxes labouring in the British Museum can dream of a success such as his. Their disciples and supporters, although shunned and shut out of academic influence can similarly hope that with the acceptance of the ideas will come fitting recognition of those who saw their merits early on, and who sacrificed career opportunities in order to advance them. The popularizers, the 'secondhand dealers in ideas' can take comfort from the hope that the patient work will eventually pay off. When the ideas are sufficiently popular to enable politicians to move, those who brought this about gain the huge psychic satisfaction of having helped to influence history and to determine events.

The popularity of this scenario derives partly from its inherent plausibility, and partly from the satisfaction it brings to all of the parties involved. In the first place, it traces through an account of how 'ideas have consequences.' It shows how work from the realm of ideas can be translated into a chain of influence which ultimately has its impact on events. Secondly, it comforts all the parties involved, the scholars, the disciples and the popularizers. Those who see the ideas triumph can claim a share in the success. Those who do not can take heart that their day will come.

It is the popularity of this familiar scenario which attaches so much importance to 'winning the battle of ideas.' If future events will be determined by the ideas which dominate in the next generation, then those who wish their vision of reality to prevail must influence it now. If it is the spread of ideas among educated opinion leaders which prompts politicians to act, then those who want them to act in particular ways must convince those same opinion leaders of the correctness of the ideas.

This is the fundamental reason why the battle for ideas is fought at two levels by those who wish to determine the future shape of society. The two levels are connected; it is by winning the minds of today's students in schools and colleges that the advocates of radical change expect to influence opinion leaders of tomorrow. A major advantage of this concentration on education is that it can be self-accelerating. A few teachers can influence many students, and when they in turn become teachers, they influence even more. Eventually it might be possible to so dominate education that an entire generation is imbued with the ideas.

Disciples and acolytes of the original scholars act to influence and infiltrate the academic world. They try to influence both the literature and the teachers. A battle is waged over textbooks, with those espousing a radical change to the prevailing paradigm trying to control the reading content of courses. News stories tend to concentrate on the remarkable (and remarkably crude) attempts to influence the minds of young children; but a more serious struggle takes place for the control of higher education materials.

The advocates of innovative thinking spend both time and resources in attempting to place their materials into the class libraries and on to the course lists of college and university courses. They establish research centres both on and off campus, and publish and promote reading matter designed for course adoptions. Some of them count success in terms of the quantity of material published, the penetration of faculty or college libraries, or the number of course adoptions for their work. Others concentrate on lecturers and scholars, holding seminar courses to attract promising ones. The content of these seminars and the speakers are such as to convert to the new ideas, or to reinforce the convictions of those already persuaded. Scholarship grants are made, essay prizes awarded, all to those who show some academic promise and commitment to the new thinking. The aim is to invest in people, and to use resources to win over the next generation.

University and college departments begin to resemble colonies as this activity proceeds. A useful person, well-placed, will secure appointment for junior people of like persuasion. Graduate students will be attracted, or steered, in the direction of those departments which emphasize the new ideas. Over a period of time a few departments acquire a reputation for commitment to a certain paradigm. Those who share it apply there and are welcome; those who do not seek academic preferment elsewhere.

The 'battle' for ideas is well-named, for the military metaphor is overpowering. One is led into seeing the struggle to capture the next academic generation as a long drawn out war, punctuated by skirmishes on different fields, a few major set piece engagements, and the dispatch of troops to reinforce critical or newly won positions. Occasionally the discreet but constant struggle surfaces, as a major institution is won over. Resignations and recriminations give a brief glimpse to outsiders of the ferocity of the battle.

One feature of the 'wilderness' period is the clan

loyalty of those engaged in the struggle to have the ideas accepted. Being in a minority, one might expect them to broaden their base of support and endorse allies who accept some elements of the new thinking. The reverse often happens, with a determination to keep the ideas undiluted and uncontaminated by deviant thinking. This can lead in turn to exclusivity, in which only those who take the master's ideas pure and unmixed are accepted. The use of key code phrases and specialized vocabulary in publications and lectures gives outsiders the impression that they are looking at something close akin to the incantations of a religious ritual.

For those who popularize to opinion leaders as well as to the academic community, success is measured in terms of coverage. The circulation figures for their publications take on crucial significance. Sales of their books are assiduously counted, not for any revenue this brings, but for the influence which is implied. A feature devoted to the scholar or his ideas which appears in an important newspaper or magazine is a major event. More people probably read the copies circulated to each other by supporters than read the original article when it appeared.

Serious radio or television programmes which cover the ideas in question are hailed as major victories in the battle for ideas. The assumption throughout is that the original ideas are being kept out by what amounts to a conspiracy of silence, and a refusal by informed commentators to take them seriously. Television or radio exposure thus represents a breakthrough, no matter how low the viewing figures might be for the programme itself, or for the channel on which it appears.

In all of this activity, as in the scientific revolutions, there are those whose careers are bound up in the struggle. In academic institutions there are some whose promotional opportunities are tied to the victory of the new ideas. Others who fail to make a mark in the conventional paradigm can perhaps gain recognition in the smaller circle which seeks to overthrow it. Directors of research institutes earn their salaries at the same time as they work to advance the cause. Writing and lecturing by both groups provide sources of additional income and opportunities to travel to international conferences and seminars.

But this is true of the academic and intellectual worlds in general. Most scholars seek to promote themselves as well as their beliefs. Most of them seek opportunities to publish or to lecture. Expenses-paid international trips are plums to be sought and rationed out carefully. If anything, direct self-interest is less true of those who work to bring recognition for the bold innovations than it is for the rest of the scholarly community.

The rebels against the prevailing orthodoxy tend to be motivated by three clear beliefs. First, they believe that the original insights put forward are essentially correct. That is, they too see the failings implicit in the status quo, and accept the analysis which undermines its validity. They are therefore very much motivated by principle itself, and like most of those who are so motivated, are ready to endure privation and ostracism in the cause of what they believe is right.

Secondly, they are motivated by the belief that ultimately their view of things will prevail and gain general acceptance. To them it is only a question of time and effort before the truths which are obvious to them are revealed to others. They are sustained in the wilderness by the nourishment which hope brings. Their firm conviction is that the day will come, preferably within their own lifetime, when the intellectual community in general will admit to the truth of what they maintained all along.

The third belief is the one least questioned. It is that when the battle for ideas has been won, events will follow in the wake of that victory. The assumption is that winning through in the world of the intellect will automatically at some date thereafter bring similar gains in the real world as those ideas are put into effect. Because they are convinced that the ideas are right, and that they will win the intellectual battle for acceptance, they also believe that the effort to achieve that victory will finally result in changes to the way in which people live.

The source of this third conviction is not difficult to fathom. All of the participants in the 'battle for ideas' are very much people of ideas themselves. The original scholar blazing a lonely trail; the disciples who take up the cause; the students and the supporters; men and women in research institutes; those who work to spread the ideas at a popular level: all of them live, to some extent, the life of the mind. Their chief concern is with ideas. It is ideas which move them, which preoccupy their thoughts, and which have the power to excite them. It comes naturally to such people to suppose that ideas are the ultimate determinants, and that to win the battle for ideas is to win thereby the battle for events.

Intellectuals throughout history have exalted the role and influence of the intellectual. That the great works bear witness to that role is hardly surprising, since it was the intellectuals who wrote them. Most men and women of ideas have taken it for granted that it is men and women of ideas who make the important steps for human progress. They downgrade the contribution of merchants and traders, of explorers and soldiers, of farmers and builders.

While many intellectuals, consciously or unconsciously, adhere to this view, its best expression comes perhaps in the words of John Maynard Keynes, a man of ideas not without influence himself. He wrote:

Practical men, who believe themselves to be quite
exempt from any intellectual influences, are usually the
slaves of some defunct economist. Madmen in authority,
who hear voices in the air, are distilling their frenzy
from some academic scribbler of a few years back.

Scholars have been mesmerized by those words, not
least because they elevate the status of scholars. Part of
their allure is that they downgrade those who appear to
exercise power and influence events. Keynes' famous
saying presents temporal power as an illusion. Those
who appear to exercise it are doing no more, he says,
than bringing to fruition the seed sown previously by a
person of intellect. The ruler wields the sceptre, but the
scholar guides the hand.

The spell of Keynes is a powerful one, at once
convincing and comforting to those whose lives are
spent in academic cloisters. It tells the intellectuals what
they want to hear, what Keynes himself believed, that
they are the real rulers. It goes some way towards
explaining why men and women of ideas never question
that victory in the world of ideas translates into victory
in the real world.

Convincing and comforting as it is to the intellectual
community, the Keynesian view is not self-evidently
true. It is by no means necessarily so that people in
authority are the unwitting puppets of former scribblers.
The familiar scenario by which 'winning the battle for
ideas' takes place is at its weakest in the final scene. The
assumption that the battlefield of ideas decides the
future of society is one which can be questioned. If it is
to be sustained, a link is needed between the intellectual
victories and the practical ones. A process has to be
shown whereby the ideas which win through to
acceptance by intellectuals are the crucial determinants
of public policy.

It is quite possible to accept the role of the innovative

scholar and his years in the wilderness, to admit the importance of the part played by disciples, advocates and popularizers, and yet question whether this is enough to influence events. Conceding even that the process outlined is a valid description of some of the battles for ideas which are won or lost, there remains a critical gap between the ideas and the reality.

The assumption by those engaged in the struggle is that the ideas are enough, and that when they gain both academic respectability and popular support it will become possible for politicians to enact them. This is the weak link in the chain or reasoning. It is weak because it is an assumption, rather than a reasoned claim backed by evidence and argument.

It is possible to argue that changes in public policy do not follow directly from victories won in the world of ideas, and that the relationship between ideas and policy is more complex than the simple model will allow.

2 Theory and Practice

> In every department of human affairs Practice long precedes
> Science: systematic enquiry into the modes of action of the
> powers of nature, is the tardy product of a long course of
> efforts to use those powers for practical ends.
>
> John Stuart Mill, *The Principles of Political Economy*

Plato's 'Republic' is one of the earliest classics of
political science. Although cast in the form of a
dialogue ostensibly in search of justice, a large section
of the book described how the ideal society might be
constituted, what its rules would be, the form of its
education and customs, and even what its myths
would be.

The vision of perfection described by Plato would
seem somewhat austere and brutal for modern tastes. It
must have seemed so at the time to his Athenian
audience. Children were to be brought up in common,
never knowing or caring who their natural parents
were. They were to be exposed early on to a tough life
designed to inculcate the martial virtues. Only the
lightest of coarse clothing was to be permitted, only the
plainest of food. Simple black bread would suffice for
the citizens of this brave new world. Strict censorship
would prevent them reading anything which might
distract or deflect them from the paths of virtue and

strength. No plays would be allowed which depicted weakness or emotional indulgence. Even music would be strictly regulated, with only the harmonies permitted which aroused suitable feelings of courage. Every aspect of life would be controlled in order that the state might be better served by its citizens.

Citizens would live communally, eat at benches, enjoy no luxuries except that of sneaking out occasionally to perform the duty of begetting the next generation of children. The job of supervising these rules would fall to what would in modern times be called a secret police, but which Plato described in more philosophical terms.

Guardians, Auxiliaries and Workers would all know their place and accept it, sustained by the 'noble lie' that they were descended respectively from the metals of gold, silver and bronze. Only a lack of appropriate technology, one suspects, kept Plato from proposing Huxley's sleep-talk voice reciting to the children 'I'm glad I'm a gamma; alphas have to think too hard, and betas have too much responsibility. . . .'

The ideal society, which produces and sustains philosopher kings is described in meticulous detail. It would be an achievement of the imagination on grand scale, were it not for the fact that such a society already existed in all of its basic elements. What Plato is describing is, for the most part, the totalitarian state of Sparta. Since Sparta was the enemy of Athens for a sizeable part of Plato's early life, it tells us much about Athenian toleration that he was allowed to exalt it as a model of perfection.

Plato embroiders and improves it in his text, but the basic pattern of Spartan life is unmistakable. The censorship, the ban on luxuries, the harsh conditions are all there. So are the ephors who enforce the rules. Spartans existed, as did the citizens of Plato's Republic, to live out lives decreed for them by the state in every detail. Sparta had existed for generations before Plato provided the gloss of an intellectual justification for it. Its rules were there in practice to govern and direct the lives of its citizens long before Plato analysed their workings and wrote about them as theory. The practice came first, and the theory followed in its wake.

What Plato did was to advance at a theoretical level the basic format of a society which already existed, and which met with his approval. Sparta may have been tough and brutal, its citizens unrefined and ill educated, but it did practise what Plato regarded as simple virtues uncorrupted by luxury as the Athenians were, and it did win wars. Indeed, the whole society more or less existed to achieve that object. Much of what we might regard as humanity was sacrificed to that end, including arts, sciences and intellectual enquiry. Plato approved of the trade, regarding the contemplation of virtue as sufficient to satisfy man's higher aspirations.

Sparta was there before Plato wrote about it. He did not invent it or set down its rules. With some changes he described them and justified them. Plato's 'Republic' is an *ex post facto* rationalization of the state of Sparta. He wrote as theory what men had already achieved in practice.

John Locke's *Two Treatises on Civil Government* were hailed in their day and to present times as classic studies in the control of absolute power. People who had previously lacked the arguments which justified limiting the powers of a ruler now found in Locke the intellectual support they were looking for. Locke set out a series of principles under which power derived from contract, and was subject to limits and constraints.

The defence of sovereign power had not been in short supply. From the old feudal pledges of allegiance, through the divine right of kings, right down to Thomas Hobbes and the need to restrain the brute in man, the justification had been available to rulers aspiring to absolute power. Now with Locke's ideas the intellectual lead passed to the other side. Here were carefully thoughtout and developed arguments deriving from first principles, which denied the right to absolute rule.

Not only was power constrained under Locke's system, it was divided to keep it under constraint. Furthermore, the rules were laid down under which dissent and resistance were permissible. Whereas previously this had involved defying God's deputy, or breaking solemn allegiances, now it was a case of justifiable action in the event of breach of contract by a sovereign.

Locke, like Plato, was describing what already existed and providing the intellectual superstructure to justify it. Despite the case for absolute power, people in Britain had resisted it under Stuart monarchs. The Glorious Revolution had already happened when Locke wrote. There already was a constitutional monarchy which accepted limits on its power, and which had been brought about by the overthrow of a legitimate sovereign who was felt to have abused his power.

Locke was writing after practice had already achieved what he now justified in theory. The British had made their Glorious Revolution, now Locke became its philosopher and spokesman. He it was who gave them the words and arguments to justify what they had already done. In elevating Locke, those who had done the deed elevated themselves. What might have been construed as the self-interest of a threatened class now became a stand of high principle, vindicated by man's moral nature and the foundations of civil society.

Locke's work, like Plato's, was derived to a large extent from what had already been achieved. His ideal of society, like Plato's, was based on a model which existed. He analysed its merits and demonstrated its virtues systematically. In doing so, he undoubtedly gave people a better insight and understanding of it. He also gave them the justification they were looking for; but the point is that they were looking for it. The world came first, the books followed.

Vladimir Illyich Lenin is credited, if that is the appropriate word, with the foundation of the first Marxist state. By leading the Bolshevik Revolution in Russia in 1917, he is widely regarded as the person who gave Marxist theory its practical application. He thereby lent some substance to the claim of Marx that his theories were a scientific account of human progress and that with them the future course of history could be predicted.

It is worth recalling some of the key elements of Marxist theory in order to measure how accurate was their predictive power. Marx had proposed that the course and development of a society were determined by economic and material factors, specifically the means of production available to it. 'The corn mill gave us the feudal lord, the steam mill the industrial capitalist.'

Different types of production required different types of economic and social organization to sustain them. The various institutions of society, including its method of government, its law and its ideology, all derived from its mode of production and all ultimately served it.

Societies progressed by conflict. Changes in the productive mode would create strains in the institutions established to fit its predecessor. They would be inappropriate to the new method. Each stage of history bred within it the seeds of its replacement. The factories required concentration of labour, for example, and this promoted class consciousness and antagonism. At each stage there would eventually come a violent clash of the prevailing state (called in Hegelian terms, 'the thesis') with its opponent ('the antithesis'). From that conflict would emerge the new state ('the synthesis'), and the cycle would begin again. The progress of history would stop when economies advanced to the stage where the final conflict produced a classless society.

It was in its day, and remains now, a fertile theory to use in the interpretation of previous ages. Its adherents are forced into Procrustean distortions by the attempt to make it account for every phase of human development throughout the entire scope of human history. They are, nonetheless, forced to do this because the theory makes no less a claim. Despite the excesses, it contains considerable insight and explanatory power.

If its central tenet is correct, then human history is working towards its inevitable destiny in a classless society. The more advanced an economy is, the nearer it is to that destiny. Here is a central prediction. Marx saw history as progress, and assumed that the advanced societies would complete the development cycle first, to reach the final phase. It is an essential aspect of his theory that the revolution will come first in the economies which have advanced the furthest.

Russia in Lenin's day was not among the advanced economies. It was in the early stages of industrialization, and was only just developing the factory system of mass production with all of the changes which this implied. Had circumstances been otherwise, it might have gone on to develop into a bourgeois liberal society, replacing its absolute Tsarist monarchy with a constitutional system characterized by democratic elements. Had it done so, it would have conformed to a large extent with the Marxist model of economic and social progress. But it did not.

Had Lenin really wanted to apply Marxist theory, he would have started in the most advanced economies, attempting to lead them into the terminal phase of class revolution as predicted on the Marxist model. If he were determined to succeed in Russia, he would have either had to wait until it reached the more advanced economic stages, or perhaps work to advance its progress toward a liberal industrialized society. In this way he would have been bringing forward what Marx foresaw as the inevitable day when its strains and conflicts would explode into the final revolution.

Lenin did not do either of these things. What he did ran counter to the Marxist theory to which he professed adherence. He became an active revolutionary, doing whatever was necessary to overthrow first the Tsarist rule, then the Kerensky government in order to seize power for himself and his supporters. He was a man of action. Instead of applying Marxist theory, he found from practical experience how a small but ruthless and dedicated band could seize control of a mighty nation and hold that power.

That he succeeded is history. It was not an application of Marx's theory; it was the establishment of an élite with a monopoly of power. Lenin did what was necessary and rewrote the theory after the event. His 'modifications' of Marxist theory are so drastic that it is now called 'Marxist-Leninism' in his honour. It is no longer a theory which predicts the course of economic and social progress, but one which tells revolutionary élites how to seize power over societies, and how to set about remoulding them so that the rule of the party élite becomes permanent.

Of course, many of Marx's terms appear in the new version. The 'dictatorship of the proletariat' is there, along with 'classless society.' None of these familiar expressions suffice to hide the new reality which Lenin created. The fact that he created what purported to be a Marxist state in a relatively under-developed economy itself led to major modifications to the original theory.

The function of these modifications is to explain, *after the event*, why it was that the revolution did not first come about as predicted in the most advanced economies, those further down the road to their inevitable destiny. The 'theory of empire' is one such explanation. Marx's revolution *would* have happened first in the economic front-runners, but for the fact that they developed overseas empires. Exploitation of these overseas empires sufficed to prop up the capitalist system, and bring the lower classes just enough extra rewards to keep them below their revolutionary potential. The workers, instead of 'expropriating the expropriators,' became, in effect, their partners in the expropriation of the product of workers overseas.

Like so many of the alterations made to Marxist theories after the facts, it has an inherent plausibility. The evidence does not bear it out, however, because investment in empire brought lower rates of return throughout most of the imperial period than could have been obtained by investment in other advanced countries or in non-empire areas such as South America.

The function of such explanations – and Lenin himself was prolific in the production of them – is to modify the theory after the facts. The theory was not applied in order to change the world. The world was changed first, then the theory was reconstructed to give those changes their theoretical superstructure and their intellectual justification.

If Tsarist Russia was an unlikely candidate in 1917 for a Marxist revolution, how much less suitable was China following the Second World War. Russia had at least the early stages of industrialization. It had its concentration in the cities, its factory workers, its dock workers, its urban proletariat. It had the nucleus of a force to fan the flames of protest and to man the barricades. The China which Mao Tse-Tung led to revolution was overwhelmingly a peasant society characterized by primitive agriculture. It did not have the industrial concentrations which even Lenin had been able to work from. On Marxist theory it should never have been able to develop the class consciousness needed for collective action. It was not a plausible candidate in any sense for a Marxist revolution. In terms of economic development it was centuries behind the advanced countries. The 'laws of history' had a long way to take it before it reached its revolutionary stage.

Even on Leninist theory, it was not a suitable country for party cadres to seize and maintain power. It lacked most of the instruments which Lenin had used. In addition to its lack of concentrations of industrial workers, it was a rural society with poor communications, and without the educated class of disaffected intellectuals to lead the workers' struggle.

If Mao had applied Marxist, or even Marxist-Leninist, theory, he would have acted very differently. Indeed, it is improbable that he would have succeeded. What he did do was to act on the basis of the circumstances which prevailed. He did what was necessary, engaging in a struggle appropriate to local conditions. His was a rural warfare, in which guerillas 'swam like fishes' between villages, attacking the enemy where he was weak, and melting away when faced by his strength.

The tactics he used were successful in China and brought his army to power. His communist revolution fitted nowhere into either the Marxist or the Leninist model. It fitted instead into the Maoist model, for he, like Lenin before him, did what was necessary and rewrote the theory afterwards. Marxist communism, which started as the inevitable product of advanced industrial economies at their last stage of development, had by this time been turned into a means whereby an élite group could take over the world's largest peasant society.

In the case of both Russia and China, the élite group called itself 'the people,' and used all of the trappings of Marxist terminology. In both cases this did not disguise the fact that the techniques of insurrection were used to bring to power a group in no way equated with the ordinary working class, and one which developed methods of maintaining its rule, even against popular aspirations if necessary.

The pattern which emerges from these examples is one in which the action precedes the theory. The cases have been ones in which advances in the realm of ideas appeared to determine events, but where the events in fact came first, and the ideas which rationalized them and justified them followed in their wake. The theory, by the time it was articulated, was describing a practice instead of proposing one.

The story of Che Guevara is a particularly instructive one because it illustrates both theory and practice. Trained as a doctor, Che Guevara took up the struggle with Fidel Castro's band to take power in Cuba in the name of the masses. The story is a famous one of the handful of followers seeking shelter and succour from the downtrodden high-hill farmers, and seeing their numbers grow against an enemy impotent to resist their form of hit and run warfare.

It was not an application of Marxism, Leninism or Maoism. What it represented was an ably-led group taking advantage of local circumstances and finding the way to succeed in the society they fought over, and in the terrain they fought in. The Batista régime, watching the enemy's strength grow, found their own will to resist sapped by their inability to get to grips with the elusive foe. When they left while they still had the chance, Castro's forces were able to impose and con-solidate the rule of the party, as in Russia and China.

Guevara was the intellectual and the spokesman, as well as the man of action. He is one of the mythopoeic figures of his age because he represents the yearning of all intellectuals for the action that most of them will never know. He strikes the chord identified by Dr Johnson when he said 'Every man who has never been a soldier feels guilty because of that fact.'

It was Guevara who rewrote the theory again to accommodate once more what had been done in practice. There was now a Latin American version of Marxism, just as there was a Russian version and a Chinese version. The Latin American brand, moreover, like the other two brands, was available for export.

This is where Guevara's story becomes instructive. Like true heroes he found it difficult to settle into the routine of ordinary life. After a brief spell in the Cuban government, he headed off to Bolivia to instigate a Castro style revolution. In this case, instead of doing what had been done in Cuba, he tried to apply the theory. He looked at Bolivia and saw Cuba. His tiny band made for the subsistence hill farmers, to repeat the Cuban experience. In fact the society and the terrain were different, and called for different tactics.

Had Guevara not been obsessed by the theory which was afterwards supplied to underlie the Cuban revolution, he might have recognized revolutionary potential in the tin miners of Bolivia. Here was a class which could have been taught about exploitation and which could have provided the growing numbers for his army. It was not to be. The hill farmers he went to save and seek support from regarded Che Guevara and the war he engaged upon as one more hazard in an already difficult existence. They betrayed him for a reward, and he was killed by US-trained Bolivian rangers.

Success came in Cuba because practical exigencies overcame any theoretical preconceptions. Castro's group did what worked and did not worry overmuch about what the theory said. The theory was rewritten afterwards, as it is after every success. Failure came in Bolivia because the theory dominated. Instead of adjusting to local circumstances and conditions, the attempt was made to put into effect a theory of revolutionary struggle. That theory had been written for a different society and a different topography. It had, moreover, been written retrospectively, with the hindsight knowledge of the methods which had gained success there.

The theory which Guevara might have applied to Bolivia, instead of being transfixed by the model which brought victory in Cuba, is that success depends upon opportunism. Men of action seize the moment to do what it takes to win in the conditions they encounter. Their brilliance is not in analysis or theoretical application. It is in seizing the chances as they come, and taking advantage of whatever becomes available. They often learn as they go along, improving by trial and error. Sometimes their mistakes are nearly fatal, as in the case of Castro. They succeed by learning from them and not repeating them.

As for the theory, this can always be written in the leisure of success. After the world has been changed there is always an interest in hearing why and how it was done. Because the theory explains the circumstances of success, being written to do precisely that, it commands the attention of men and women of ideas by supplying rationality to the events.

The role of theory in the above events is an interesting one in so far as its status is concerned. The theory is that which, had it been devised and known about in advance, would have explained that which eventually came about. Instead of predicting what will happen, it supplies an *ex post facto* rationalization for what did happen. Its role is thus one of interpreting events after they have happened.

Of course, the theory claims to predict future events. It appears as a modification of Marxism which explains all that has occurred so far, and on whose basis future action can ostensibly be taken. The factual situation is that each new circumstance requires yet more modification to the theory. For a theory to be acceptable, it must explain the past. It must enable one to 'retrodict' what did in fact occur. It should also be susceptible to tests of its predictive power. If it fails every time, then rewriting the theory after each event begins to resemble rewriting history. The theory, in other words, begins simply to list what has occurred rather than to make it understandable by analysis.

There is, curiously enough, an earlier version of the Marxist approach which does allow room for men of action as well as the logic of ideas. Frederick Wilhelm Hegel was one of the most potent influences on Marx. He had proposed, a generation before Marx, that human history was set on a certain course towards the emergence of reason. He did not use the term to mean human reason, but rather that some kind of logical determinism was moving mankind through inevitable stages of social development toward a predetermined goal. He it was who devised the dialectic of progress in which the conflict of 'thesis' and 'antithesis' produced the 'synthesis' of the next stage.

Marx adopted much of the Hegelian system, adapted to a different conclusion, and with the base of economic determinism grafted on. Although Marx left little room for individual will in his system, Hegel had recognized the role played by great men in history. In his version there was space for the 'World Historical Figure' who has the honour of ushering in each new stage of history when the time is right. Thus Alexander, Caesar and Napoleon all have the function of bringing about the next phase of history. It might be the end of Greek city states, the end of the Roman republic, or the emergence of the modern state.

Hegel's version appears to have the attraction of an underlying theory which nonetheless allows opportunists to win victories for it and rewrite it along the way. Unfortunately, Hegel's theory is totally retrospective. There is no way of predicting when these 'World Historical Figures' will come, who they will be, or which ones will succeed. They are only identified as such and named after their success. In other words, Hegel's theory is like that of Marx, to be modified by every major event which history throws up. Like Marx's, it allows only for *ex post facto* rationalization after the critical events have already taken place.

The clear implication of the foregoing analysis is that major advances in political theory come only after practice has already established them in the world. The writer who appears to be engaged in putting forward a radical innovation at the theoretical level may in reality be setting down the intellectual basis for something which has already come about. The message is that the practice precedes the theory. The textbooks are engaged in description, albeit under the guise of prescription.

There is nothing anti-rational in such a suggestion. It is consistent with the respectable view that more knowledge is gained in the world by trial and error than by the computation and application of complex formulae. The formulae codify and amalgamate what has been learned. They unify what would otherwise seem disparate and unconnected pieces of knowledge.

The experience of advances in political theory suggests that the process is similar, with the writers and thinkers setting down in analytical form what has already been learned in the real world. But an important question arises from this insight. If we accept the primacy of practice over theory as a source of political innovation, where does this place the battle for ideas?

If theoretical ideas follow from and interpret the changes which have already taken place at the practical level, then 'winning the battle for ideas' loses importance as a means of influencing events. It is downgraded from a struggle to determine the future course of society into a struggle to decide how changes shall be interpreted. The battle becomes a battle between competing explanations, rather than a contest to decide future outcomes. If theory really does follow in the wake of practice to supply its rationale and its intellectual superstructure, then the battle between prevailing theories and innovative ones becomes a contest to decide how events will be interpreted.

The events themselves take place as people seize opportunities to achieve goals. Only afterwards does theory come to place the successes into the context of a new political framework. To call the motives which move people by the name of a political theory is to elevate them too high. They may be no more than the ordinary passions which people act from, such as greed, the lust for power or fame, or the desire to help others and make a better world. It is sufficient for the moment that some people act in innovative ways and produce a new reality. The events which they cause need to be explained and understood.

The lonely scholar, labouring away in the wilderness with the new and unacceptable idea, is more likely to be providing a theoretical basis for interpreting recent events than proposing a leap into an unknown future. It is more likely that recent events have left existing explanations and interpretations inadequate to deal with them. The innovative scholar has realized this, and has produced an innovative theory to accommodate those recent events.

The intellectual battle is as bitter, the struggle as intense and drawn out. But the victory when gained in the world of ideas can no longer be seen to pull events automatically in its tow. The battle in the world of events may have been fought and won on the field of practice. The assumption made by intellectuals, and distilled in the words of John Maynard Keynes, was that when the ideas triumph, rulers will act as their unwitting servants and handmaidens.

The reverse may be true instead. It may be that men and women of ideas, thinking themselves quite exempt from any influences, are in reality the slaves of some defunct man of action. Scholars who fancy they hear voices in the air suggesting new ideas may be doing no more than distilling the practical experience of those whose impact is made upon the real world.

3 Illustrations from Democracy

Although it is evident that in many cases the events lead the way with the explanatory theory following, it could be argued that this model is not applicable to democratic societies. The men of action might take the lead where public opinion is of little consequence, but where governments need a wide measure of popular support to gain power and implement policies, it could be crucially necessary to win first the battle for ideas.

Plato wrote in praise of the oligarchic government of Sparta. It is true that the Athens in which he lived and wrote was a limited democracy, but Plato's ideas were not adopted there. He was idealizing a form of social organization which already existed, and his work did not lead his own society to emulate it. It is of note that when military defeat led Athens into a temporary period of oligarchy approved of by Sparta, many of Plato's friends and relatives participated in that government, although Plato himself was soon disaffected by it.

Plato did make the attempt to influence a real society, by taking the post of advisor to Dionysius, then Dion of Syracuse. In both cases he attempted to shape the society concerned by direct input through the ruler, rather than by convincing the citizens. The attempt to found his Republic in the temporal, as opposed to the ideal, world foundered on both occasions, and Plato narrowly escaped the fate, typified by Che Guevara, of those who approach society with a preconceived theory.

The Glorious Revolution which instituted the constitutional monarchy given its justification by Locke was not achieved by democratic means. It was, in effect, a *coup d'état* brought on by those who feared the designs of a Catholic king armed with absolute power. Informed opinion was divided. Indeed, the myth that James I had 'abdicated' (by being forced to flee) was put forward as the justification for giving away his throne, and the constitutional Protestant monarch, William III, was obliged to share the throne with his wife Mary, who was closer to the Stuart blood line. Both of these moves were designed to assuage those opposed to the *coup*.

The events set in motion by Lenin, Mao and Castro all took place in non-democratic societies, with no need to win the battle for ideas. All that they had to win was power, and then institute the means to maintain it independently of popular opinion. It is significant that there are virtually no cases in which Marxist or communist governments have come to power on a majority vote, and none at all in which they have left it by such means.

It may be that the cases cited all took place in societies where informed opinion counted for little, and that the formula whereby the action precedes the rationalization of it is simply not valid in a democratic society. It could be that 'winning the battle of ideas' is an essential prerequisite of change wherever informed opinion is of consequence.

When the American constitution was adopted in 1789, it was in a society with a strong democratic element, and certainly one in which informed opinion counted. Yet the constitution which emerged from the convention was not one for which arguments had been fought and won, for the most part. Many of the delegates had not been empowered to do what they did.

Just as it had been a minority of Americans who had fought and won the war for independence from Britain, so it was a minority who turned the Articles of Confederation into a federal constitution. Again, the event had some of the elements of a coup, with a few leaders pushing through a constitution to give a strong and central identity to the United States. As in the other cases examined, its theory and its justification came after its success. The *Federalist Papers* were not written in order to persuade informed opinion to do the deed; they were written afterwards to provide a retrospective rationalization. In this respect they stand in the same relation to events as do the *Two Treatises on Civil Government* by Locke. The argument did rage after the event, as it did in Locke's time, and there was a battle of ideas. But it was once again a battle for explanation; a struggle to justify what had been done.

There are two recent cases from democratic societies which merit close attention; they are the administrations of Margaret Thatcher in Britain and Ronald Reagan in the United States. Both deserve study in the context of the present argument because each is alleged to provide an example of how previous victories in the battle for ideas made possible their election and the policies they were able to implement.

While there are important and obvious differences, relating in some ways to the different constitutions and societies under which they serve, there are similarities so striking that some latterday Plutarch would have no difficulty dealing with them as 'parallel lives.' The coincidence in time inevitable leads to a comparison, with Mrs Thatcher's winning her first election in 1979, and Mr Reagan his in 1980.

There is a further and highly significant parallel. In each case there had been a predecessor of the same party elected on a broadly similar mandate. The predecessors were not immediate: in each case there were intermediaries. Richard Nixon took up office as President of the United States in 1969, Edward Heath as Prime Minister of Great Britain in 1970, and each left office in 1974. Gerald Ford and Jimmy Carter separated Mr Nixon from Mr Reagan, while Harold Wilson and James Callaghan separated Mr Heath from Mrs Thatcher.

The significance of Nixon and Heath is that they were elected to do what Reagan and Thatcher were elected to do. The difference is that they did not do it. Whether or not their lives ran close enough to each other to attract a Plutarchian comparison, neither of them implemented the programme they were elected upon. Each achieved some notable and perhaps lasting accomplishments, but both are currently remembered more for their failures than for their successes.

A look at the rhetoric of their election campaigns, and the manifestos on which they stood, show striking similarities. The thrust of the Nixon stand was anti-big government, freeing US business from some of the regulations which stood in its way. The burden of government, expanded hugely under Lyndon Johnson's 'Great Society' programme was to be lifted. Foreign policy would assert national interests.

The media and contemporary US historians remember the election as dominated by the 'peace' issue of withdrawal from Vietnam, with Eugene McCarthy's upset victory in the New Hampshire Democratic primary effectively knocking Johnson out of the race. In history, as opposed to memory, Johnson won that primary, and both Nixon and Humphrey went into the election opposing immediate withdrawal of US forces, defusing it as an issue.

It is striking today to realize how conservative was the tone of the Nixon campaign of 1968. It is even more striking to examine the manifesto on which Heath's Conservatives fought the 1970 election in Britain, and to look back to the Selsdon Park Manifesto which immediately preceded it. The familiar sentiments call for rolling back the state, denationalizing public industries, cutting the costs of government and its involvement in the economy. The breath of free enterprise which blew through the Nixon election programme found an echoing breeze in the British election which followed.

Nixon in America and Heath in Britain were both elected on a mandate broadly hostile to collectivism, in favour of more space for enterprise, more freedom from regulation, and less burden of taxation. Nixon was elected twelve years before Reagan, Heath won nine years before Thatcher. It did not take those intervening years to convince the electorates on both sides of the Atlantic of the merits of the stance. In each case they voted for it the first time.

The significant fact is that both Nixon and Heath won. The voters were sufficiently in favour of the anti-government and pro-free enterprise ideas being put forward to elect their proponents into office. If it took a battle of ideas to reach that stage, it had been won by 1968 in America and by 1970 in Britain.

Given the programme on which they were elected, the clear way in which this was put forward during the campaign, and the mandate given to it by the voters, the subsequent behaviour of both of the two administrations requires some explanation. Neither of them did what they said they would. Both to some extent performed more of the policies which they had opposed during the elections.

In the United States Nixon further limited the freedom of the market by introducing wage and price controls in Stages One, Two and Three. Regulation was extended under his term of office. The judicial activism of government agencies, such as the forced bussing prompted by the Department of Justice under Civil Rights legislation, continued, and was extended in a major way into the cities of the Northern states. An entire new agency was set up to handle 'legal services,' which meant, in effect, providing public funds for a department to regulate by litigation.

The size and cost of government increased, and the total burden of taxation increased. Inflation dragged many people into higher tax brackets which had originally been intended only for the very rich. Most disturbing of all to those who supported the manifesto on which the President had been elected, the pattern was intensified whereby federal agencies in effect made law without reference to Congress by the use of detailed rules to interpret broad statutes. American individuals, businesses and corporations found themselves assailed by a minutiae of law put into effect by the Food and Drug Administration, the Occupational Health and Safety Administration, and the alphabet soup which made up the federal agencies.

While this was happening in the United States, its parallel was unfolding in Britain. The Heath administration had been committed to a large degree of denationalization. It managed to sell the state-owned Carlisle brewery, taken into government hands in the First World War to discourage drunkenness among munition workers, and to dispose of a state owned travel agency. These tiny acts of denationalization were outweighed by the government's takeover of the ailing Upper Clyde Shipbuilders and Rolls Royce, the aero-engine manufacturers.

The Heath government introduced its own wages and price controls, in the British case via Phases One, Two and Three. It reorganized local government into huge bureaucracies remote from ordinary people, and without the old names and local loyalties. It debased the currency by a huge increase in the supply of money, nominally to fund a 'dash for growth,' but in fact funding a stampede towards paper fortunes made in speculative property deals. The phrase 'U-turn' entered the political vocabulary to describe a government which turns in the exact opposite direction to the one it started upon.

The obvious question to be answered is why both of these administrations, given majority support in the elections for a conservative programme to limit the government's power and scope, should not only have failed to implement such a programme, but should have done the opposite. If the battle for ideas had been won to give them that majority support, why did events not follow in its train?

Several explanations have been advanced, with varying degrees of sophistication, to explain this event which happened in two major countries at roughly similar times. The simplest is also the least plausible; it is duplicity. This explanation would have us believe that neither Nixon nor Heath ever believed in the ideas on which they were elected, or had any intention of trying to implement them. On the contrary, the-argument runs, they saw that the battle for ideas had been won by the advocates of less government and free enterprise, and simply cashed in on that sentiment in order to secure election.

The argument is implausible because both leaders in fact made early attempts to introduce at least some parts of their promised programme, and only later in their terms of office did they make the U-turns. This same fact probably defeats the second argument, a slightly more subtle version of the first. This is that both Nixon and Heath were at heart members of the governing class, and shared its general values and preconceptions.

While they might play with the rhetoric of radical change, they were determined in fact to keep to the kind of politics which was understood by the business and financial community, and with which they felt comfortable. Although this version is rather more polished than its primitive counterpart, it again fails to explain why they both started on one set of policies and then changed to another. Surely the time to reassure the business and financial leaders was at the start of their terms of office?

A third explanation, and one advanced most often by disgruntled former supporters whose aspirations had not been realized, was that neither of the two men was 'tough enough.' This criticism is often accompanied by the assertion that they should have struck earlier and harder, while their mandate was hot. It might be true, but an examination of the personality and record of each of them reveals an extraordinary strength of character.

Nixon showed considerable resilience over a year and a half of relentless Watergate investigation and media abuse. A weaker man would have broken much earlier. Heath showed then, and since, a strength of will and a determination which characterize a reluctance to give way on anything. The description of them as 'not tough enough' simply does not fit. It tends, in any case, to be used by supporters disappointed that the millennium does not arrive in the first week of a new term of office. It has been used of both Reagan and Thatcher, of whom it is no more accurate.

There is a fourth explanation with the advantage that Mr Heath, among others, appears to subscribe to it. It is that things look different in opposition. When one looks from the outside, ideas are put forward, and plans laid. Government itself, however, is a learning process, and leaders soon come to realize just which things are possible and which are not. In other words, the promises made in opposition should not be taken too seriously; they represent more of a declaration of intent. It is assumed that once in government, leaders will have to modify their plans to fit in with political realism.

On this model, both Nixon and Heath soon found out

that some of what they had promised just could not be done. Both of them concluded that it was not realistic in modern times to think in terms of less government. With the world and society growing ever more complicated, government, too, has to increase in complexity and scale. With more international interaction and interdependence between nations, governments can no longer afford to stand back from national industries.

A series of several similar assumptions builds up into a picture in which it is simply 'unrealistic' to expect conservative programmes such as those promised by Nixon and Heath to succeed in the modern world. This view is one which was quite widely held in the bureaucracy of government in both countries, and was at the time generally espoused in such media in both counties as aspired to be thought of as enlightened. This explanation was the most plausible, and perhaps the most widely believed, until the advent of the Thatcher and Reagan administrations showed that it was possible to implement major parts of a conservative programme and to make serious efforts to fulfil election promises.

A more complex version of the above explanation suggests that while the battle for ideas had been won, it had not been won in the right places. Even though the ideas were acceptable at a popular level, and to an extent sufficient to propel their exponents into office, perhaps the battle had not been won among opinion leaders. The attempt to implement them, on this version, was met by fierce resistance and incredulity on the part of an intellectual class whose approval was needed by government.

Thus, although the public and the party leaders were persuaded, the intellectual community was not. The policies were scorned in the academic world, in the powerful echelons of the Civil Service and among the influential media commentators whose opinions are valued by administrations. Even with a popular mandate, the Nixon and Heath governments were unable to fly in the face of what appeared to be virtually all informed opinion. The battle for ideas had to be won in that group before success would come.

An attractive feature of this explanation is that there did appear to be a disparity between the popular opinion which returned the Nixon and Heath governments, and the views of the intelligentsia. In Britain John Braine on television pointed out the contrast between the scorn which an educated BBC audience accorded to his views, and the results board which showed the country at large voting for them. In the United States, the Vice President Spiro Agnew was castigating the 'effete corps of intellectual snobs' and the 'philosophical eunuchs.'

Despite its truth content, this disparity between popular and intellectual opinion falls down as an explanation for the failure of Nixon and Heath to carry out their programmes because it was still true for their successors. Academic and intellectual opinion leaders had not been won over by the time of the Thatcher and Reagan governments. The 364 economists who wrote to *The Times* in England denouncing Thatcher economics typify an opposition to her views among educators and intellectuals. Polls in America contrasted the huge support enjoyed by Reagan among ordinary citizens with the equally huge majorities against him among informed commentators.

If the hostility of the intellectual community had been sufficient to thwart Nixon and Heath despite a popular mandate, why was it unable to stop Reagan and Thatcher? The battle for ideas which had been won among ordinary voters in Britain and America by the time of the 1968 and 1970 elections had still not been won among the intellectual classes by the time of the 1979 and 1980 elections.

The experiences of the Nixon and Heath administrations are very revealing for those concerned with the
battle for ideas. On the conventional, and rather
attractive, model, the advent of Reagan in America and
Thatcher in Britain represented success in the struggle.
The long years in a scorned minority had paid off; the
patient and diligent effort had achieved its objective.
Now those once mocked ideas became standard
currency, and leaders espousing them were carried to
office on a popular upswell of sentiment in their favour.
Only then did it become possible to act.

What appears as a classic illustration of the importance of making the ideas acceptable at all levels, and as
an inspiration to others to put in the same kind of
dedication, melts away when the evidence is examined.
If the battle for ideas had not been won at a popular
level in 1968 and 1970, how is it that Nixon and Heath
were elected on a platform constructed of those very
ideas? If the battle had not been won among the
intellectual classes in 1968 and 1970, how did that differ
from the situation in 1979 and 1980?

There is a vital ingredient missing from the recipe.
Nixon and Heath were elected with a popular mandate,
albeit with opposition from 'informed' opinion, on the
basis of a programme to curb big government and
promote free enterprise. They did not do so, for the
most part. Reagan and Thatcher were similarly elected,
roughly a decade later, also with a popular mandate
and lack of endorsement by the intellectual classes.
Their programmes also pledged to cut government and
boost private enterprise. They implemented substantial
parts of those programmes. If the contrast cannot be
explained by differences in the characters or the
preconceptions of the participants, and it cannot be
glossed over by talk of what was or was not 'realistic' at
the time, the explanatory gap remains to be filled.

One possible way of filling that explanatory gap

would involve the supposition that both Nixon and Heath were badly equipped to do what their supporters expected of them. This would suggest that they were sincere in their declared election programmes and that they were not lacking in strength of character, but that neither of them appreciated the magnitude or complexity of the task which faced them.

The prevailing view of the day contained the implicit assumption that changes in events follow automatically upon changes in ideas. Both Nixon and Heath probably shared the general view that reforms came about by being wanted and proposed. Since there was general support for their programme, both assumed that when it was introduced in the legislature it would be put through and would achieve the desired changes. When it failed to do so, they concluded that the ideas were inappropriate to the real world, and looked instead for alternative policies which would succeed.

Both were victims, in a sense, of the 'battle for ideas' outlook which assumed that it was enough to muster general support for free market ideas and opposition to big government. They both had the will to make a radical departure from past practices, and they enjoyed a climate of opinion generally favourable to such action. Neither of them, however, knew what to do.

The point is that the battle of ideas takes place at the level of generalities. Concepts such as 'free market' are set in opposition to others such as 'big government.' The debate takes place in the realm of theory and abstraction. Practical evidence is drawn from the world of experience to support or confute positions laid down in theory.

Detailed academic studies might be performed which show that the record of government-owned steel industries, for example, is poorer than that of privately owned ones in other countries. The results might show that the state-produced steel costs more per unit to produce, that manpower is used less productively, that delivery dates are not met, and that quality control is nowhere near as effective as for its private counterpart. Other theorists might even step in with suggestions as to why this is so, and to explain the reason for the practical outcome.

Activity such as this might establish a case against state ownership of steel industries. Indeed, empirical and theoretical studies had established just such a case against state ownership of industry in Britain by the late 1960s, if not earlier. Similar work in the United States had shown the baneful effects of regulation on the wealth creating process and the crowding out effect of government spending.

All of this might motivate popular opinion and political leaders with the determination to change things; but none of it tells them what to do. It is one thing to know that a state-owned steel sector is inefficient and inferior. It is quite another to know what to do about it.

The response of the simplistic supporter of private enterprise is to say: 'Get rid of the state steel industry.' That this is a difficult and complex task requiring detailed knowledge of sophisticated techniques does not occur to him. He elects a government to get rid of state steel, and watches with mounting impatience as months, perhaps years, go by without action. He wants to know why, and suspects weakness or duplicity. He resolves next time to elect someone tougher who will go in harder on the first day and actually do it.

Meanwhile, the government he helped to elect becomes increasingly frustrated as it tries to find a way of doing something about the state steel industry. Every suggestion seems to promise dire consequences. Figures are produced by its Civil Service to show that it will be less costly to continue subsidies to state owned steel than it will be to support the hundreds of thousands of people who would lose their jobs otherwise. Bleak scenarios are set before ministers in which supporting industries are forced to close. A domino effect is predicted in which bankruptcies and closures follow one upon the other. The government hesitates and reconsiders.

It is not attracted by the 'hair shirt' strategy urged upon it by its most ardent supporters. This, in essence, claims that any thing worth doing in politics is bound to produce unpleasant effects and unpopularity to begin with. An incoming government therefore has a duty to do everything all at once in the teeth of an outcry of enraged opposition. It should then sit back and ride the storm of unpopularity and possible violence, until the long-term beneficial effects of the market have had time to work through and show people the wisdom of the government's deeds. With luck, and if the government's programme is not delayed by opposition and constitutional processes, this might come about before it has to seek re-election.

It is unfair for supporters of the Nixon and Heath governments to criticize them, as they do, for not adopting that strategy. In the first place, it took the experience of office to make them realize the problem. By the time they realized that they lacked a technique, it was already too late to implement the 'hair shirt' solution. Secondly, it must be said that the checks and balances of democratic societies, the separation of powers and the space provided for a voice of opposition, are all designed precisely to prevent such tactics being used.

The Nixon and Heath administrations are remembered more for their failures than their successes not because they did not want to implement their programmes, nor because they lacked the support for them, but because they did not know how to do it. They might have known that free markets were a good thing,

but they did not know how to get them. They might
have been persuaded of the case against big government, but they did not know how to make it smaller.

The suggestion is thus that technique fills the gap
between ideas and events. The knowledge of how to
implement policies to achieve political objectives is no
less important than the selection of the priorities to be
sought. On this explanation, the reason why Reagan
succeeded to a large extent in areas where Nixon had
failed is not that opinion had been won over in the
meantime, or that the 1980s were more suitable for such
attitudes than the 1970s. It was that the Nixon administration did not know how to do it, but the Reagan team
did.

In a similar way on the other side of the Atlantic, the
Heath government's U-turns were brought on by its
lack of techniques to implement its original policies. The
climate of opinion had not changed substantially at
either the popular or the 'informed' level between the
election of Heath and Thatcher. Neither local nor
international developments had made centralist policies
any more or less appropriate during the intervening
years. What was different was that the Thatcher
government paid considerably more attention to the
details of policy. They had a conception of what was
needed, as did Heath's administration, but the Thatcher
team also knew how to do it.

The crucial difference between Nixon and Reagan,
between Heath and Thatcher, was policy itself. The
early 1970s saw the return of governments with a broad
grasp of the principles of free market economics, but
which were forced to turn their back on those principles
for want of detailed knowledge of how to put them into
practice. The early 1980s, by contrast, saw the return of
governments versed to a greater extent in the technical
details of how the principles could be applied.

The difference reflected itself in a self-conscious

appreciation of technique by the later administrations. The earlier ones, faced with their inability to implement their programmes, had turned back to the old paradigm. The new governments, when early attempts failed, tried different techniques to achieve the same objectives. Instead of reversing their course, they both learned as they went along, discarding techniques which proved ineffective, and repeating ones that worked.

The factor which makes the difference between failure for the Nixon and Heath governments and success for those of Reagan and Thatcher is not one of the personnel, of the movement of ideas, or of the times in which they operated, but appears to be one concerned with the ways in which policy is implemented. The later teams were very much more concerned to have a battery of policy techniques developed, techniques, moreover, which showed acute sensitivity to that which is politically acceptable.

This leaves unanswered the question of why it happened that the early conservative programmes lacked policy techniques to enable them to be implemented, whereas the gap had been at least partly filled by the time of the later ones. To some extent the one may have been the cause of the other. That is, the experience of the failure of Nixon and Heath may have engendered in their successors a determination not to repeat the process. The experience of that false dawn of the early 1970s might itself have led to the development of policy techniques which would take later governments to success in the 1980s

It may have been so. Just as there were those in the early attempts to achieve a free market programme who 'learned' from the failure that such ideas were no longer relevant, so there may have been others who took a different lesson, resolving to try in alternative ways if the chance came again.

There is an alternative explanation which may be true

either in conjunction with the first, or independently. It is that opinion in the early 1970s lacked a coherent theory of policy application, and thought that the task of political leaders was simply to 'implement' ideas. Some time during that decade, perhaps spurred on by the Nixon and Heath experiences, came the realization that it is not ideas which are implemented, but policies, and that there is a substantial gap between the idea itself and the policy which puts it into effect.

There were developments, in other words, which laid open to question the fundamental assumption that ideas have consequences of themselves. The awareness came instead that the battle for ideas is only a part of the story; on its own it will lack the power to change events. During the period between the first try to implement free market programmes and the second, there came the understanding that ideas and policy have a more complex and interactive relationship than was formerly grasped, and that without the detailed policies to give them effect in a way which succeeds, the ideas may change our thinking, but they will not change the world.

4 Scientists and Engineers

We praise the pure scientists who add to our understanding of the world. They give us insights into the universe and help us to predict what we shall observe there. Some gain recognition and reward instantly, for others the appreciation takes time. The great discoveries of pure science are not like the insights which great political thinkers give us into the organization of society. In the case of scientific hypotheses, there is an established procedure by which theories must survive tests which can be replicated before the process of acceptance begins. There is no such agreed methodology for accepting the work of political thinkers.

The social and political theorists are, however, like the pure scientists in one important respect. They try by their insights to increase our understanding of the world we live in. From Plato and Aristotle, through Adam Smith and Edmund Burke, Karl Marx and John Stuart Mill, down to thinkers such as Friedrich Hayek in our own time, they can change our perception of the world.

In much the same way, thinkers such as Isaac Newton, Sir Robert Boyle and Lord Kelvin change the way we look at the world. Thanks to their contributions, it appears to us to be more unified and more comprehensible. The pure scientists change our understanding

53

of the world; they do not, however, change the world. It may look different after they have done their creative work, but it is the same world as it was before.

After the pure scientists have put forward their ideas, a second group of creative minds comes to build machines which operate on their laws. The activity is no less creative, but its function is to take the insights of the pure scientist as the starting point, and to construct engines which work on their basis. Just as we honour Newton, Boyle and Kelvin, so do we also honour the engineers who use their work to build the machines. James Watt, George Stephenson and Isambard Kingdom Brunel have their place in humanity's hall of fame, no less than the pure scientists whose work provided their starting-point.

With Newton we understand motion and optics, with Boyle the behaviour of gases, with Kelvin the dynamics of heat. We could list many others, and the area in which they extended our understanding. But it is to James Watt that we owe the working steam engine, to George Stephenson the locomotive, and to Isambard Kingdom Brunel the suspension bridge and the trans-oceanic steamship. The pure scientists change our understanding of the world; it is the engineers who change the world itself.

It takes a second type of thinking, no less original, no less creative, to devise the machines which will operate on the principles uncovered by the scientists. With Boyle we understand gases under pressure; with Watt and Stephenson we make it work for us. The scientists have interpreted the world; the point is to change it.

Of course, the work of the pure scientist is an essential precursor of the work of the engineer. Without the great creative insights our engineering would be no more than a few rule of thumb devices developed by chance and improved by experience. The ancient Chinese and the Romans did reasonably well on such a basis, but the leaps and bounds of modern technology are made possible by a firm grounding in theoretical understanding of the workings of nature.

The pure scientist is essential, but so is the engineer. Without the second stage of creativity we would be left with a much richer understanding of the universe as we tilled our fields with wooden ploughs.

There is a parallel between the work of the pure scientists and that of the great social thinkers. To some extent Montesquieu and Locke resemble Hooke and Joule. The fact that human society is the subject of study in one case makes for important differences in what can be achieved, but the creative insights are still there to enrich our understanding. We feel after reading them that human society is more comprehensible than it was, and that we understand some of the principles which underlie it.

This understanding does not, of itself, change it. Just as with the pure scientists, the world remains the same after the social theorists have made their pronouncements upon it. It takes a second group of creative minds to put the flesh of practice on to the bones of social and political theory, just as it takes engineers to build machines based on scientific theory. The great scholars who analyse our societies and their laws need their engineers before the insight can alter the reality.

It is one thing for us to understand a principle, but quite another to make it work to our advantage. This applies no less to the study of society than to the study of nature. We honour our political theorists as we honour our scientists, for the insights they give us. But we should recognize that policy engineers are needed to make machines out of the theory, and that the activity is by no means automatic.

No one would suppose that after the work of Newton, Boyle or Kelvin, the machines which operated by their laws would simply emerge. If they did, we would be waiting still. We know that it takes the application and work of creative minds. The machines do not happen; men make them. The same is true of political theory. The advances made at the theoretical level do not translate themselves into working policy. If, after the pioneering work of Adam Smith or Friedrich Hayek, we waited for a change in events to follow automatically in its wake, we would be waiting still.

It is as true of public policy as of pure science: the theorists change our understanding, the engineers change the world. Policy is an intricate process which requires skill, sensitivity and creative intelligence. It does not just happen, any more than machines do.

The 'battle for ideas' in political and economic theory can be likened to the disputes which take place in scientific theory. Scientists put forward competing theories, and they and their supporters fight to gain recognition for them. No doubt much of the decidedly unscholarly behaviour takes place in these contests as typifies academic infighting in general. Even though there are procedures for testing, these can occasionally be faked, hushed up, or ignored and denied publicity. The struggle, however fairly it is conducted, is for mastery of explanation. It is a contest between conflicting interpretations of the universe.

Ideas at the scholarly level in politics and economics are also engaged in a battle for acceptance, and it is also a battle for explanation. At the end of the struggle, it alters how we look at things. It does not alter the things themselves. For that we need policy engineers to construct the instruments we can use to have an impact on the world itself.

There is an intellectual fashion in Britain, and a regrettable one at that, which affects to sneer at the role of the engineer. The very term 'pure science' is elevated as though engineering were somehow impure. It is assumed that the work of the pure scientist is at a higher level, more academically detached, and therefore more holy than the work of the man in overalls with grease stains on his hands and clothes. This is an intellectual fashion which arises partly from the priorities of our system of education, and partly from the legacy of a class system which accorded more status to an office job with clean hands.

Other, more successful, countries have no such scale of priority. They recognize that the creative requirement of the inventor is not less than that of the theorist; and they admit the social utility of the former. They honour their inventors and engineers as the British once did, and reap the reward of seeing their top talent move into that area.

Perhaps it is the preoccupation with 'pure' research which has led to the primacy of the notion that the 'battle for ideas' is what changes events, and for the essential role of the policy engineer to be overlooked. This is particularly unfortunate in view of the fact that the engineer's role in the application of social, political or economic theory, is possibly more important than that of his counterpart in the world of material things.

It is usually the case in the realm of technology that the work of the pure scientist comes first. The theoretician achieves the breakthrough in understanding, and the engineers, mechanics and inventors come at a later stage to build their creative ideas upon that base. It is not universally so. There are cases in which a working machine produced by an inventor prompts the theorists to re-examine their models of the universe. There were, after all, primitive working machines before the discipline of theoretical scientific study was established.

The ancient Chinese and Romans had crude, rule-of-thumb working machines long before the physical laws on which they operated were known. In their case it was only much later that the pure scientists were able to say why the machines worked as they did. There have been more recent cases in which an engineer has produced a machine which ought not to have worked according to known laws. The presence of the machine has turned the attention of scientists back to those physical laws in order to restructure them to explain why it was able to function successfully.

These are exceptions to a general rule. In science it is usually the theory which comes first, and the machines which are built upon it. In the field of public policy, however, there is no such general rule. Inspection reveals the opposite pattern. In general it is the practice which comes first, and the theory which is later elaborated to interpret it and to fit it into an explanatory framework.

The cases referred to all fit comfortably into this pattern. The Republic of Plato set out the general style and many of the detailed rules of the comparatively successful society of Sparta. The attempt to apply the theory of the Republic to Syracuse failed. Locke's *Two Treatises on Civil Government* delineated a theory for the already accomplished limited monarchy of the Glorious Revolution. The *Federalist Papers* argued the case in principle for a constitution of the United States already decided in practice. Lenin's revision of Marxism justified in theory what Lenin had done to win power, and showed retrospectively why it had been done that way. The same is true of Mao Tse Tung's modification of Marxist-Leninism, and of the theoretical additions necessitated by the success of Castro's revolution. In all of these cases it was the policy which was applied first, and the 'pure' theory which came afterwards.

In policy, as in science, it is the engineers who change the world and the theoreticians who change our understanding of it. The major difference is that it is usually the theorists who come first in science to pave the way for the creative engineers. In political theory the policy engineers usually change the world first, with the academic theorists coming after them to explain things.

There is an interaction between theory and practice in both science and political theory. Once a valid theory has been put forward to explain the observations and to accommodate the practical cases, it might itself inspire some new practical applications. The study of case histories, on the other hand, can lead to modification of a supporting theory, as practice reveals facets previously unsuspected by theory.

The relationship is not cause and effect one way or the other. There is a complex pattern of feedback between the two, operating in both directions. While theory tends to lead in science, and practice tends to lead in public policy, the same type of interactive relationship between theory and practice is to be found in both fields.

In a hypothetical case in science, and perhaps a typical one, the original insight produces a general theory. On the basis of that general theory, innovative machines are devised and constructed. Some of those machines might point to circumstances not covered by the theory, leading to modification or extension of it to fit them in. This, in turn, might inspire newer types of machine.

A similar hypothetical case could be described in the field of public policy, as typical of its realm as the scientific example. An innovation is introduced, bringing practical success. The success brings it before the attention of the scholars, who apply creative insight to delineate the theory which accounts for its performance. That theory may, in turn, lead to other applications of the principle underlying the first success.

In each case theory and practice feed from each other, pointing those with creative imagination in the directions which might be fruitful. While in science the general theory usually comes ahead of the machines, it need not. And while in social innovation the practice usually precedes the explanatory theory, it need not. These are general tendencies rather than universal rules, and there are easily recognized exceptions to both of them.

That said, there is an important corollary which follows for the field of human studies. If it is true that the practice usually comes before the theory which interprets it, and also true that theory on its own does not promote change without the creative activity of policy engineers, then it follows that the role of theory is of less significance in policy change than it is in the study of nature.

The battle for ideas might be equally intense in both disciplines in so far as the scholars and their supporters are concerned. Indeed, it might be more intense in political theory because of the impression that it is a battle for power over the future course of society. Despite this impression it is a battle in both fields over interpretation. Since the engineers tend to follow the pure scientists in the field of nature, victory in a struggle for interpretation might at least influence the generation of machines which are built upon the foundations of that general theory.

This is less likely to happen in political theory. With those who engage in policy engineering generally leading the way, the outcome of the conflict of ideas is likely to be of less consequence. It is more likely that the future has already been shaped by practical action, and that the battle is taking place to supply a contextual theory to cover it. The ideas are important because the way we look at our world is important; but it is the outlook over the long term on which they have their greatest impact, rather than on the policies which will be implemented in the immediate future.

Once the role of policy engineering is appreciated, it

becomes possible to account for the difference in the performance of the Nixon and Heath governments on the one hand and the Reagan and Thatcher governments on the other. There was, as already shown, no difference in the acceptability of the ideas between the administrations of the 1970s and those of the 1980s. They were sufficiently acceptable at a popular level both times to elect parties committed to them, and sufficiently unacceptable at the intellectual level each time to call forth widespread denunciation in academic and 'informed' circles.

The difference in performance could be attributed to policy. The Reagan and Thatcher administrations were much more equipped with the detailed mechanics of policy implementation, and aware of the need to develop even more practical policies in office. While the manifestos contained the same generalizations each time, the later governments had detailed policy options in preparation to put those generalities into effect.

Both Nixon and Reagan platforms referred to cutting the burden of government, but the Reagan team understood the mechanics of tax cutting, and had ready a detailed set of policy proposals which were designed to overcome some of the obstacles encountered previously.

Both Heath and Thatcher manifestos mentioned the desire to return state industries to the private sector. But whereas this remained only an unfulfilled wish of the Heath era, the Thatcher team went in with some conception of the policy problems, some notion of possible options, and a determination to learn from successful ones which techniques could succeed in a modern democratic society. The result was that in the Heath years more industry entered into the state sector, whereas the Thatcher years were characterized by its accelerating withdrawal from it.

The differences which some observers have sought in

the character or temperament of the participants, in their preconceptions, in what was realistic at the time, or in what opinion leaders were prepared to accept as reasonable, are now attributable to policy itself, to its mechanics and details. The first two leaders did not know how to do it; the second two did.

As a result of the experiences of the Nixon and Heath terms of office, some of those who supported their declared programmes decided to seek tougher and sounder standard bearers for those causes in the future. Others took a different message. Some who had been involved closely with those first attempts, either as participants or close observers, took the lesson that more subtle and more intricate policies would be required if they were to succeed in the future where they had failed in the past.

With the benefit of hindsight it seems as if the policy details were the deciding factor. It is true that Reagan and Thatcher appeared to those supporting their programmes to be both tougher and sounder than their predecessors. This is largely because unlike them, they did not abandon and then reverse those declared intentions. In other words, the success of the policies put into effect enabled both Reagan and Thatcher to remain true to their original programmes in a way which was not possible for their predecessors. It is because the policies were successful and could be repeated and extended that the leaders implementing them seemed stronger. It is not because the leaders were stronger that the policies were more successful.

The foregoing analysis suggests that a crucial switch in strategy took place some time in the 1970s among some of the elements which had supported political ideas conducive to the free market and hostile to the expanded domain occupied by government and the growth of government spending. Before the 1970s the argument had been fought on the level of principle.

That is, the emphasis had been on pointing out the evils wrought by collectivist policies, and of the superior virtues of the market economy. Books and papers were published, lectures delivered, seminars held, all designed to sell the case for free enterprise and to undermine centralist planning.

That the Nixon and Heath governments were elected on the basis of platforms strong on those themes attests to the success of that campaign of persuasion. That they did not succeed attests to the value of the maxim that one should not put one's trust in princes, nor indeed in the ideas which they profess to espouse.

The 1970s saw the emergence in both Britain and the United States of a new concern with policy itself. Many who supported a free enterprise programme continued as before to promote market virtues in general, and to criticize and expose the flaws of collectivist policies. Some continued to aim at academic opinion, others at political leaders, and some at the informed public. The new element was policy research, in which the detailed mechanisms of policy proposals were put under scrutiny, honed and polished to maximize their chances of success.

Part of the reasoning behind this new action was an appreciation of the time lag between the election of a new government and the preparation of its legislation. The process could take a full year, with a further year allowed for delay in preparation caused by civil service procrastination and obstruction. By the time the legislation could be put through in the following year, the end of a term of office would be approaching, and the government in power reluctant to take risks with unpopular policies.

One of the ideas which lay behind policy research was the idea of short circuiting the delays by having developed policies worked out in advance and ready for immediate action by an incoming government. The

view was current that some of the toughest fights
would have to be fought first, and that a new government would have to be ready for them.

A further strand which led to the development of
policy research in the 1970s was the appreciation that
the civil service establishment enjoyed a virtual monopoly of practical knowledge. Outsiders might advocate
ideas in general, but only within the bureaucracy of the
various departments of government was to be found
the experience and the expertise to set events in motion.
The result of that monopoly was that the civil service
view tended to prevail. Even the strongest willed
minister with clear ideas of what should be done was
alone against a united phalanx of expert opinion
proclaiming this to be impossible.

The policy research teams took action in part to end
that Civil Service monopoly. By advance preparation
and detailed study of technique, they could offer the
minister an alternative source of suggestion and initiative, and override the effective veto which the Civil
Service had until then possessed by virtue of their
exclusive command of detail.

A third intended result of the policy research was the
breaching of the credibility barrier. Whereas general
ideas might be dismissed as 'irrelevant' or 'unwork-
able,' a detailed policy proposal merited more serious
attention. It would be harder to claim that certain things
could not be done if there existed detailed plans and
mechanisms for accomplishing them. Ministers who
might otherwise have been persuaded that the prevailing paradigm was the only possible one would now be
armed with worked-out alternatives showing this to be
untrue. The detail given to the method of application
lent credibility to the idea underlying it.

One of the important insights which led to the
development of policy research was the realization that
some techniques would be more successful than others,
and that investigation could show which they were.

Instead of assuming, as previously, that victory in ideas would lead on to victory in events, some of those who advocated free market programmes now engaged in the work of identifying which policies would be likely to succeed. To do this involved them in consideration of the whole theory of public policy, so they could construct policies designed to overcome the hurdles which it placed before them.

The understanding that different ways of attempting to achieve similar objectives could be more successful than others led to competitive evaluation of policy proposals. The policy research workers began to test hypothetical scenarios to discover which proposals would attract support, and which might alienate popular opinion. Adjustments were made, details refined. A series of policy proposals gradually emerged during the 1970s, quite different from the broad advocacy of free enterprise ideas which had characterized the 1960s.

There were still groups, societies and institutes which carried on the work of winning converts to market solutions, and spreading disillusionment with the record of collectivism. But now there were new kids on the block. In both the United States and Britain there were established institutes whose function was not the advocacy of free enterprise, but the investigation and preparation of the detailed policies which might secure it in practice throughout the different areas of government. They were an important difference between the situation of the 1960s and that of the 1970s.

The new institutes took as their starting point the failure of the nominally free enterprise governments of the early 1970s to put market-oriented ideas into practice. They learned how the political system worked, and how to solve the problems it posed to would-be legislators. They researched ways in which choice and enterprise might be extended in practice, as well as advocated in theory. They gave policy-makers what they were looking for: policies.

PART II
THE PUBLIC SECTOR

5 Public Choice

The 1986 Nobel prize for economics was awarded to Professor James Buchanan of the United States. Buchanan, along with Professor Gordon Tullock and others, developed over many years the 'Theory of Public Choice.' First at the Virginia Polytechnic Institute, and more recently at George Mason University in Virginia, the public choice theorists put out a stream of monographs, research papers and articles in economic journals. The constant theme which ran through their work was that people behave in political life in a very similar fashion to their behaviour in economic life.

The 1970s saw the rise to prominence of several schools of economic theory, not all incompatible with each other, which gave theoretical refutations to the central tenets of the Keynesian system, beginning by then to be discredited in practice.

There was, first of all, a return to respectability of market economic systems in general, and a revival of the neo-classical ideas. The rise of the monetarist 'Chicago School' led by Milton Friedman continued remorselessly throughout the decade, pointing to the relation between the supply of money created by government and the rate of inflation. Friedman, himself a Nobel Laureate in 1976, was an articulate and eloquent critic of governments bent on economic inter-ventionism.

Less visible was the slow rise of the 'Austrian School,' whose leading modern exponent, F.A. Hayek, received the Nobel prize in 1974. The emphasis of this school was on economics as a process, rather than as a series of equilibria, and one driven mainly by the aspirations and actions of individuals. A characteristic of 'Austrian' economics is its rejection of macroeconomics and its insistence that the reality lies in microeconomic activity.

Other schools and their offshoots introduced new concepts into economic analysis. 'Rational expectations' rose to prominence; while the celebrated Phillips curve sank into the swamp of 'stag-flation,' as countries managed to achieve simultaneously the high unemployment and inflation which were supposed to trade off one against the other.

It was, and perhaps still is, a period typical of the scientific revolutions described by Kuhn. The prevailing paradigm had collapsed under the weight of contradictions and anomalies, and scholars searched for something to replace the 'Keynesian consensus.' Kuhn describes such periods as those when the most creative work is done. It was certainly a creative period for economics.

Against this background of ferment, the public choice school was slowly rising in esteem as the quality of its work and the consistency of its outlook made itself felt. It never gained popular acclaim, and although it was regarded with respect, it was treated as tangential to the developments which were taking place in economic ideas. There is a reason for this. Public choice theory is not fundamentally a theory of economics, but of politics. It would fit happily into the old study of 'Political Economy', but sits uneasily in the classroom of 'Economic Science'. It applies economic ideas to political behaviour, and shows how certain economic principles can be used to explain and interpret behaviour in the political realm.

There had been a dichotomy between politics and

economics. That is, most scholars had supposed the two to be fundamentally different types of activity. When people engaged in economics they did one set of things; when they moved over into politics they did another. The public choice theorists have shown that the two are more closely related, and that people behave in politics as they do in economic activity.

In economics people make decisions on the basis of their goals. They respond to their own hierarchy of values, trading off some things in return for others. They might trade valued leisure time in exchange for even more valued additional income. They buy and sell in the market. Entrepreneurs enter the picture, linking investors and producers, sellers and buyers. Information has its price and is bought and sold. Scarcity increases value, as does proximity in time and place. When many people want something in limited supply, price goes up in response.

All of this is a familiar world, and has produced innumerable analytical works investigating its apparent laws and producing the insights to bring unity to what seems initially like random disorder. Politics was studied differently. Scholars had assumed that it was an altogether different type of activity. People were assumed to make decisions collectively, competing for majority support for their views. It was supposed that decisions were made intermittently at elections, and that minorities gave way before the majority will, except in areas protected constitutionally.

A major insight of the public choice school was the appreciation that political activity proceeds in very similar ways to economic activity. People act to maximize their advantage. They make the decisions which pursue their objectives. They make trade-offs. Instead of intermittent voting taking place at elections, the reality is of a constant series of 'votes' as people take actions to influence the political process.

The public choice theorists established that there is a kind of marketplace for votes. When they are in short supply they command a higher price and have to be bought more dearly. Some of particular value are bought at higher prices than others. The vote, in other words, has economic value and is traded as such. The majority does not simply overrule the minority. Rather does the minority trade its votes for an acceptable recompense. People trade the vote, which has an economic value, for something they consider to be worth more. It is like other economic exchanges.

All of this may seem rather abstract and philosophical. It appears to say more about the way people behave in political life and activity than it tells us about economics as such. Its value lies in part in its ability to predict the behaviour of groups within the political process more accurately than any of the conventional models. By assuming that the general rules of economic behaviour also cover political activity, it is possible to gain a much more realistic picture of what goes on in political activity than can be obtained by the traditional picture of politics as a series of decisions made collectively.

Far from seeing minorities give way every time before the will of the majority, public choice theory tells us why it is so often the other way round, that the minorities collectively have their way at the expense of the majority. The closure of one ailing factory may have very few votes at stake. But to those voters affected it matters crucially. Their representatives are prepared to pay a high price for support on so crucial an issue. They will trade support for others in exchange. Thus coalitions are put together which succeed in satisfying the various minorities on the issues which matter to them, even though this might be at the expense of the general good.

It costs little to support or subsidize each particular minority. On each issue, therefore, those who benefit are prepared to pay a higher price in terms of support than those who will eventually foot the bill. It matters more to the former than to the latter. Political reality is constructed not upon the merits of the individual cases, but on the arithmetic of traded support. People act in order to maximize their reward from the system, just as they do in economics. The reward need not be material; it need only be whatever they count as important.

Public choice theory in effect breaks down the majorities we see in political activities into their constituent elements. It shows how they are assembled of groups trading with each other to gain what matters more for them in exchange for what matters less. It shows how minorities on a particular subject trade votes with others in a shifting pattern of support which really does evoke the smell and sound of the market-place.

Terms already familiar to students of the United States Congress, such as 'horse trading' and 'log rolling,' are seen to apply to groups in society, as well as to elected representatives. Every election presents packages; part of politics consists of the assembly of packages whose attractive features are more important to many groups of voters than their unattractive ones. Not that the activity is confined only to occasions when actual votes take place.

Even between elections groups trade support with each other, supporting some Bills, acquiescing in some and opposing others. Sometimes opposition is powerful enough to merit being bought off. All of this wheeling and dealing is seen as an important part of political reality, and makes politics more comprehensible than it would be on the simpler models which place more emphasis on rational decision-making than on quasi-economic exchanges.

Public choice theory has shown itself to be an extraordinarily powerful tool when it comes to predicting the behaviour of the various groups operating in the public sector of the economy, and the outcomes which they collectively bring about. It sees bureaucrats not as public servants who dispassionately implement the policies of elected leaders, but as a distinct interest group or series of groups with a strong interest in those policies.

Workers in public sector industries or services are recognized as groups in a position to influence very strongly the level and the quality of those services, and to have a conscious interest in the level at which they are funded. Those who manage state operations have an identifiable stake in the total size of the operation, its manpower levels and the range of its activities.

Even legislators cease to be simply the elected representatives of the public, and emerge instead as yet another distinct interest group with its own priorities and advantages to pursue. Activities which bring visible credit to legislators from voting groups, for example, are of greater benefit to them than activities which gain no visible credit, no matter how much more worthwhile they might be.

The interest of trade union leaders operating in the public sector does not lie in producing the best possible level of public service at the lowest possible price. It lies in maximizing the level of subscription to the union, which will normally mean maximizing its membership. This can, of course, operate against the interests of the public at large who are the supposed beneficiaries of the service.

When the voting public itself is broken into interest groups, each pursuing the objectives they value, some features of the supply of public goods and services in democratic societies become more explicable. It is usually in everyone's individual interest, for example, to maximize their own consumption of goods and services which are paid for collectively. They can exert pressure through the political system to increase the level of services they receive, and groups which receive services form more distinct and more effective groups to trade with than does the general mass of taxpayers which foots the bills. The tendency of democratic societies to oversupply public goods and services can thus be understood in terms of the pressures within the system.

In a hypothetical case there might be ten people in a village who seek an improved level of maintenance for their road. Ten is not a powerful political group, but there are others who would welcome improved roads for their own area. There is thus the basis for a coalition composed of those who seek road improvement for their own areas, and who are prepared to seek general road improvement in order to secure it. Politicians will be able to bid for the support of that group by promising to increase the level of road maintenance. Even those whose own roads do not need improvement will probably not oppose very strongly the principle of road improvement, since they do not generally perceive the costs it imposes upon them to be sufficiently large to arouse their opposition. The cumulative effect of this activity might well be a level of road maintenance higher than necessary, and certainly more than people would spend if they had to part with the funds directly, instead of through government.

The general approach of the public choice school is to treat political activity as if it were economic activity, and to recognize that it is subject to similar inputs. It is very useful in this context to treat those groups which operate within the political framework as if they were businesses working in an economic environment. It is a good predictive tool to take it for granted that they are each trying to maximize their advantage within the rules which prevail. Just like businesses, they seek opportunities, they try to increase the benefits which accrue to them, they compete for a share of the market, and they act always to lower the effort and sacrifices which have to be put in to secure a given output.

Just as business corporations struggle against each other for a market share, so do the bureaucracies of different ministries compete for the allocation of funds. In a similar way, the power play which goes on within corporations as senior executives vie for position and prestige finds its parallel in the civil service as department heads within a ministry struggle for advancement. A treatment of the bureaucracy which looked only at the stated political objectives and the response to them would miss the crucial element of the personal stake of the people involved, whose lives and careers were affected by the decisions.

The behaviour of businesses in pursuit of economic objectives has a major impact on the economic outcome; the same is true of the groups which behave like businesses within the political context. They have real power to influence events. Civil servants can assist or delay public policy. They can even thwart it if it threatens one of their vital interests. Public sector workers can undertake or threaten strike action to put pressure on legislators. The outcry from a public deprived of essential services is something to which politicians are particularly vulnerable, since popularity is their stock in trade.

Trade union leaders can threaten non-cooperation by their followers in order to secure agreements which maximize the job security, and which optimize the working conditions, for their members. Groups of the general public in pursuit of specific benefits for themselves can use protest to bring pressure on legislators, and use demonstrations to bring similar pressure from the media.

Members of the legislature who wish to be re-elected have to watch for signs that impending action on certain issues, or the lack of it, will bring the wrath of the electorate upon them. They, in turn, put pressure on the executive and influence its determination to proceed with, or abandon, parts of its programme or to undertake new initiatives.

All of these pressures upon the political system are very real. The will of governments, by contrast, is a feeble reed. It might set out a course in its manifesto and embark upon a programme, but it has no choice but to respond to the pressures which it encounters. Part of the art of government is perhaps knowing what can be done, and seeing when there is too much resistance from the interest groups affected for a policy to succeed. It has, after all, been described as 'the art of the possible.'

The insight that politics is a marketplace is an explanatory device. Like so many of the explanatory theories of economics, it is at its most useful when it is pointed backwards. That is, we can look at what happened and interpret the events in the light of the theory. With public choice theory we can begin to see why some political programmes were derailed, and why others succeeded. Very often it comes down to the fact that the groups who stood to gain as a result perceived the benefit as small, whereas the potential losers stood to lose big, and were ready to pay a high price to prevent it. That high price need not be paid in money. It can be paid in time and effort, in sacrifice, or in terms of what is traded to secure the support of other groups.

Public choice theory helps us to understand what would otherwise be a curious and incomprehensible fact: that minorities can be benefited more readily than majorities. On the conventional political paradigm, one would expect the majority to vote itself the benefits at the expense of the minorities. The public choice model, however, points out that to benefit a majority it means that an amount greater than that benefit must be taken from the minority. More crudely, to give a dollar to each of the majority involves taking more than a dollar from each of the minority. And the minority will squeal more loudly. Conversely, to benefit a minority requires less than that benefit to be taken from the majority. When the many support the few, the few receive a lot but the many give only a little each. The blame bestowed by the many is light, but the praise gained from the few is heavy.

This explains the fact that even though farmers now constitute a fraction of the numbers they did a century ago, they receive many times the state benefit. Indeed, it is typical of the advanced countries that the farmers are now in a small minority, and are supported with huge subsidies from the more numerous urban tax-payers. In less developed economies where agriculture still employs a majority of the population, it is typically the farmers who are taxed or forced to sell at artificially low prices in order to subsidize urban minorities. As the farmers decline in numbers, their ability to command support increases.

The case illustrates the general point explained by public choice theory; that it is easier to benefit minorities than majorities. It cost less to do so, and they value the benefit sufficiently highly to justify the trade-off to legislators.

Not all minorities count equally in the political process, nor do the actual numbers within them make up their most important element. On public choice theory, the value they place on the benefit makes them ready to trade accordingly. A group, small in actual numbers, might value their benefit so highly that they are prepared to pay a high price for it; that is, they might be ready to trade a great deal of support which potential allies find worth having.

The visibility of minorities is important to their

success. There are cases in which minorities stand to gain a great deal from a particular decision but are unable to influence it effectively because they do not present a visible group with which influence can be traded. For example, if a school is threatened by closure, the parents of the children who attend it form a highly visible group. They can meet and demonstrate, write to their representatives, hold street marches and be interviewed on television. Where the issue concerns the possible opening of a new school, however, the group of future parents who might want to use it are not as visible and do not count for as much politically because their support is difficult to trade.

A further factor which adds to the importance of minority groups is their ability to make trouble. Social workers might be more numerous than electric power technicians, but a potential disruption in social work makes less trouble than interruptions in the supply of electric power. This means that the power technicians count for more, regardless of the objective value of the contribution they make to society compared with that of social workers.

To trade effectively in the political marketplace, a minority group must be self-conscious. That is, it must identify its group interest and its status as a minority seeking particular benefit from the system. The minority of conservationists seeking to block the building of a new housing estate in their area form a clear and identifiable group. They know who they are, and know what their interest is in the matter. They can make their views known to legislators, attract publicity and cause trouble.

Those who might benefit from a new housing estate might well be more numerous, but they are not self-conscious. They do not know who they are. They might live all over the country at the moment, and not appreciate how they might be the direct beneficiaries of new housing in the area concerned. Public choice analysis tells us that the former group, being aware of their position and what they stand to lose or gain, will be more effective, other things being equal, as traders in the political market than the latter group.

It is easy in retrospect to see the features of American politics which made the emergence of public choice theory more likely to take place there than in Britain. The United States is a more fragmented society, composed of people who identify themselves as members of sub-groups within that society to a much greater extent than in Britain. This does not mean that public choice theory is not applicable in Britain, or that its explanatory power is any the less: it simply means that the roots of it are less evident. Many of the groups which trade influence and benefits in the political market in Britain have tended to be based on categories of employment.

There is a long-standing tradition in American politics referred to as 'building constituencies.' It means appealing to sufficient numbers of groups to win a popular vote when they are added together. Majorities in American politics have often been thought of as collections of minorities put together for the purpose. The coalitions which characterize the main American political parties may shift and change, but the principle is one of satisfying enough interest groups to build a majority out of them.

The US parties make calculated appeals to such groups as 'Jews,' 'Blacks,' 'Hispanics,' 'Women,' 'Veterans,' 'Organized Labour,' and 'Farmers.' Co-alitions are forged out of such groups, and they shift and change as the groups move across the political spectrum towards where they perceive their interests to lie. One of the classic mistakes of American politics, made by Senator Mondale in the 1984 election, is to secure the support of minority leaders, rather than that of their members. The leaders tend to emerge because of their militancy, and may not reflect the general views of the minority groups they appear to represent.

It is easy to see, as it always is with hindsight, how observation of the role played by minorities in American politics led the public choice school to the insight that their behaviour in the political realm was characteristic of economic activity, with votes being traded for benefits instead of cash for goods and services. It gives a far more accurate picture than the previous idea that minorities supported parties and candidates which they thought 'represented' them.

It is also more productive because it does not deal only with the traditional and permanent groups commonly perceived. While a person's status as a 'Black' or a 'Hispanic' does not change, it is possible to belong in addition to different and changing minority groups on a whole series of issues. Depending on one's residence, one might be part of a group supporting more subsidy for highway maintenance or the construction of a new bridge. A person's job might place him in the group supporting particular industries, perhaps against foreign competition. A tenant might be part of a group in favour of rent control, whereas a home-owner might look to lower property taxes.

The behaviour of all of these shifting and changing groups in the political process comes within the ambit of public choice theory, as does that of the elected representatives at all levels of government who react to their pressures and trade votes and influence with them. Some of the products of democratic government seem irrational and counter-productive when we try to explain them on the conventional political model. Analysts have been perplexed at the apparent inability of societies to correct obvious wrongs. A great virtue of the public choice approach is that it gives us a paradigm into which such behaviour fits, and within which it can be interpreted in terms of a market of political influence. Some of its most useful research has given us revealing insights into the structure and operation of the sector of the economy which comes under the direct responsibility of government.

6 The Public Sector

Public choice theory is particularly effective at explaining features of that part of the economy in which the goods and services are paid for out of taxation and produced by the direct responsibility of government. There are aspects of the public sector of the economy which seem very difficult to explain or to understand on any of the conventional political models.

There is, for example, the tendency towards over-production in the public sector. When people pay collectively for their goods and services, they consume more than they do when each makes payment individually. Public choice theory points the way. There is always a demand for more service. If there are no restraints, people prefer to have the bus service run twice a day instead of once, they choose to have even more street lighting, even better roads and more of them. When there are no restraints, this is almost regardless of use, and therefore the demand is potentially infinite. In an extreme case, people might want empty buses to pass every half-hour on the off-chance that they might wish to catch one. Without restraint, this is a reasonable preference to make.

There are restraints, of course, with cost featuring among those which limit such preferences. When people pay directly for goods and services, they have to allocate limited resources, and limit their demand for each in consequence. In the public sector of the economy the restraints are less effective because they are felt less strongly and because they are less visibly connected to the supply of goods and services.

A minority in an area might demand an improvement in their service. Its shortcomings could occur to them spontaneously, or a candidate for elective office might raise with them the prospect of an upgrade in their service. The benefit of such an improvement is valued, whereas the fractional additional cost which this imposes is of less consequence. The group may be small, but their desires can be added to those of others who seek improvements in their own services. In this way there can be a general demand for more service, without any significant pressure to restrain it. The groups trade support for benefit in the political marketplace, and there is no equivalent support coming from those who object to the cost.

The result of this is to have public goods and services supplied in greater quantities than individuals would have chosen had the decision rested with them individually. This does not mean that the services are higher in quality or that they respond to the demands and needs of consumers. It simply means that people spend more collectively through the political process than they would choose to spend individually. When they have to pay directly for the service, they demand less of it than when it is provided through the public sector. The public sector is thus responsible for a misallocation of goods and services which would seem irrational without the insights of public choice theory.

It is not only consumers who perceive benefit from overproduction of goods and services in the public sector. Naturally enough, those who administer that production acquire responsibility and status as the service expands. Those who are employed in it gain

promotion opportunities and the opportunity to increase earnings as more demand is made for their
services. The legislators themselves stand to gain the
support of the groups whose services are over-pro-
duced, without losing that of the general taxpayers who
fund this activity. The result is that of a massive one-
sided support for additional service, with scarcely any
effective pressure against.

The service, while being produced at greater levels
than would be demanded or supported by individual
consumers in a private market, is by no means responsive to their demands and needs. It responds instead to
the pressures of the political ˙process. In a private
market, the consumer can limit the quantity of any
goods or services purchased by deciding to spend
resources elsewhere. The supply is limited by what the
customer is prepared or able to pay for it. In the public
sector the consumer is not able to limit the quantity of
supply or the amount paid for it.

In the private sector, the consumer selects the goods
and services which meet his or her requirements, and
rejects those which do not. As a result of this process
the goods and services tend to meet consumer preferences. Those producers who fail to do so risk bankruptcy
if customers go elsewhere.

The public sector is subject to totally different
pressures. The consumers have no choice but to pay for
its production because the funding for the most part
comes out of taxation. Consumers have no effective
alternative, first because the public sector is often
characterized by monopoly, and secondly, because
when they have been forced to pay for the public
supply, very few of them can afford to pay yet again for
a private supply. This means that consumers have no
opportunity to make economic inputs into the public
sector. They have periodic political inputs, but these
form part of a very large package in which the spending

on any particular item of public goods or services is very small indeed.

Consumers thus have very little impact on public goods and services. The political system favours over-production, but it does not favour consumer responsiveness. The producers, on the other hand, exert very considerable influence on the service. Those engaged in the administration of it at management level, and those employed directly in its production, all have a direct stake in the type of service which is produced.

The bureaucracy of a public service has an interest in a service which is run in a way convenient to administer, and which maximizes the career opportunities for the administrative and managerial class. The workforce has an interest in a service which minimizes the effort and discomfort of the employees, while maximizing job security and reward. Both of these groups are in a position to bring real pressure to bear on the system. Unlike the consumers who have no alternative but to take what is supplied, these two groups both have influence to trade. Both can make life difficult for the legislators.

The bureaucracy has the power to impede, to delay and to thwart changes which would adversely affect their own status and position. The workforce can interrupt, or threaten to interrupt, the service, and bring public protest down upon elected leaders. The result is that the public services tend to be 'captured' by the producers. By this is meant that over a period of time they tend increasingly to meet the needs of the producers rather than those of the consumers. The producers have real power within the system; the consumers do not. The producers have more influence to trade than the consumers.

Little by little over the years, the service ceases to be one which satisfies the needs and requirements of the public as a whole, and becomes one directed to

achieving what the limited class of producers prefer to
see done. This 'producer capture' is explicable and,
indeed, predictable, in terms of public choice theory,
but would be very difficult indeed to explain on more
conventional political models. Why should the citizenry
choose to establish a service which will slip beyond
their control and divert their resources toward the
satisfaction of the group of people employed within it?
It would seem extraordinary without the realization that
the process involved giving some groups extra bargaining power in the political market place at the expense of
the general public.

The products of producer capture are plain to see
throughout the public sector. Services which exist
nominally for the benefit of the public are increasingly
geared to the benefit of those whose livelihood is gained
within them. The Post Office provides a very typical
model. The second Saturday delivery disappears. The
Sunday collection is ended. Post offices cease to open
on Saturdays. The telegram service disappears. None of
this is the result of pressure by consumers. On the
contrary, it is probably the opposite of what consumers
want. But it does make life easier for the producers if
they do not have to work at weekends.

Throughout the public sector the tendency is for the
convenience and needs of the producers to take priority
over those of the consumers. None of this is immediate.
It is a pattern which builds up over the years as the
pressures are exerted and the results of them emerge.
The garbage collectors call in the early morning and
wake householders with the noise they make. This is
because they have negotiated working agreements
which specify that they are to be paid on a 'task and
finish' basis. What is supposed to be a fair estimate of
the time for a task is calculated, and the number of tasks
expected in a working day is calculated accordingly.
The calculation is contested and argued every year,

until it is such that the workforce can start early in the morning and finish their day's work by midday. This would be virtually impossible in the private sector because firms would find the costs reflected in prices, and the public would turn to cheaper competitors. The public sector, however, rarely allows the customer the luxury of alternative choices, and is itself unlikely to go bankrupt in the normal run of events. The result is that agreements are negotiated over the years which increasingly put the conditions of service into the hands of those who produce it. Many of the specifications written into conditions of work would be incomprehensible without any analysis of the pressures exerted on the system. The working agreements which typify the public sector find no counterpart in private business, except perhaps in the production of newspapers and television programmes.

It is inconceivable that a private clinic would wake its patients before six o'clock in the morning because the staff found it more convenient to clean the hospital in the early morning. Nor is it plausible that they would keep patients waiting for several hours in corridors awaiting X-rays or other tests, or keep them waiting for similar periods to be taken back to their wards, all because the porters who performed this service had imposed rules designed to improve their own conditions of employment. Yet both of these practices can be found within the hospitals of the health service produced in the public sector. The difference is not caused by the fact that the private clinics have more money. It is caused by the fact that they have not been captured by producers, and therefore give a high priority to meeting the requirements and the needs of their customers.

If one feature of public sector supply is the prime consideration given to the convenience of the workforce, another is the tendency towards overmanning. The public sector is generally less efficient than its private counterpart, in that it takes more resources to produce each unit of output. This is established by comparison. The unit costs of the public sector supply can be set alongside those of equivalent industries or services in the private sector; the unit costs can be compared with what they were before the service was taken into the public supply; or the contrast can be drawn between what is produced in the state sector by one country and in the private sector by another.

Comparison shows a repeated pattern of higher expenditure for equivalent output when goods or services are produced in the public sector. It takes more people, other things being equal, to produce state health, state steel or state transport, than it does to produce their private counterparts. Public choice theory tells us why.

It is generally in the interests of producers and consumers to have efficient manning levels. Producers in a competitive market keep their costs down by making more efficient use of labour, and thus can either increase profits directly or keep prices down to attract more custom and augment their share of the market, and the lower prices benefit consumers. But the public sector does not usually operate in a competitive market, and does not usually allow its consumers the luxury of choice. The normal incentives which lead to the efficient use of labour are thus absent, and other pressures dominate.

It is in the interests of management to have responsibility for a large workforce. The additional responsibility will bring extra reward. The workforce perceive it to be in their interest to have overmanning. On the face of it, it appears to mean that each worker has less to do, and that there are more jobs available, and thus greater job security. For those who negotiate on their behalf, this perception is also a reality. It is not in the interest of union activists to concede reductions in manpower achieved by more efficient use of labour. Lower manning levels equal lower union membership figures. Public sector negotiations are marked by a notorious reluctance by the unions to accept new equipment or new working methods which will generate job losses.

Although there might be a desire on the part of government and the administration of the public sector goods and services to achieve efficiency, it normally takes extreme measures to attain it. It is usually easier to concede to the demands of those with real power at the expense of those without it. This means giving more to the producers at the expense of the consumers where the public sector supply is concerned. An American executive of the National Association of Solid Waste Management Operatives declared at their 1986 annual conference that the real tourist sight in London was not the royal family or the historic buildings; it was the sight of five men on the back of a garbage collection truck, picking up sacks by hand and throwing them into the back. He found this sight more historic than the buildings.

The degree of overmanning and the costs which it imposes upon the general public as consumers may be seen by what happens when contractors are brought in from the private sector to perform a public service formerly carried out by a workforce employed by the state. The contractors are able to perform the same task more cheaply and with less manpower. They do not achieve this by making the employees work harder; they do it by making more efficient use of their labour. It might involve new types of equipment or more often, better management techniques.

They are able to achieve these working conditions because they compete with other contractors and face bankruptcy if they lose their market share. The work-force accepts these conditions in the private sector because their jobs are at stake if they do not. An interesting feature of the switch from public supply to private contractors is that many of the workforce which move across to the new private firm express more job satisfaction than they enjoyed in the producer dominated state sector. Although their work is managed and used more efficiently, and manning levels are lower, they find new opportunities for earning bonus pay for extra work, and new chances for promotion to upgraded jobs carrying greater responsibility.

One feature of the public supply of goods and services which is not predictable on conventional political theory is that it will be characterized by chronic under-capitalization. There appears to be no reason on the surface why people would want to provide services for themselves which lack adequate capital to maintain themselves. Given that the funding for each service represents a small item to the taxpayer, it is difficult to see why they should be under-capitalized to the extent to which they are. The tendency towards over production has already been noted; why is there no similar tendency towards over-capitalization?

The answer is to be found in terms of the pressures which are exerted on both the current and the capital side of the account. The funding for every service is limited by what legislators feel that taxpayers can tolerate. Although each recipient of a benefit values it more highly than he or she objects to the incremental payment which sustains it, there is a general background of interest to keep taxation to the levels which the pressure of those services require.

On the total funding there is a stronger pull towards the current side of the account. Current spending sustains the provision of existing services and the payment of those involved. Capital spending, on the other hand, sustains future services. The pull on the current side comes from a public which will protest if there are service cuts, and from a workforce which can interrupt the service if their demands are not adequately met. There is no such pull on the capital side because the beneficiaries of future service can exert little current pressure. They are a diffuse and unidentifiable group who do not readily perceive their loss when capitalization is cut.

The parents of an existing school threatened by closure can exert pressure to trade in the political market; the future parents who might benefit by expenditure made now on a new school cannot. For the most part they do not themselves know who they are, nor do they perceive the connection between today's capital spending and the benefit which will accrue to them tomorrow.

Given the unequal balance of forces pulling at total funding, it is always easier for legislators and administrators to seek savings on capital expenditure in order not to cut into current spending. It involves less political cost to postpone the purchase of new equipment or the building of new premises, than it does to oppose pay claims or to implement service cuts. Over a period of years this lopsided pressure results in a constant decline in the proportion of funding devoted to capital spending within the public sector.

The effect of this can be seen in terms of the tendency of the public services to be characterized by out-of-date and poorly maintained equipment. The private sector industries cannot afford to fall behind in the race to modernize and make use of the latest technology. Companies which do so will lose out in the marketplace. In the political marketplace, however, the gains are to be made by cutting into capital expenditure, which has few self-conscious beneficiaries, in order to fund current spending, which has many.

The phrase 'private affluence and public squalor' was coined to describe adequately funded private goods and services, but what were seen as inadequately funded public ones. It might be applied to the state of their equipment, because the public sector will tend to be under-capitalized regardless of its total level of funding. Even if vast extra funding for capital projects could somehow be justified and supported politically, it would not find its intended target. Rather would it be distributed heavily toward the current side as the pressures there exerted the same pull upon it as they have applied to previous funding.

One result of this is that we see a sleek and modern private sector alongside what seems to be a shabby and out-of-date public sector. Equipment in the public realm is made to serve longer than it should. New purchases are postponed, and the consumers have to accept services which seem years behind the times in terms of the technology they use and the modernity of their equipment. It might be puzzling to account for on conventional models of political decision-making, but becomes readily explicable in terms of the economic nature of political markets. Current spending has more traders than capital spending.

The public choice model is particularly effective in accounting for the behaviour of the bureaucracy. The traditional model sees the bureaucracy as the instruments of government, which itself reflects popular will within certain limits. On this basis comes the picture of the dedicated and dispassionate Civil Service whose function is to put into effect the policies determined by their political masters.

While civil servants may indeed be dedicated, and may form an essential and valuable part of the 'machinery of government,' the public choice model in no sense regards them as machines. They are people, and are motivated by aims and aspirations similar to those which motivate other people. They are a distinct minority group with assets of value to trade in political markets. By treating them as if they operated like private businessmen to maximize their advantage, we obtain a much more detailed picture of their response to given situations, and a more comprehensible account of their overall behaviour.

In the bureaucracy, reward comes partly from seniority, partly from responsibility. It is in the personal career interest of each of them to extend their responsibility and status. It is against their interest to preside over a reduction in the size of their department unless there are compensating advantages to offset the reduction of responsibility which this would imply. On the contrary, the bureaucracy will be more likely to suggest new areas of departmental activity calling for expansion of both budget and personnel.

A hypothetical programme might start with a real demand from a certain section of the public. It might be instigated by a candidate for elective office suggesting the new service in an implicit trade for supporting votes. The group might use protest and demonstrations to bring the matter to government attention, or it might be taken up and highlighted by the media. At some point it is taken up by legislators, who in turn put pressure on government to do something about the problem.

This is the point at which the Civil Service comes in. They will be asked to study the alleged problem, and to propose some means of dealing with it. It is very much in their interest to add new programmes to their field of responsibility, and even to compete with other departments to be the one selected to do so. This is the origin of the process known as 'empire building' within the Civil Service, and under which they act to expand their own areas of activity, the size of the staff under them, and the salary scale open to them.

The process parallels that of senior executives in a private corporation, who will compete with each other for influence and status within the firm, each seeking to have as large a number as possible responsible to them and dependent on them. Just as it is routine in the private sector to expect executives to move into new areas and to suggest moving into new markets, led by their own section of the company, so does the bureaucracy mirror this pattern of behaviour. While they may indeed be dispassionate and dedicated, a more accurate explanation of the way they behave is generated by the assumption that they behave like businessmen, bidding and trading in a political market instead of an economic one.

The difference introduced by public choice theory is that it deals with the bureaucracy as an interest group and takes into account their own motivations. Instead of treating them as the traditional view does, in the role of referees standing outside to administer the rules in a fair and unbiased way, it treats them as players in the game, as yet another group dealing and trading in the political market. It recognizes their interest as participants, as well as their role of administrators.

The tendency of the public sector to undergo steady expansion in democratic societies is not only explained by the interest which the bureaucracy has in expanded responsibility. Nor is it only accounted for by the perception of greater benefits than costs on the part of their recipients. There is more to the public sector than the administration of the direct transfer of benefits, with gains by both administrators and recipients. Everyone whose livelihood comes from public funds is part of the public sector.

The list includes automatically all members of the armed forces and the police. It includes all of those employed in state health or state education. It includes not only those directly employed in state-run industries, which might include mines, railways and even automobile manufacture. Added to these must be all those who are employed in industries dependent for their survival on state subsidies.

Even this list is far from complete. On it must be included those employed by different levels of government, county and city. Thus employees from street sweepers to architects, from park keepers to lawyers, must all feature as part of the public sector. All of the above have a vested interest in seeing spending in their particular section kept up or increased. Each may object to the costs in taxation which fall upon them because of increases elsewhere, but each will fight their own corner more strenuously than they will oppose the spending elsewhere. Collectively they constitute a powerful force for the steady expansion of public sector operations.

Shrewd politicians have understood, centuries before the articulation of public choice theory, that it might be possible to forge a majority out of such groups. From the point of view of an elected representative, there is great advantage in having more than half of those who vote dependent upon the state for their livelihood. Whether they are public servants, public employees, or public beneficiaries, if there are enough of them to constitute a majority, they will generally elect politicians who live and trade by redistributing benefits in the political market.

The process may be self-sustaining, perhaps self-accelerating, even though it is probably against the interest of most of the parties involved. It causes them to sustain a higher level of consumption of most services than they would have chosen themselves, and there is the additional cost imposed by producer domination of those services, under-capitalization and over-manning. Adding the cost of the layer of bureaucratic control, it can be seen that people are voting for more services than they want, and at prices higher than they need pay. But once again, the loss set against each programme is tiny, compared with the large gain brought to them by their own benefit. The pattern of trade in political markets leads people to act individually in ways which can be opposed to the general good, including their own.

One group which has nothing to trade with in the political market is the next generation. It brings no current gains in terms of support, and can therefore strike no bargains. There is a strong tendency, therefore, for gains to be offered to this generation at the expense of the next one. By persuading today's voters that their benefits will be paid for by tomorrow's voters, today's support is gained, while tomorrow's support is of no account.

In democratic societies there is a marked tendency in pensions and social security for benefits to be handed out which bear no relation to payments made by the recipient. Typically, a new and generous scale of benefit is introduced which is justified on the basis of higher payments. The immediate beneficiaries naturally support it. Those of whom higher payments are required support it on the basis that their own promised benefits will be higher still. These, in turn, will be funded by their children and grandchildren who at the moment have no say in the matter.

Even simple demographic calculations are sufficient to show that the system can only be sustained, and the promises met, by a burden upon tomorrow's taxpayers which they may well refuse to accept. The morality is that of the chain letter, with those who embark upon it paying now in the belief that there will be more who will embark upon it further down the road to pay them in return.

John Maynard Keynes said that 'In the long run we are all dead.' In his case it is true, but the cornerstone of the system of pensions and insurance is that it will also be true of those who made gains by introducing and extending it. They make their gains now in today's political market, and by the time tomorrow's generation emerge to perceive themselves as losers, today's politicians will be beyond their reach, safely transformed into statesmen.

Any politician who tries to tackle the problem before it reaches its crisis point will come up against the expectations and the interests of the promised beneficiaries. The formula of asking people to pay more now and receive less later is not one likely to command much value in the political market. Observers have often noted the short-sightedness of politicians, and of their failure to plan for the long term, even when trends can clearly be seen to be unfolding. The answer in public choice terms is that future stock is discounted. The only value it holds in the present is the concern of today's voters that their children and grandchildren will inhabit a tolerable world; but this concern is difficult to set much value upon when politicians are so intent on focusing people's concern entirely upon today's world.

The features of the public sector of the economy which appear both irrational and counter-productive to observers armed only with the conventional paradigm, become susceptible to prediction and interpretation when the public choice model is brought to bear upon them. That people act unwittingly against their own interest is explained in terms of the relative value set upon their own benefit as opposed to those of others. That people collectively contrive by their behaviour a situation they would not have accepted by choice is explained by the value which votes and influence command in the political market.

The public choice model does more than make the present system comprehensible. It also sets out a detailed and clearly woven pattern of explanation which tells why and how that system has been able to resist so many of the attempts made to reform it or to improve it.

7 Response of Bureaucracy

The features of the public sector which run counter to the general interest have long been noted. Its comparative lack of cost-effectiveness, its inefficiency, even its frequent lack of adequate capital funding, have been the subject of many studies. The way in which it fails to respond to consumer demands and needs, or takes an excessive time before it does respond, reluctantly and sluggishly, have also been noticed, both at the level of anecdote and in more serious statistical studies.

In a similar way, the tendencies of the bureaucracy to behave in particular ways have also been documented. The 'empire building' which goes on within departments, the struggle between them to take on areas of responsibility, and the constant pressure towards expansion of the state sector, are known not only at the level of political science, but in popular humour in addition. One of Britain's most successful television situation comedies took as its theme the behaviour and attitudes of the Civil Service, and assumed that its audience would understand the fundamental truth which lay behind its humorous exaggerations.

Before the public choice type of analysis was put forward, there was a general assumption that the problems within the public sector and the bureaucracy which administers it are accidental, and not essential facets of the system. That is, the adverse features were

99

thought to reflect instances where the public part of the economy had gone wrong, and done things it was never intended to do. Indeed, this is true, but the supposition was that these were contingent activities which could be eliminated, rather than inherent defects of the system itself.

On the face of it, and at a straightforward level of rationality, it seems that defects can be identified and corrected by the appropriate remedial measures. If the public sector is overmanned, then its manpower levels should be trimmed. If it uses antiquated and dilapidated equipment, it should be re-equipped with new material. If it is inefficient and non-cost-effective, new management techniques and working practices should be brought in to improve it. If there is insufficient response to the needs and requirements of consumers, some mechanism should be put into place which will bring those to the attention of the management so that changes can be made accordingly.

The assumption throughout is, on the face of it, the reasonable one that if there are faults they can be corrected. The same has been thought of the bureaucracy itself. Again, the adverse practices have been identified, and the assumption made that it is simply a question of introducing remedial measures. The bureaucracy tends to be larger than that sustained by equivalent private sector operations, so it should be cut down to size. There seems to be a totally excessive amount of paperwork and duplication. In which case new systems should be established which make much of it no longer necessary. If bureaucrats are prone to build empires, then circumstances must be established in which they can no longer do so. If departmental responsibility is always pushing out to extend its range of responsibility, then measures should be adopted to limit it.

All of these responses, like those to the defects within the public sector as a whole, take the commendable standpoint that what is wrong can be put right. If the attitude was fundamentally sound, one would have expected the public sector to be very much better than it is, however. After all, the deficiencies observed in the public sector and the bureaucracy have been identified for some time. Many studies have been published to document them, and they have been written of as well-established features of the system. Occasionally the studies have themselves suggested measures which could rectify the defects identified. The question arises as to why, after being studied and known about for so long, and with remedies suggested, the adverse practices should still be a feature of the public economy.

The answer is that the remedies failed. Although they were tailor-made to remove specific defects, they did not succeed in doing so when they were implemented. The reason for their failure is itself instructive, and it is well worth charting the course of them as they are applied.

It is not a difficult thing to recognize that part of the public sector is over-manned. Simple comparison with private counterparts will reveal it. The attempt to reduce manning levels meets with more resistance than it encounters in the private sector. In private industry there is the ultimate threat of closure; there are limits beyond which the workers cannot push without losing everything. Private firms must be competitive, and occasionally cut manning levels. This is opposed, but accepted after some negotiation concerning the conditions because it is in the interest of the workforce as well as the management.

None of this is true for the public sector. There is not normally a risk of closure or bankruptcy, nor any need to be competitive. It is not in the interest of either workers or management to acquiesce in cuts in manning levels. Workers value the security of a job in the public sector, especially when it is accompanied by fringe benefits more generous than private industry could afford, including perhaps index-linked pensions. It is not in their interest to accept any job cuts. Union leaders lose unless they keep manning levels, and potential membership, to a maximum. Management, normally paid on the basis of responsibility, will lose if they end up in charge of a smaller operation.

The capacity which workers, union leaders and management have for thwarting any attempt to impose job cuts is immense. They have control over the service itself, and access to the media via protest and demonstration, and access to the general public and through them the legislators via strike action or the threat of it. The level of resistance encountered in practice to job cuts is such that a great deal has to be endured in order to achieve a very little. Legislators soon learn that the costs in political terms exceed the gains in economic terms.

Attempts to deal with capital depletion in the public sector fare a little better, but not enough to solve the problem. A lop-sided pull of influences makes it easier for capital funds to be raided in order to concede demands made on the current side for services and salaries. After a time the serious erosion of capital stock becomes apparent, and remedies are called for. Difficulties arise because the problem is treated simply as if it were simply there, without cause.

The attempt to solve it by voting additional funds for capital spending is like trying to cure a sickness by working only on the symptoms. Any new funds are subjected to exactly the same pull as the previous funds. The extra cash intended for the capital account is used instead to relieve pressure on wages. It becomes yet another source of finance, making it easier to concede to the wage demands of the workforce. The unions themselves, at some critical impasse in negotiations, will suggest that the purchase of new equipment or the building of new premises can be delayed by a further year or two in order to free extra cash needed to break the deadlock.

The lack of consumer input is dealt with by the establishment of new institutions designed to represent their interests. In the private economy, consumers express their needs and requirements by their purchases, or by the lack of them. Firms respond to what customers want to buy, otherwise those customers go to someone else who will. There is no need for institutions to tell industry what consumers think of their service. In the first place they say it by their spending patterns, and in the second place the industry concerned will do its own market research to find out what it should be doing.

Because consumers cannot express themselves by purchases or the lack of them in the public sector, 'consumer watchdogs' are set up to represent their interest. When the Post Office decides to raise the price of first class mail, the official body which is supposed to represent the Post Office users tells them what 'the public' thinks of the idea. The actual public has little chance to express its opinion in the absence of alternative mail services. The Post Office, meanwhile, may or may not pay whatever attention the users' council merits. It has no power to influence events, and is not elected by the public nor is representative of it. If it were, it would probably be worse, giving the illusion of democratic control where there was none.

There is a sense in which these watchdog bodies are 'captured' by the industries and services they are established to monitor. They study the industry over the years, negotiate with it, and come to understand its problems and difficulties. Very subtly, their role switches from representing the public to the organization to one of acting as spokesman for the organization to the public. A watchdog is less effective if it has dined for years at the same table as the intruder it is supposed to guard against. The real public does not take the trouble to learn about any problems and organizational difficulties which Honda might be going through. They are not interested. If Honda fails to deliver the right quality at the right price, they buy Hyundai instead; and Honda knows and accepts this.

Attempts are made to deal with the problems of the bureaucracy, as they are with those of public sector goods and services. They start from the same disadvantage, in that they derive from a standpoint which treats them as contingent; that is, one which regards them as unfortunate features which have somehow attached themselves onto the system and which have to be removed. The standard practices and procedures of the bureaucracy give rise to features immortalized by C. Northcote Parkinson in his famous laws. But the books would not have become humorous classics were it not for the seam of truth which permeates them. The same is true of the 'Yes Minister' series on television. Foreign audiences often wonder whether to regard these works as humour or as a species of social documentary.

Knowing the practices is one thing; correcting them is another. Given that the procedures of the Civil Service are more complex and cumbersome than those of private industry, one possible solution might be to study the practices of the private sector and to introduce them into the public bureaucracy. In many of the advanced economies the public sector administration has been subject to detailed and repeated study of its operations. Experts from the private sector have been called in to do management efficiency studies. Time and motion specials have examined the practices and procedures. Critical path analysis has been applied to their work. The phrases which are in vogue change from time to time, but the cycle of study and report continues.

Recommendations are made, expressions of intent are declared. The practices continue, perhaps with some token and temporary improvement in some areas. Departments might be amalgamated, some abolished, with their functions transferred elsewhere. Yet at the end of it there is still a bureaucracy which engages in empire building, expansion of operations, extension of areas of responsibility. Reform of the Civil Service is like a tide which washes backwards and forwards, but the rocks are still there each time the tide recedes.

The fundamental error of this method of examining faults and seeking to apply corrections is that it assumes that the public sector is capable of behaving like the private sector. Most of the adverse practices of the public sector are made evident by comparison and contrast with the private sector. In other words, private industry is used as the base model by which the public sector performance is judged. Where the latter falls short of the former, the attempt is made to transplant the techniques of the one onto the other: to make the public sector behave more like its private counterpart.

There is no reason to expect that it should be capable of doing so. It is a totally different kind of animal. The mistake derives from the assumption that it can be made to do what the private sector does, but in the absence of any of the forces which make the private sector behave in that way. The public sector is subject to pressures upon it and within it which are totally different from those which bear on the private sector. This is why it behaves differently.

A great deal of the study and research of the public choice school has been devoted to minute examination of those pressures and to the consequences which follow from them. It may well be that the motivating forces within both public and private sectors are the ordinary aims and aspirations which people have in common. Their desire to maximize their advantage and to improve their position in life, their conditions of work, and the rewards which accrue to them may indeed be common to both sectors; but the rules and conditions which prevail in each are so different that these same motivations will inevitably produce different outcomes.

The failure to recognize the structural differences is the source of the error. The public sector is different because the forces operating upon it make it so. No one designed it that way; but the group interests and pressures produced that outcome. The private sector is not a rational creation of man. It is certainly man-made, but not according to some preconceived plan. It does what it does as a result of the interplay of many different human activities. The features which make it as it is are such things as freedom of choice, competition, the ability to allocate one's resources according to preferences, and to limit consumption to what one is ready to pay for.

Many of these features are either not present at all in the public sector, or operate there to a very much less degree. The outcome in the public sector is therefore very different from that which emerges in the private economy. The features referred to play an important role in the structure of the private sector by limiting the degree to which individuals can operate the system to their exclusive advantage. Because there is choice, price is restrained. Because consumers can withdraw demand, the service cannot serve only the needs of the producers. Because expenditure is limited to what people will willingly part with, the quality of what is on offer must be sufficient to attract it.

It is a significant aspect of the public sector that the factors which impose restraints and disciplines upon the pursuit of exclusive advantage are by no means as effective. One would expect the public sector to be characterized by the pursuit and the achievement of advantage to its participants at the expense of the general public. The state sector of the economy behaves as it does not because of any accidental features which have crept in by chance during its growth, but because of inherent structural aspects of it.

The reason why the attempt to transplant private sector practices does not take is that the pressures which sustain those practices are absent. The public supply of goods and services is less cost-effective than private industry can achieve because it does not have to be efficient. The pressures leading towards efficiency are weak compared with those which lead towards over-manning and to the adoption of restrictive practices.

The desire to have more capital spending, more modern equipment and new buildings is weak compared with the pressures which pull available funds towards the current side of the account. The feeling that consumer interests ought somehow to be taken account of and safeguarded becomes no more than a pious wish in a system where most of the forces lead to the satisfaction of producer needs and desires at their expense.

A similar pattern repeats itself in the public bureaucracy. At the base-line is the fact that public administration does not operate like private manage-ment, nor does it achieve its levels of efficiency, because it does not have to. It faces none of the penalties which fall upon inefficiency in the private sector, and faces instead pressures which lead to expansion of staff and extension of function. The top executives of private firms might similarly compete for influence and try to expand their own areas of influence. The difference is that in the private sector there is the ultimate test in the market. If it results in better sales or greater savings or a more competitive company, it may last. Otherwise the pressures will take it out. There is no equivalent market test by which to measure success in the Civil Service.

All of the various attempts to improve the public sector and to eliminate some of its adverse features have it in common that they are derived from the performance of the private sector, and they assume that the public sector defects are accidental ones, and are susceptible to removal. The public choice style of analysis suggests that both of these characteristics make it unlikely that such attempts will succeed. In the first place, without the pressures which sustain those features in the private sector, there is no reason why they should be kept in place in the state sector. Secondly, the examination of interest groups and the consequences of their motivations suggests that the major disadvantages of public sector supply are necessary, rather than accidental. That is, they are an almost inevitable consequence of the way the public sector is set up and of the way in which it operates.

To put it in the terms of public choice theory, the problems in public sector supply are a by-product of the political market. In the economic market the goods and services which are traded bring one type of result. In the political market the votes and support which are traded bring quite another. The features which make the economic market successful and responsive to the general good are absent from the political market. In their place are features which make it successful and responsive to the minority interest groups which trade within it, at the expense of the general good.

The same features which enable minority interest groups to pursue their advantage in the public sector to the detriment of the general good also enable them to resist successfully the attempts which are made to graft private sector methods and practices onto their operations. Bluntly, it is against their interest to accept such practices and limitations, and they have the power to oppose any attempt to apply them.

Once again, a hypothetical illustration can be used to

trace some of the techniques and practices which thwart the attempt to make the state sector behave more like private industry. Whether these are applied consciously by the participants, or whether they emerge as a result of the unconscious desire to protect the privileged position they enjoy, is not relevant. The fact that they are applied and that they are successful is what matters.

The case might be one which occurs from time to time in which the study of government operations shows that there is opportunity to make savings, to achieve the same output or better, while cutting back on the inputs. When the political decision is made to seek major economies, it signals the start of infighting between the various departments as each one struggles to make sure that the cuts are imposed elsewhere. Even if some departments are finally selected as the ones to bear the brunt of cost savings, there is still a struggle between the operations which come under their ambit, and an effort made to make sure that someone else has to take the painful medicine.

With each department fighting to maintain or increase its budget, the pressures which they collectively bring to bear on government militate against major savings. The top bureaucrats in each department produce projections to show the dire consequences which will follow from major budget cuts. The ministers in turn fight within the cabinet for their own departmental budget, using briefs prepared by their civil servants. Other cabinet members know even less than the minister does about the working of other departments. They are not in a strong position to evaluate the figures.

What starts as a simple attempt to cut out wasteful spending has already turned into a fight between ministers at cabinet level, with the pressures building up for compromise and for scaling back the degree of saving originally postulated. The process is repeated on a smaller scale inside each department, with sections putting their efforts into justifying their appropriation, rather than on seeking opportunities for saving. The bureaucrats are perfectly aware that it is not in their interest to have less spending within their section, or on their overall departmental budget.

Two methods have been tried in an attempt to overcome the pressures which lead each section and department to seek to maintain its own appropriation and make the cuts fall elsewhere. One is the device of imposing the cuts equally across the board, and requiring, for example, that every department reduce its spending by perhaps five per cent. The other method is to impose total cash limits on each department, and leave it to the department itself to determine how these shall be achieved.

Both of these methods acknowledge that civil servants will fight to defend their own appropriation, and attempt to contrive a way of making this ineffective. If everyone has to accept an across-the-board cut, this could eliminate the tendency of each department to pass the buck, and try to make the burden fall elsewhere. This will at least prevent, in theory, the struggle at cabinet level as ministers act as mouthpieces for their departments and oppose each other in order to keep up their own funding.

Similarly, cash limits on each department are designed to confine the battles within the ministry. The theory is that each section must struggle against the others for its budget, with the overall ceiling of the cash limit as the final aggregate. Instead of each section justifying its own total, and sending the minister out to fight for the total demanded, the cash limit predetermines that total and internalizes the struggle.

Behind both of these strategies lies the assumption that if unnecessary spending and wastage can be identified, they can be eliminated, or at least curbed, if only sufficient discipline can be brought to bear. The idea is that across-the-board budget cuts or cash limits impose an overall ceiling which cannot be broken through, and under which the departments must learn to live. They will have to cut down on duplication and excessive administration in order to carry on the work of the department at less cost.

The reality is different. The bureaucrats find it easier in practice to push through the limits than to achieve savings within them. Ministers respond to the suggestion of across-the-board cuts with the response that this is fine in general, but should not apply to the essential work of their own department. There should not be cuts in the vital area of health, for example, or education, or pensions, or social security. It would be false economy, they say, to attempt cuts in environmental spending. Security would be threatened by defence cuts. A highly public defence of each department's essential work turns what was designed to be a cut falling equally on everyone into the more familiar picture of a cabinet fight for privileged position. This is a scenario in which bureaucrats feel comfortable, and which they know how to manipulate.

With cash limits the response is twofold. First, there is direct opposition to the limit imposed on each department by its Civil Service. They supply budget figures showing the impossibility of keeping within them. Secondly, after some degree of cash limit has been approved by government, they respond with pressures which burst through the limits. As each individual case comes up for consideration, the circumstances will be contrived to ensure that the original appropriation is exceeded.

It might be, for example, that the cash limits were used to set a maximum pay increase below any figure acceptable to a vital workforce, such as teachers. The resultant labour dispute puts pressure on the government, and when a compromise seems acceptable to the work force, the minister asks the cabinet for the increase in the cash limits of his department required for him to meet it. In this way the cash limits can be broken through by means of a series of separate incidents, each one of which presents a compelling case. The notion that the extra cash for each one might be met from savings elsewhere within the department is not a viable option. It will simply transfer the pressure elsewhere. The only option which does not do this is one which raids the capital account to fund increases in current spending.

Although the idea behind across-the-board cuts and cash limits is that administrative wastage will be curbed, the pressures are such that it is easier to overturn the policy than to achieve the savings. Exceptions are made to the across-the-board policy in favour of particular departments; extra funding is allocated to those which find situations force them to exceed the cash limits. The bureaucrats have much experience in contriving situations which will achieve this.

If one took public servants at face value, on the conventional political model, one would perhaps expect them to seek savings in order to give better value for money. Thus one might expect to see public money saved by the adoption of more streamlined practices and working methods. Some sections might be closed, with their workload taking up the slack in others. Unnecessary or unproductive activity might be sought out and eliminated. The end-product would be the achievement of the outputs of the department at somewhat less cost in inputs; this would represent an increase in efficiency.

Using the public choice model which treats the participants as traders in a political market, working like businessmen to secure their own advantage, a different pattern is expected. It is the one which conforms much more to the reality of experience. When the cuts are imposed, the plans presented propose to achieve them not by administrative savings, but by cuts in services. Instead of office work facing the brunt of the economies, it is those who receive the services who face the burden. Furthermore, the cuts which are proposed are commonly in sensitive and valued areas, with a vociferous and articulate public as their recipients, and with high media visibility.

When the proposed cuts are announced, there is an immediate outcry from those whose services are threatened. The media respond accordingly, and the ministry feels itself under pressure as the protests mount. The government in turn experiences the unpopularity increases, and its members begin to show political concern. Legislators receive hostile mail, and opinion polls show how much support there is for maintaining the service. The saving to be achieved seems too small a gain to justify the losses being incurred at the political level. The government calculates that it can afford to lose only a certain level of support before the exercise is no longer worthwhile, and its enthusiasm for the savings diminishes. This was, indeed, the effect intended by the civil servants when the cuts were proposed.

Public choice analysis suggests that the proposed cuts will tend to be in services rather than in administration, and that they will be proposed first in those services which have effective supporting groups. The effective groups are those which perceive their benefit, value it highly, are visible to the media, and which have articulate spokesmen and the capacity to cause trouble for government. The benefit might be an indirect one, in that it might not be the supposed recipients which constitute the interest group, but those whose livelihood is made in representing them, and who are thus major beneficiaries of the programme under threat.

Economies in the health service might involve hospital closures or the suspension of life-saving operations in certain areas. Cuts in the education budget could reduce the number of mathematics teachers. Reductions in the naval estimates might cut the number of ships. The pattern is similar throughout. It is that proposed cuts will be offered first in the most valuable area of service, and that in which the government is at greatest vulnerability. It is a consequence of this that economy campaigns have rarely been sustained for long, and have rarely achieved major administrative savings. In general, the cost in terms of effort and unpopularity proves to be more than the results justify to those seeking to achieve them. A mountain of bitter and debilitating struggle against administrative obstruction labours to bring forth a mouse of cost saving.

A fictional episode of *Yes, Minister*, the television comedy series on the Civil Service, showed the result of cost cuts in the health service. The hospital had the same administrative staff, as busy as ever, but it had got rid of all of the patients. No administrative savings had been possible, even though the service had been eliminated entirely. Anyone who supposes that it is only in fiction that bureaucrats respond in this way should study the record of the US Customs and Immigration Service. When a cut of 10 per cent was announced in its appropriation, its director responded by immediately taking off duty all of the officers whose job it was to stop drugs coming into the country through the airports. No administrative saving was offered, just the most valuable service, and the one government was most vulnerable on. This was considered an extreme case, and the officer in question lost his job. He was not dismissed, however, just transferred to another department.

PART III
MICROPOLITICS

8 From Critique to Creativity

Public choice theory is a critique. It is an analytical tool which enables us to understand and to explain why it is that some things happen in the public sector in the way that they do. It enables us to trace the interests of the various groups involved in the formulation and practice of public policy, and through them to anticipate or to account for the responses evoked by it. Equipped with this approach, it becomes possible to see why it is that events take place which would be otherwise inexplicable or even irrational. It shows us immediately why it is that conservative programmes should labour under the difficulties they have met. The essence of the traditional conservative formula is that of curbing the role which government plays in economic life and the costs which it imposes upon its citizens. It seeks to reduce the size and scope of government operations, to decrease the regulatory burden which it places upon business, and to stop it pre-empting so large a share of the funds with which individuals and businesses would otherwise determine their own priorities.

All of these aims run counter to the interest of most groups involved in the process of public programmes. They might indeed be of benefit to society as a whole, to the wealth-creating process, and they might even leave the overwhelming majority better off than they would otherwise be. None of this is sufficient to take them into the realm of practical politics. All of the aims singled out as part of a conservative approach to government oppose in some measure what the groups perceive to be in their vital interest. Each minority can be shown that its own benefit is under threat from the reduction of expenditure in general. While they might support in theory such a general cut in expenditure, they each fight to retain their own programme more strongly than others will fight to cut it.

The bureaucracy recognizes immediately that a conservative programme constitutes a real threat to its opportunities to move to higher salary scales by extending the area of responsibility and the size of the staff controlled. Their interest lies in there being more numerous public programmes and bigger ones. The prospect of a cut in activity and in spending is one which they will take action to limit, if not to thwart.

The source of a major conservative complaint can now be identified. Conservatives have often made the observation that state power and spending are extended rapidly under collectivist and centralist administrations, and more slowly under conservative ones. They speak of a 'socialist ratchet' by whose turns the size of the state moves in one direction only: it increases. If a government of conservative inclination managed to achieve a brief holding action, preventing an increase in state power while it held office, this was regarded as the best which could be hoped for.

To their supporters, as well as to those who participated in such administrations, this was a puzzling and an irritating phenomenon. Lacking the insights of public choice theory, they did not know wherein lay the explanation. With the help of that analysis, however, it is now possible to see why this should have come about. With opposition from each group which perceived a state benefit coming to them, and with the workings of a bureaucracy directly opposed to the central planks of the conservative programme, the explanation emerges. It is not that the proposals are 'irrelevant to the modern world,' or even 'impractical in the real world.' It is that they are politically too difficult to push by the will of government against the entrenched pressures which act in the opposite direction.

It now becomes possible to interpret the comparative failure of the governments of Richard Nixon in the United States, and of Edward Heath in the United Kingdom. Neither of them had any kind of effective technique to set against the pressures which militate against a conservative programme. Although both went in with a climate of ideas favourable in theory to less government and less costly government, neither had any sense in advance of the practical difficulties involved in implementing such a programme, or of the tactics which might be needed to overcome them. Both subscribed to the notion that events followed ideas, and neither had the benefit of the public choice school of analysis. It was there, but it was in its early stages and had not yet attracted sufficient attention.

The failures which attracted such a variety of explanations are seen much more simply in the light of public choice theory. The programmes set out what government wanted to do on the one side, and were faced by the real forces inherent in the system on the other. The result was that under both the Nixon and the Heath administrations, both the regulatory power and the role played by government in the economy increased; as did, of course, its cost.

In the absence of a valid model to account for behaviour in the public sector, neither government had any idea of what it was up against. The senior advisers and experts on which it relied to implement policies were the very people whose interests those policies threatened. Both governments found wages and prices were rising faster than it wished, without understanding the pressures which pushed them in that direction. Both brought in legislative controls on wages and prices, vastly extending bureaucratic authority, although not bureaucratic power. The strongest government in the world has never been able to do more than build temporary dams against the real events which wages and prices represent. When they burst through the flimsy barriers of government desire, they soon assume the natural level dictated by demand and scarcity.

In the final analysis, neither the Nixon government in the United States nor the Heath government in Britain really knew the constraints upon political action which are imposed by the self-seeking behaviour of those who are its participants. Had they realized how much opposition would be generated by interest groups who saw their perceived benefit threatened, or by the bureaucracy which saw its own career opportunities challenged, they might have attempted very different policies and achieved a different result. At the very least, the comparative failure of their declared programmes would have been attributed correctly to their failure to deal adequately with the political system.

The public choice approach explains both the remorseless rise of the state sector over the years, and the failure of attempts made at different times to reverse it. Indeed, it also explains the fatalism of those who regard it as evil, oppose it in principle, and yet think that nothing whatever can be done about it. This is all it does, however. The public choice school has provided a new method of analysis. It provides a critique; it shows us what is wrong. The question arises as to whether its findings can be built upon.

The new analysis at least teaches politicians their limits. It enables them to predict in advance the policies which are unlikely to work. If no more than this were to be achieved it would be useful. It would save the disappointment of hopes and the raising of unreal expectations. By understanding how interest groups would react within the system, political leaders at least can avoid the policies doomed to fall foul of them. Thus public choice analysis, although only a critique, already offers the political process a means of winnowing out in advance the policies which will fail. It saves, thereby, the debilitating and divisive struggles, and enables politicians to lower their sights to more realistic goals. All of these are worthwhile achievements in themselves, but they all tell politicians what not to do. None of them tells governments how to implement the policies which they think are correct.

If public choice is a critique, there is a creative counterpart implicit in its findings. If the prevailing political system acts to thwart certain types of policy, perhaps others can be constructed which work with the pressures it imposes, instead of trying to override them. Given that those pressures are known of in advance, and given that the source of them can be identified, the possibility emerges that policies can be devised which either work with them, circumvent them or overcome them.

On the face of it this seems unlikely. The interest of the minority groups lies in receiving specific benefits funded from general taxation. The interest of the bureaucracy lies in an augmented and more costly state sector. It would seem to require remarkable policies to set those interests to work for a reduction in state subsidies and benefits, and for a decrease in the production of goods and services in the public sector. On the face of it, the policies would have to make people work directly against their own interest.

There are, however, several possible ways in which this apparent contradiction can be resolved. That is, there are several routes by which people might be prevailed upon to acquiesce in or support policies even though the effect of those policies might lead to an overall reduction in the volume of benefits for privileged minorities, and to an overall reduction in state power and state spending.

One possibility is that people might surrender the benefit which they presently enjoy, if an alternative benefit is available to compensate them. People will fight to retain their benefit, other things being equal, because its worth to them is more than its perceived cost to others. They might, however, part with benefits as part of an exchange which they felt left them ahead. This means that the gains they receive for giving up the original benefit must be larger than it was, and be perceived to be so. It might well be that most people would gain if the benefit transfer system was ended; but this would not work because it is difficult to make this evident. They feel the gain strongly and the cost of funding the gains of others weakly.

If there is to be a policy which offers a trade-off, the new gain must not only be larger, but must seem obviously so to its target recipient. There will be no political gains from the trade unless people feel it leaves them better off. It should be possible in some cases to construct policies designed to replace benefits by altern-ative ones perceived to be larger. Although on the face of it this appears to tighten the ratchet one more turn by increasing the total amount of benefit transfer, this need not be true. The new benefit can be different in character.

It might be possible to construct policies under which people are ready to accept the loss of a state benefit because they perceive more advantage for themselves through the acquisition of a private benefit which seems larger. In this case the system of state benefits is eroded by the substitution of a private benefit in exchange.

Again, there could be cases in which people will give up a long-term and continuing gain from the state in return for a one-off gain which is larger, but which ends the system. It might be possible to create policies under which people are offered a substantial and immediate gain as an alternative to the continuing benefit. If they value the larger benefit now, and if its nearness in time outweighs the ultimate accumulated value of the continuing benefit, there is the basis for trade.

If people accept the loss of a state benefit because the policy places a perceptibly larger private benefit into their hands in return, then the policy can diminish the role of government. If people regard a one-off benefit now as an acceptable substitute for a continuing state benefit, then the policy which supplies it can gradually reduce the cost of government in the future, even if it has to increase in the immediate short term. Neither of these two approaches should be surprising. Once the public choice thinking is taken on board, and the political system is regarded as operating like a market, then normal market transactions such as these should be taken for granted.

In private economic markets people trade gains every day, giving up that which they value less in return for that which they value more. This provides the basis of free exchange. It is also a daily commonplace in the private economy that people trade off the long term against the short term. Some will give up spending power now in order to acquire regular income in the future. Others give up future income in exchange for a cash sum to be spent in the present. Such transactions are routine in economic markets; yet policies which embody them as part of a systematic approach seem novel in a political context.

All that the above policies do is to bring to the surface the principles of exchange which are already there and functioning in the political market. They start with the recognition that there is such a market, and then enter it with intent to trade. Instead of trying to oppose the forces and pressures within that market by no more than the will of government, they use those very same forces to achieve more acceptable outcomes.

The two approaches considered so far form only the beginning of a battery of techniques derived from the same principles. With the acceptance that a political market is operating comes a range of different types of policy specifically designed for that market. The conflict of ideologies on the conventional model of political activity is now supplemented by the interplay of interest groups and the development of policies tailored for the market situation of each of them. Instead of facing head on the opposition of the various groups which perceive value in their state benefits, the new policies seek to trade in the market, offering where possible something of greater perceived value which nonetheless makes possible a reduction in the size and scope of government.

There may be cases, of course, in which a group is enjoying a position of such power that they can command a benefit greater than any which can reasonably be offered in return. This leads to an alternative range of possible policies. Perhaps a new group can be established and built up which will outweigh the first. It will then be a potential trading partner with a policy which does take on the original group. The loss of votes and support among that group will be more than offset in the political market by the gain of those from the new group. Legislators will then feel able to act to curb the benefits enjoyed by the original powerful group, in the knowledge that they are gaining more support from the new group.

It could be that policies might be constructed to circumvent and neutralize the power of the original group, before attempting to deal with the benefit they enjoy at the expense of society. Once their power has been undermined, so has their capacity to command and retain so high a benefit. If their ability to cause trouble declines as their power diminishes, they have less to trade with and less need be given in exchange for it.

The common thread which links these new policy approaches is that they are the creative counterparts of public choice critique. If people do indeed trade in a political market, this limits what governments can hope to achieve by conventional means. But it opens up the prospect of a new style of policy formulation geared to the workings of that market, and which can succeed by using its mechanisms where others failed by opposing them.

Such a style of politics, if it could be achieved, would start from the base-line of public choice critique. Its origins would lie in an understanding of why previous policies had failed. By tracing through the analysis of the public choice school, the way in which the interest groups proved too great an obstacle for the conventional policies would provide the starting-point for a new series of policies. The new policies would contrive circumstances in which the interest groups would pursue new objectives made available to them, be outweighed by more powerful groups created to offset them, or find the power which sustained their benefits eroded. All of these could, in theory, lead to a reduction in the role of the state as the agent which rewarded some at the expense of others.

It is apparent immediately that there is a radical difference in the style of political activity which this implies. It involves a minute attention to detail. The benefits enjoyed by the various interest groups must be traced through by public choice analysis, as must be the influence and support traded. Only after the current position has been thoroughly understood can the task begin of constructing policies which can use its forces to change it. This is a creative exercise. There are no ideological formulae which automatically produce the correct answers. There may, indeed, be no correct answers; only better solutions and worse ones.

The dramatically different feature of this type of policy generation is the scale on which it takes place. It has to go right down to the level at which individuals give expression to their preferences in the political market, and has to trade at that level. The difference is as great as that which separates macroeconomics from microeconomics. The former deals with the large aggregates and statistics which may, or may not, represent real events. The latter deals with the choices which are made by individuals seeking to fulfil their aims. It takes account of the incentives which are present, and considers the trade-offs which people make, and the circumstances under which they make them.

It is often a feature of economists that they might recognize the prime importance of microeconomic factors, but do not extend this to the political arena. It is not uncommon to hear economists whose analysis derives from microeconomic study calling for such things as 'the end of state industries' or 'the abolition of all subsidies.' They tell British Prime Ministers to 'abolish the National Health Service', and American Presidents to 'end the food stamp programme'. Political leaders know that they cannot achieve these things simply by wanting to do so, and regard such cavalier advice as out of touch with political reality. The ideas considered in public choice theory suggest that they are right to think so.

Just as many economists find that study at the micro-level is needed for a more accurate picture of economic reality, so it could be argued that the equivalent might be useful in the field of politics. If it is true that people bid and trade in political markets as they do in economic ones, then study at the micro-scale might give a more meaningful picture, and might even lead to more practical solutions.

The suggestion is that there is a 'micropolitics' just as there is a microeconomics. Microeconomics considers the behaviour of individuals and groups in economic markets; micropolitics looks at it in political markets. Moreover, just as microeconomics is closer to the level where decisions and actions are taken in the economic markets, and is thus closer to real events, the same is true of micropolitics in political markets.

It is easy to talk on the macro-scale about ending state industries or abolishing all subsidies, but governments are not going to follow this advice because they cannot. Governments might know all of the defects of the National Health Service or the food stamp programme without being able to do a thing about them. Macro-politics proposes the broad sweeping remedies which are not implemented, and which fail when they are tried. They fail because they take insufficient account of political reality, of the decisions made by individuals and groups which trade for advantage in the political market.

Micropolitics, on the other hand, involves the formulation of policies which acknowledge the findings of the public choice theorists, and which use them to redirect the behaviour of the individuals and groups involved. Instead of trying to act on the large scale against the benefits which groups enjoy at the general expense, micropolitics sets about creating policies which alter the choices people make by altering the circumstances.

Even though consideration thus far has taken place at the level of theory, several characteristics have already emerged marking the approach to policy formulation as quite different in both style and content from the conventional approach. In the first place there is the implicit assumption that politics is not only concerned with a battle of ideas. Taking its lead from the public choice findings, micropolitics takes as its starting-point the assumption that self-interest plays a large part in the attitudes which people take towards public policy.

Given that people trade in a political market, they will regard policy in the light of its possible effect on the value of what they trade. Thus it is quite possible to have general support for a particular ideology from a group, only to find them thwarting in practice any attempt to apply it to their own circumstances. People who work in the public sector might think government is too big; but few think their own section of it should be reduced.

A second major difference lies in the attitude which is taken by micropolitics towards the various benefits which minority groups receive from the state. The conventional free market attitude is to regard them as illegitimate, and to seek their removal. Given that people defend benefits, and that there is little trade to be had in return from those who fund them, this always arouses both resentment and hostility from the groups whose advantage is under threat, and usually fails.

The attitude of micropolitics is to accept that the benefit is there, and that it will be defended, whether or not it has any claim to legitimacy. If people are to acquiesce in its removal, they must be offered something of greater advantage in exchange, or their power to sustain that advantage must first be eroded. The point missed on conventional analysis is that the status quo itself is regarded as a source of legitimacy. If something has long been enjoyed, the recipients regard it as an entrenched value, and a part of established society. They will fight to defend it, feel aggrieved at the innovation which threatens it, and find a suitable ideology to justify their stance. This is, in broad outline, the situation behind the struggle for American independence; they were fighting to preserve advantages already enjoyed against new encroachments upon them, rather than to claim new and untried benefits.

There may be a valid case for argument about the legitimacy of certain benefits. Such arguments may be important at the theoretical level, but there is no reason to expect them to result in the removal of those benefits. A change in circumstances is more likely to be effected by policies which lead to those benefits being traded, than by a direct confrontation seeking to abolish them. It is not that micropolitics ignores the moral issues, rather that it is more sympathetic to the point of view of those who receive benefits from the state. By getting down to the level at which decisions are made by individuals and groups, and by examining the incentives, it studies the way in which they see their situation. It recognizes their claim, without conceding it, that tradition is itself a source of legitimacy, and seeks to construct policies which offer something in return for the loss.

Not only is it less confrontational than conventional policy, it is less holistic. It does not seek to implement the vision of a market economy right across the board in the shortest possible time. Rather does it seek to find policies here and there which can make inroads. It seeks to create a situation in which state benefits and transfers are gradually traded off for things which are perceived to offer greater value. In place of the broad sweeps it offers the fine detail. It involves close study of each situation, and the formulation of policy designed to achieve success in that area. It is thus more piecemeal and more gradual.

In order to succeed it tends to work with the grain of entrenched interest groups, instead of against them. Sometimes it will contemplate an increase of state expenditure in the short term in order to set it on a downward path in the future. Sometimes it will make available what seems like an unfair benefit to a select group in order to encourage it to trade in an even more unfair and more long-term advantage.

Not only is it less holistic, it is less coherent. It does not seek to apply everywhere and at once the simple principles of markets free from subsidy or government interference. These are more in the realm of long-term goals than indicators for policy formulation. Micropolitics produces different policies in almost every area, because it starts with the view that every area presents different problems. The interest groups, the character of their benefit, and its past operation vary from one section of society to another. There is no simple formula for dealing with them. On the contrary, the detail will be different for each case. If the problems are different in each area, then so must be the solutions.

Micropolitics does have coherence, but it is that of consistency of approach. The policies and recommendations change between one field and another, but the method by which they are produced is the same. It begins with a detailed analysis of the status quo, of the various advantages and benefits enjoyed, of the nature of the interest groups involved, and of the power and the pressures which they are able to deploy. From there it proceeds to the construction of policies which will offer trade-offs in benefit, alter the structure of power between different groups, and set up incentives to lead individuals and groups to accept circumstances which lead to the long-term diminution of transfer gains and to a reduction in the proportion of goods and services supplied from the state sector.

The micropolitical approach is more conservative than conventional free market policies precisely because it is more piecemeal and more gradual. It rarely produces policies designed to achieve sudden change and immediate impact. Rather does it attempt to set in motion chains of events which lead ultimately to the desired goals. These chains of events are the trades and exchanges which are made in the political marketplace. Instead of ignoring these trades or seeking to end them, it works with them, making offers available which seek to influence the outcome which results from them. Traditional or long-standing benefits are not attacked, but bid for on the basis of more attractive offers. Individual groups are invited to exchange a continuing state transfer benefit for a short-term gain or an equivalent private sector advantage.

The process takes time. It takes society as it is, and introduces policies here and there to change it gradually but remorselessly in the direction of less subsidy and less government direction of the economy. The cumulative result of this political approach is to increase the degree of spontaneity within society, to expand the area of decision left outside of the ambit of government and within the realm of choices made by individuals and groups. While not a revolutionary programme by any means, it does seek steady and consistent movement in one direction.

It is one thing to have a picture of what an improved society might be like. It is another to analyse the workings of society as it already is. The role of micropolitics lies in the territory in between the two, in the area in which policies are formulated to change the world as it is into what it might become. The world might be improved if there were less government involvement in the economic processes, less regulation, and less pre-emption of the funds which people can allocate to their preferences. Wanting it so does not make it so; nor does persuading others of the merits of it. Policies can make it so, however, if they can be crafted in such a way as to persuade people to relinquish their state benefits for alternative gains, or to remove the leverage which some groups have over society in a way which attracts support rather than hostility for the government which does it.

There is a clear distinction to be drawn between this approach and simple gradualism. Gradualism involves moving in small steps and slow ones. The small steps might be taken against the grain of society, with the supposition being that if they are small enough, they will not evoke opposition large enough to prevent their success. Fabianism is an example of this, in that the idea was to achieve socialism, then an unacceptable goal, by a series of stages each of which would be small enough to pass without the opposition that the final goal would arouse.

Micropolitics is not the same as gradualism. The policies created within its framework are not designed to be tolerated, but to be preferred to the prevailing state of society. Some of its changes might be large if groups and individuals in large numbers opt for the alternative advantages offered. It has no concept of a final form to society, only of a process moving in the direction of less subsidy and government involvement in the economy. Whatever society emerges as a result of that process will be one resulting spontaneously from the interplay of different decisions and actions, not one decided by planners to be superior. Furthermore, it is basic to its approach that it uses the existing pressures in society, creating the circumstances needed to redirect them.

Its changes may come about gradually, but it is not gradualist. It does not seek to do the same things as conventional policies, only more slowly. It seeks to create new policies to do different things. Even more to the point, it seeks to do them in different ways. It does not start out with a list of things to be done, and then proceed to do them slowly. It starts out not knowing what is to be done, but armed with a technique for creating policies in response to the various situations which it encounters. It is an approach, not a set of priorities. In place of a list of policies to be implemented is a means of generating policies.

All of this is at the theoretical level. We understand from the work of the public choice school why it is that the response to conventional policies comes as it does. We appreciate that it is because they fail to recognize the political market in operation, or to accommodate themselves to it. It emerges that there might be the possibility of a system of policy generation starting from the base line of that analysis and not subject to those objections because it does take account of the political market and operate within its framework. Such a system would, it seems, enable policies to be created piecemeal, each in response to a different situation. Its unity would be that of method, rather than of content.

The question arises as to whether theory translates into practice to produce such a system. Is there, in fact, a micropolitical approach capable of achieving what theory claims to be possible? The short answer is yes. There is such an approach, already working in practice. It emerges from the critique of conventional policy by the public choice school, and seeks to make good the deficiencies which that analysis points to. The appearance of micropolitics has led to the formulation of policies to achieve successfully what previous attempts have failed to bring about. It has led to the ability of conservative governments to achieve at least a partial success for their declared programmes. It has set in motion a worldwide chain of events as the results of its policies have become apparent.

The difference sought between the governments of Nixon and Heath in the 1970s, and Reagan and Thatcher in the 1980s, can now be explained. There was not, as seen, any intervening victory in the battle for ideas, nor sufficient character differences on the part of the principal actors. There were no changes in the world to make policies impractical at one time suddenly practical at the other. The change was in policy. The later governments were equipped with a range of policy proposals created from the micropolitical approach. They knew what they wanted, like the earlier governments, but unlike them they were equipped with some of the policies which might bring it about. The emergence during the 1970s of a radical new method of policy formulation led to the later governments having available to them a range of detailed applications. Instead of running headlong into the opposition of interest groups under threat, they were able to introduce policies which offered such groups the opportunity to trade for greater advantage.

The conservative programmes of the early 1970s met with failure. Those of the early 1980s met with some successes. The difference between the two was policy technique. It was the entry of ideas concerning political markets into the activity of policy formulation.

9 Problems, Non-Solutions and Solutions

It is instructive to compare the differences between conventional policy suggestions and those which emerge from a treatment of the political process as a market. The divergent approach is easily illustrated by looking at the measures with which both political styles propose to treat long-standing problems.

There are many parts of society and the economy which are regarded as real problem areas by those who advocate conservative or free market solutions. The provision of local government services presents one such area. The basic problem is that the gradual accumulation of services by local government authority has led to an extension of the state into economic processes, and all of the problems attendant on public sector supply.

Local government services are typically provided by the elected government of the authority, administered by its bureaucracy, and manned by a labour force employed directly by the council. The services are financed out of local authority revenue, which has been made up from the business rate and the domestic rate, both of which are effectively property taxes, and from a central government grant making up about two-thirds

135

of the total. Both the finance and the production of local services are thus provided in the public sector of the economy.

As the analysis of public operations has shown, this has involved the public in paying for services without having the ability to control the level of supply or the quality of service. The long-term tendency has been towards oversupply of quantity, decline in cost effectiveness, overmanning, depletion of capital, capture of the service by its producers, and lack of any inputs of consumer preference. The high costs have provided a real handicap to local business enterprise, and the high property taxes have fallen very unfairly on certain classes of home-owners who in many cases were only a small minority of the electorate.

The patterns within the political market can be traced. The small proportion who paid rates counted less in number than those who perceived themselves as beneficiaries at their expense. The local businesses had no votes to trade, and the system failed to impose penalties on authorities which reduced their own tax base because it made up the shortfall from central funds. Candidates for local office had an interest in offering the highest possible number of services perceived of as free at point of consumption.

Two solutions were put forward on the conventional paradigm. One, which merits brief consideration, was for a reorganization of the whole system of local government. The hope was that amalgamation into larger units would make possible economies of scale and new peaks of business efficiency in the provision of services. This was implemented in the early 1970s and achieved exactly opposite results. The new areas were too large and remote to sustain any influence at all by electors. On the contrary, such interest there had been was diminished. The new giantism left voters with the feeling that the new authorities were too large, too powerful and too remote to influence. Inefficiency and wastage increased, and abuse quickly became endemic. Under the new arrangement, some local authorities found they had funds to spare to bid openly and with cash for the votes of minority groups within their area, and proceeded to make grants and subsidies available for a variety of causes whose main linking thread seemed to be their dependence on the politicians who had done this for them.

An alternative suggestion was put forward many times. It proposed to counter the lack of consumer pressure by introducing user charges for local services. Under user charges, the service would continue to be provided by the local government authority, but would be paid for by the customer directly at the point of consumption, instead of being funded from general revenues. This aimed to make customers feel the cost of each service in a way they never did when funding was provided out of taxes. By having to part with actual cash, the citizenry would be aware of how much each service was costing, and would put pressure on the area authority to provide value for money in each case.

The added advantage offered by user charges was the possibility which would exist for customers to limit the quantity of service to what they were prepared to pay for. It was taken for granted that user charges would have to meet most of the costs of the service, and that provision would be gradually geared to what people were prepared to pay. For example, if the costs of garbage collection were assigned to user charges, it might well be found that when people had to pay for the service directly, they would choose to pay for only one collection a week instead of two, or perhaps even for one every second week. The supply would then be adjusted accordingly.

On the face of it, user charges offered a considerable degree of consumer input where none had existed before. By having them pay directly, they would appreciate the cost of each service in a way which central funding never achieves, and could control their own consumption. At an economic level, this offers advantages. People would exert the pressure of the purse upon the system. They would not have a choice between suppliers, but they would at least be able to decide how much was supplied.

On the level of political markets, user charges are considerably less attractive. In the first place, they leave the production of the service entirely within the state sector, taking only the finance of it into private hands. This means that all of the consequences of public supply continue unabated. The comparative inefficiency, over-manning, capital depletion, lack of choices and producer capture are all features of production within the state sector. To take the finance into the private sector does not necessarily mitigate their effects.

No less critical is the objection that most people perceive the benefits of service more than they perceive the burdens of cost. While the laudable aim is to make them feel the burdens of cost, there is no reason why they should want this. Many people think that 'other people' pay most for the services they receive, and do not appreciate that they are paying themselves through direct and indirect taxation. The estimated charges which would have to be levied for fully-costed services might well attract their angry opposition to any such scheme.

Of course, the corollary of user charges is that the taxation which currently pays for the services from local and national sources should be remitted. People would then have it to spend for themselves on the services, or not, if they saw fit. Giving people their money back instead of the free services runs counter to the findings of public choice analysis, that each group values its services more highly than others resent paying for them. In other words, user charges work against the grain of the political marketplace instead of along with it.

There is a further point to be made concerning its political impact. User charges require the price of services to be set by the local authority. The price may indeed be set on a full cost basis at the outset, but it must be subject to annual review by the local legislature to keep abreast of cost increases at least. This means that legislators have to consider price increases for services, and decide on them. At this point they come under great pressure from every minority group which thinks it has a deserving case, or whose lobbyists and spokesmen do so. They are asked to exempt the unemployed from the increases, and perhaps senior citizens or those on social security. They are called hard-hearted if they fail to do so.

Minority groups at this point can be bid for in the political market by candidates who pledge to offer them the service at special subsidized rates, and the pressure is felt to reduce the full impact of cost increases. Over a period of time it is quite possible for what started as a full-cost user charge to finish up as an ever more nominal charge, with the balance borne by subsidy to support target groups of the population. In this way political pressures can make user charges self-reversing, by exposing those legislators who would impose real costs to the brunt of electoral unpopularity.

To prevent this might require an Act of Parliament to remove discretionary power on user charges. This would attract in its turn a storm of political opposition from councils which saw their powers taken away, and minority groups which saw their benefits threatened. For their failure to recognize the strength of political markets, user charges are probably a non-starter, and have not, in fact, started.

As an alternative to the introduction of user charges,

the exponents of micropolitics developed the idea of inviting private businesses to bid for the provision of public services. This is known as 'contracting out' services into the private sector. The process involves the local authority retaining responsibility for the services, and continuing to pay for them out of public funds received from local and national sources. The difference is that instead of providing its own staff and labour force, the local government authority pays private firms to perform the services, having them bid against each other to secure the contracts.

Just as user charges proposed to take the finance into the private sector and leave production in public hands, the use of contractors involves transfer of the production to the private sector, while leaving the funding still public. It does not give members of the public individual control over consumption, as user charges are designed to do, nor does it give them any more choice between suppliers than either user charges or the municipal system. What it does do is generate competition between would-be suppliers.

Under contracting out, firms have to bid against each other for local service contracts. Thus competition is introduced, and the suppliers have to keep down the cost of the service and keep up its quality. Failure to do these will result in the contract going to other firms. Typically, the contracts are for a small number of years, perhaps three, depending on the type of service. The businesses which submit tenders have to keep efficient, and remain abreast of up-to-date technology and service techniques. Any which fail to do so will find the contracts going to firms which do keep competitive.

The result is that most of the features of public sector supply are removed. The inefficiency, the overmanning, and the capital shortage are all far less common in the private sector, for the very simple reason that firms which permit such practices lose business to those which do not. Producer capture is very much more difficult in the private sector because of the possibility of business being won by firms which satisfy the consumers instead, and because of the consequent risk of bankruptcy.

The result is a service for the community provided at less cost. The savings achieved by contracting out local services are found normally to lie in the range between 20 and 40 per cent, depending on the service and the country. In Britain the early savings were calculated by the Institute for Fiscal Studies to have averaged 22 per cent. This is probably an underestimate because savings are not usually as high in the first year of contracting out. The figures represent the difference between the cost of the municipal supply and the price of a private replacement for it which includes the profit of the firm and the taxes it has to pay.

There is thus a gain to be had by legislators short of the funds to do all they would like to do, and a public which does not like to pay more than necessary. Contracting out has the potential to offer a benefit if it can be implemented in a way which meets the requirements of the political market. This is by no means an easy task, and requires policies to achieve it to be constructed on the base of public choice analysis. The different interest groups must all be taken into consideration.

The public is concerned about the quality of the service which it receives. Any move towards the use of contractors must therefore aim to achieve at least as high a service quality. This can be accomplished by means of a tightly-drawn contract with penalty clauses specified and performance bonds posted. There is also public concern to have its wants considered, and many firms take care to initiate market research when they win local authority contracts, in order to keep apprised of public demand.

The local bureaucracy is at risk of losing position and reward if its responsibilities move out to the private sector. This makes it especially important for councils which contract out to move their managerial staff up to the work of contract monitoring and enforcement. This creates opportunities for higher grade work to replace the responsibilities lost.

The labour force employed by the council is most at risk, and can offer fierce opposition to the introduction of contracting out of work. This is why councils often specify that their own displaced workforce shall have the first opportunity to apply for the new jobs created in the private sector. Many councils also neutralize potential opposition from their direct labour force by a policy of no forced job losses. They make it a policy to reabsorb their displaced workers elsewhere within their establishment, letting them take up vacancies which would otherwise be filled from the outside. Yet another policy is to offer voluntary redundancy at terms sufficiently generous to induce enough workers to take them up on a voluntary basis.

The union leaders are the most difficult to deal with because there is little the council can offer them to compare with the power they enjoyed over a producer-dominated service. In general the offers and conditions to the employees must be sufficiently attractive to go over the heads of the union leadership and seek support directly from their members.

The practical experience of using contractors for local services in Britain is that they will provide the service with perhaps 10–15 per cent less manpower. Those who are displaced can be reabsorbed and sometimes re-trained. Workers who take jobs with the new firm find the jobs upgraded in skill, and more opportunities for promotion. Job security is lower in the private sector, and pension benefits are not as high, largely because no private firm can afford the index-linked pensions provided in the state sector. On the other hand, take-home pay is as good, and so are other fringe benefits. The workforce is not worked harder, but used more productively, and many have spoken well of the transition.

While the saving in costs might be very important to hard-pressed legislators, too much should not be made of its appeal to the public. Other things being equal, they prefer the lower costs and taxes which contracting out brings, but they perceive the service more directly than they appreciate the costs it imposes. This is why quality control is essential to successful contracting out. If a new and attentive service can be introduced, consumers will prefer it to the often shoddy and arrogant service which resulted from producer capture in the public sector.

This, in turn, requires the application of several detailed techniques. Many councils use pre-qualification of tenders, going through the list of bids to winnow out those incapable of attaining the required standards. The final selection is made from the list of those who are deemed sufficiently competent and experienced. Many seek professional help in drawing up contracts, and nearly all require performance bonds to be posted so that if the firm defaults or goes bankrupt, the service is safeguarded. A further device uses cash fines in the event of work not meeting the required standard, something which no council has achieved from its in-house services. The possibility for corruption in the award of contracts exists, of course, but to a far lesser extent when the bidding process takes place publicly than existed before with a municipal service largely hidden from public scrutiny.

The methods of micropolitics show clearly through the process. An analysis identifies all of the groups in the political market in question, and traces the perceived benefit they receive. A policy is then constructed to offer as many of them as possible a bigger gain from the new method than they enjoyed before. All possible objections are anticipated, and the policy is structured so that most of them can be dealt with in advance. The result is a policy which succeeds, and whose success promotes the confidence in it to have it applied elsewhere.

Contracting out of local services is not the free market solution. It is a success, in that it brings better services at less cost. It achieves some free market goals in that it removes production from the public sector and replaces it by private sector activity and enterprise. It introduces competition in both service quality and price, and encourages innovation and efficiency. Advocates of a macropolitical approach would, and do, criticize it on the grounds that it does not go far enough. They point out that a true free market situation would have the individuals within a local government area making the decisions about which business to employ for their services, and how much service they wanted. This is a just criticism, in that the use of private contractors does not achieve a totally free market. The finance is still provided collectively, without the possibility for individual choice. The problem is that public choice analysis suggests that the attempt to achieve a totally free market will fail because of the pressures of the interest groups involved, whereas the attempt to introduce contractors can succeed. While the advocates of a total solution were still attempting to win the battle for ideas, the micropoliticians meanwhile managed to take the use of private contractors to such a stage of success that the British government felt confident of enough support to mandate local authorities to seek outside bids.

The contrast between the solution developed by micropolitics and the alternatives supplied from the conventional paradigm, notably the introduction of user charges, shows how very much the former is involved in the practical world. Its concern with bringing the idea to reality through the political market shows itself in the detail which it devotes to the development of techniques which can circumvent possible obstacles. It does not seek to apply a blanket solution, but to tailor-make a policy for each situation it encounters. It often succeeds because the policies fit better when they are tailor-made.

The field of public education in Britain affords yet another area in which public sector supply has induced serious problems. Some 93 per cent of British children depend on the state sector and none other for their primary and secondary education. There is a theoretical alternative in the shape of the fee-paying schools, but since all have to pay through taxes for the state system, only the minority who can afford to pay twice over have effective access to private schools. The fee-paying schools are regarded as expensive, though their fees correspond roughly with the costs of state education, by the time that administrative overheads at national and local level have been included.

Most parents have had no effective choice within the state sector of education. Their child is allocated a place at the nearest state comprehensive school, and while there was added a possible alternative choice of schools, this could be prevented by a local authority citing "the interests of education' as its reason. Many of the problems of public supply made themselves evident. Parents were dissatisfied with the quality of education, and saw decline in standarads met not by a determination to improve, but by the attempt to prevent measurement.

Many of the characteristics of producer capture were evident. The quality of the service was judged by inputs, rather than outputs. Thus the attainment of the children did not count, but class size and ostensible level of teacher qualification did count. The cost and size of the administrative establishment grew huge as a share of the total supply. Attempted cost savings did not hit wastage, but bit instead into capital and equipment, and into essential services.

Parents were forced to pay through taxation a sum they could not control for an education in which they had no choice and no opportunity to exercise their preferences. For a high cost they received a poor service. Uniformity prevailed instead of variety and choice, and the educational priorities were decided by the producers rather than the consumers. These priorities included what many parents saw as political indoctrination rather than education.

To restore market pressures to education and give space for input by consumers presented a problem for policy-makers. People were used to the system of education free at point of consumption, yet were dissatisfied with its product. One set of solutions turned to the private schools, and sought ways of making it easier for ordinary parents to have access to them, and for an increase in the numbers of children they taught.

Among suggested policies was the idea of making school fees deductible against tax, thereby lowering the cost in real terms, and giving more people access to fee-paying schools. A similar variant proposed giving a rebate on taxation to those who opted out of state education by choosing a private school. The theory behind this was that such parents were saving the state the cost of educating their child, so perhaps a small incentive would encourage more to do so. If the rebate were finely judged, the state could save more by not having to educate the children than the cost of the rebates from taxation.

All of the proposals which centred on the private sector of education suffered from the fundamental weakness that the numbers who stood to gain from its expansion were too small. The evidence suggests that there is a lobby from the middle classes which would like access to private schooling to be easier financially. Polls indicate no strong resentment from the majority of parents; they seem to favour allowing choice to those who can afford it. Thus it might be politically possible to increase access to private schools. The trouble is that even if private school places were to double, this unlikely event would still leave 86 per cent of parents trapped in the state sector. Reform, for most parents, must mean improvement of the state sector.

Advocates of free market solutions have long supported the idea of education vouchers. Instead of giving parents a free place at a state school, under a voucher system they would instead receive a voucher equal to the value of that place, and would be free to spend it at the school of their choice. The voucher takes the place of cash. Instead of receiving money back from the state and having to spend it on schooling, the parents receive a piece of paper which works like cash with the important proviso that it cannot be diverted for other uses. The voucher scheme thus deals with the possible objection that if parents had to pay the cash themselves, they might spend it on gambling or drink instead.

The voucher scheme is by no means designed to bring about a full free market situation. There are still subsidies and transfers, in that taxpayers who are not parents continue to pay taxes and do not receive vouchers; so non parents support parents. Moreover the amount of the voucher specifies a minimum sum to be spent on education, denying parents the choice of going below that sum. It is possible that a black market might develop in vouchers, with illegal trade for cash taking place, so that parents would have such a choice in practice; but this would be in defiance of the voucher law, not a result of it.

The aim of the voucher scheme is to introduce market pressure. By choosing where to spend their vouchers, parents would be choosing the types of school they wished to proliferate. Unpopular schools would not receive enough voucher income to pay their way, and would face contraction and possible closure. Popular schools, by attracting extra demand, would gain additional voucher income to enable them to expand. They would, moreover, serve as a model to the other schools. Gradually, education would take the form which parents wanted for their children. It would slip out of the hands of the producers, and under the control of consumers expressed by their choices.

There are several variants of the voucher scheme, but most allow parents to add to the value of the voucher in order to purchase a place at a more expensive school. This implies that parents can choose private schools if they wish, making up any difference between their fees and the value of the voucher. It also implies that some state schools will choose to offer an education which is more expensive than that offered by others. The net effect is to bring more money into education, and to bring its output ever more into line with what parents want and are prepared to spend vouchers and cash upon.

The voucher scheme has many attractive features and would, if it could be achieved, be a vast improvement on the effective state monopoly of education. Unfortunately, the evidence suggests that the voucher scheme cannot be introduced. Despite its undoubted economic strengths it has political weaknesses which tell heavily against it. In its modern form it has been discussed at various times for over sixty years. It has been seriously investigated by Conservative governments in Britain, but never introduced. Even the combination which saw strong supporters as Secretary of State and junior minister at the Education Department was insufficient to bring it into practice.

In the first place, there is very strong opposition from those engaged as producers of education. Teachers' organizations resist it, not wishing their members to be exposed to market forces. Ministry bureaucrats are fanatical in their opposition, recognizing correctly that it would transfer power over education to parents. The parents themselves are easily alarmed at the prospect of losing the free place at the local school. They fear that they would have to pay large extra amounts to secure a decent education.

The voucher system cannot really be introduced gradually. Despite talk of experimental schemes, it would have to cover all of the schools within a very large area to be effective and to allow for real variety and choice. It would be prone to sabotage by those determined not to lose control over education. It is a holistic scheme, which makes its changes all at once. Parents would find pieces of paper arriving through the mail in place of their free school place. Schools, as well as the parents, would suddenly face uncertainty. It is easy to characterize it as some theoretical scheme, never properly tested, which would put the education of children at risk. Governments have tried to push voucher schemes through, but always have had to retreat in the face of political pressures exerted by interest groups.

An alternative proposal, owing a great deal to micropolitics and its style of policy formulation, proposes three separate reforms, each of which can be justified independently, but which together constitute a new system. Firsty it suggests that parents should have an effective choice, and proposes complete open entry within the state system, so that a child can be sent to any school which will accept it.

This policy is calculated to be popular with parents. Many of them are trapped by location into the catchment area of a bad school. Choice of school would enable them to escape. This choice in the absence of open entry is limited to those who can afford to move house into the catchment area of a good school. Indeed, it is not unknown to have a premium of several thousand pounds for houses on the side of the street in the good school area, compared with identical ones opposite them. The policy of open entry still leaves parents to cope with problems of transport to and from school, and would see good schools heavily over-subscribed and unable to accept many of their applicants. However, it represents an improvement, and is a popular one.

The second leg of the reform is a policy of making schools much more independent in operation. The board of each school, strongly representing parents by means of a ballot, would acquire control over school policy. It would have power to hire the headteacher, and to give the headteacher powers to hire and fire staff with the board's approval. The school would determine its own policy towards discipline and academic emphasis, subject to inspection of the achievement of its students in a core curriculum.

With such a reform, schools would show much more variety, putting alternative approaches to education into practice. This, in turn, would give reality to the choice between schools. This policy is popular with parents, who like the idea of being able to influence the school's approach. It gets a mixed response from teachers, with headteachers broadly in favour because of the increased status and responsibility it gives them, and other teachers being more divided. Some recognize opportunities for advancement and increased earning, others see job security threatened. Guarantees over terms of employment and grounds for dismissal might do much to assuage such uncertainties.

The third part of the change calls for direct funding of schools on the basis of the number of children enrolled. The present system funds them out of taxation through the administration of the local authority education committee. The reform would cut the local bureaucracy out of the picture, permitting schools to opt out of local authority control, and allowing schools funds direct from the centre according to enrolment. Of course, this incurs the hostility of the local education committees, but these are very small, and have little to trade in the political market. There is more support from the central bureaucracy, which perhaps sees more openings for its members in the administration of such a scheme, and sees no potential job losses or drop in status for them.

It is proposed that the funding by numbers should be based on the cost of the education for each age group, and might have exceptions to allow a higher rate for inner city schools with language problems, and for isolated village schools with less economies of scale. Two groups who might have felt threatened by the move over to direct funding are thus taken care of. Parents as a whole have nothing to lose by direct funding of schools, and gain the saving which results by eliminating an entire layer of administration, leaving more available to be spent on actual education.

Once all three legs of the proposed reform are in place, it will be evident that their combined effect is to establish a market in education. Because schools are then controlled by their governing boards, they pursue a variety of different educational priorities and vary in quality and type of education. Because parents have open entry, they choose for their children the type of education they prefer. Because schools are directly funded according to the numbers enrolled, schools which attract extra demand gain extra funding. The schools which are unpopular with parents either make changes or face closure.

One great advantage of this micropolitical reform is that each of its steps can be supported independently by different groups, yet the combined effect of them produces the change. No sudden change is forced upon parents against their will, in that for those who want nothing more than the free place at the local school, this is still available. Choice is there for those who want it; no one is forced into it. Of course, as the system developed, increasing numbers of parents would take advantage of what it offered. Extra techniques have to be incorporated into the new system to allow for the establishment of new state schools where there is demand for them, and to attract additional sources of finance from the private sector.

This policy does not produce a total market situation. Indeed, it does so less than the voucher scheme, in that it is concerned only with the state schools. It leaves the fee-paying schools as they are, unaltered by the new system, and not participating in it. It is aimed straight at the state system on which 93 per cent depend, and aims to improve it by transferring power from producers to consumers. The schools are still state schools, still funded out of tax revenues for the most part. New schools founded by parents and teachers are also still state schools, attracting the direct funds from the centre.

Despite these shortcomings, the new system offers major changes. The state schools become independently run, even though they stay in the public sector. Parents have choices which determine where the funds should go to pay for their child's education. Schools must respond to demand in order to attract the enrolment on which their budgets depend. The clear boundary which exists under the old system between the state sector and the private schools blurs a little under the new system. Forces and pressures are set in motion whose effect is to bring gradual improvement in standards of education achieved within the state sector. They are brought in by means of reforms calculated to command the support of some of the groups which have a direct interest in state education.

There are key differences between the voucher

scheme and the new approach. One of them is that the new policy does not involve the use of vouchers. The money follows the child as its parents make choices between a variety of schools. Another difference is that the alternative proposal represents practical politics, working with the grain of the political market. It is capable of being brought in by stages, and of developing gradually into a system of education which shows more flexibility, more variety, and more responsiveness to the wants and needs of parents. It may not be perfect, but it is a viable solution to the problem. And it is significant that, whereas the voucher system was rejected for years, the new system was in the Conservative election manifesto of 1987, its elements introduced in the Queen's Speech following the Conservative win, and similar proposals outlined for Scotland a few months later.

10 Practical Details

Although the programmes of the Conservative governments of 1970 and 1979 in Britain were very similar, the practical details of their policies were very different. It could be claimed that the later government has knowledge of the failures of the earlier one; but this would only have told it what not to do. The cause of failure could easily have been attributed to lack of will, to inappropriate times, or to lack of relevance to the modern world.

A major feature of the intervening years between the two governments was the rise to prominence of the public choice school and its description of how political markets operate. That analysis formed the starting-point for several organizations committed to innovative policy research. They developed new ideas which were not available to the first government, but which were beginning to circulate by the time the second one took office.

The change in thinking is best exemplified by a comparison of the approach to several key issues, showing how drastically it moved over the period from the late 1960s to the late 1970s. The early attitude was one of determination to put the slide to socialism into reverse by imposing conservative alternatives, even though this meant incurring major hostility from the groups which stood to lose. By the end of the period it had changed to a search for new techniques which could be implemented in practice by giving people more gain from them than they had enjoyed previously.

The attitude to state housing illustrates the point. Some 35 per cent of the population lived in publicly-owned homes, usually at highly subsidized rents, and in places with maintenance costs which were higher than revenues. The average income of the council tenants, as most of them were, was higher than that of people living in privately rented accommodation. There seemed to Conservatives to be an obvious unfairness in requiring those who were buying their homes to pay higher rates and taxes so that others could be given cheap rents.

Conservative candidates in local as well as in national elections had advocated bringing rents up to economic levels, but found the average council tenant on the whole seemed to prefer subsidized rents to economic ones. The result was that the council estates formed a vast block of opposition to reform of the housing system despite its constricting effect on the supply of houses and the very adverse effect it had upon mobility. People were reluctant to move for fear of losing their coveted position on the waiting-list for a subsidized public rental property.

As with so many other cases of minority benefit, those in receipt of it valued it more highly than the others resented paying for it. The bureaucracy of local government had built empires on the administration of council housing. Local councillors had carefully built majorities out of it over the years. The vested interests were locked into the prevailing system, and proposed reform would always arouse their hostility.

The new policy did not abandon the idea of economic rent, but it placed its emphasis on giving council tenants the right to buy their homes. While council tenants liked subsidies, many of them liked even more the idea of becoming home-owners. To foster their support, the policy provided for sale below market valuation. If they had lived in the house for two years, then a 20 per cent discount was given off the market value. This rose to a maximum of 50 per cent off to those who had lived there for twenty years. Attractive though subsidized rents were, the prospect of owning their own home and collecting a capital gain of several thousand pounds proved more attractive to many council tenants.

A new offer had appeared in the political market, and support of some groups shifted accordingly. The new offer was worth more to some than the subsidies had been. Pressure was now felt by local councils to sell homes to tenants. Some resisted and deliberately tried to obstruct the policy, but support was sufficiently high for the government to introduce a 'right to buy' which compelled local authorities to sell if tenants asked. The discounts were increased first to 60 per cent then to 70 per cent maximum off market price.

By September 1986, over one million of the five million tenants had already bought their homes, and legislation was underway to encourage those who rented council flats to do likewise. The new group of home-owners already formed a powerful new force in the political market. The Labour Party, which had all along been opposed to the sales, acknowledged this fact by doing an about-turn. It not only rejected the idea of taking back the homes into state ownership, it pledged itself to continue with the policy of discounted sales.

Council officials saw their empires crumble, while elected local councillors saw their captives slipping away. The pressure of the interest group was too large. The government was working with the political market this time, by offering them more. The transfer of power and property which this accomplished was huge. The value of the houses sold was in excess of £10 billion, after discounts had been given. Between 1979 and 1986, one-fifth of all tenants of the state had chosen to buy their homes. Meanwhile, the policy research had turned to finding new ways of increasing the number who could be persuaded to buy in the future.

The difference between the two approaches illustrates starkly the distinction between trying to impose an economic market by an act of will, and attempting to introduce more market characteristics by means of policies which recognize and work within a political marketplace. The old approach tried to override the interests of the council tenants by removing the subsidy advantage which they had long enjoyed. The new method sought to offer an exchange with something of greater value. The result was that the opposition to the first approach turned into enthusiastic support for the newer one. Not only were large numbers of homes brought into the private sector and subjected there to real prices and maintenance costs, but substantial political support was gained in addition.

The private rental sector in Britain has been reduced to only a few per cent of the total number of homes. The reason, quite apart from the competition of subsidized council houses, has been the twin policies of rent control and security of tenure. There is an active market in high prices business rentals, where neither of the policies operates because the lessee is a corporate entity and not a person. Individuals and families in private rented property have proved to be an effective interest group, more numerous than the landlords, and more suitable material for the activities of the charitable organizations and lobbyists.

The result has been that benefits have been awarded to tenants at the expense not only of landlords, but of future tenants as well. The effect of the policies has been to dry up almost completely the supply of new rental properties. Future tenants form no more an effective interest group than do landlords. Just as landlords are few in number, so future tenants do not perceive their loss.

Rents have been fixed by law below the market value, and owners have been denied the ability to reclaim their property, even when they wished to live in it, or in cases of major payment default. Since tenants are allowed to take possession of someone else's home, and live in it at less than its economic worth, sometimes at less than it costs to maintain it, it is difficult to see how this differs from theft, except for the obvious difference that it is not against the law. People who perhaps inherited an extra home from their parents are unable to let it out for fear that it might be lost to its 'tenants.'

Given the need for a healthy private rental sector, Conservative governments have tried to make headway with the repeal of rent controls and security of tenure. The mere mention of the idea has always brought outraged reaction not only from tenants, but more effectively from those whose livelihood derives from representing them, or whose ideology opposes private property. It has always provided the cue for demonstrations and media stories about the hardship it will cause to tenants. The hardship of landlords does not feature because they are typecast into the role of the rich who exploit the homeless desperation of the poor. If there were to be a patron saint of landlords, Ebeneezer Scrooge would be a good candidate in the eyes of the media. The proposals have never managed to proceed very far in consequence.

A free market in private rentals would bring more property onto the market, and probably lead to the stabilization of prices and a greatly increased supply of property. Unfortunately, as with so many other cases, the ideal and fair solution is unobtainable by conventional means because of political obstacles. The groups who have advantages will fight more hard to keep them than the others will to remove them.

The solutions suggested by micropolitics are certainly not fair. They centre on protecting the advantage of the current generation of tenants, but permitting new leases to be offered outside the scope of rent control and security of tenure. The thinking is that the current tenants will have no reason to oppose the move, since their own advantage is not threatened. On the other hand, a situation will have been created in which all new tenancies would be free from the restrictions. As the current tenants moved out or died, the properties they occupied would be relet with market leases. Some might even be bought out with cash sums. The numbers in protected tenancies would diminish over time until all rentals were in the free market.

The result would not be fair to current landlords, any more than the present system is fair, but it would at least diminish the unfairness steadily over time. It has the hallmark of practical politics because it is tailor-made to neutralize the opposition of the group whose opposition might thwart it. The lobbyists would still oppose it, but they are small in number, like landlords. In the absence of troops of tenants to march behind their banners and feature in television horror stories, they are ineffective.

A further suggestion emerging from this type of approach has been that there should be separate classes of landlords, each subject to different degrees of control. For example, the small landlord who lets one or two properties for a time is in a very different class from the professional landlord who commands many properties to draw income from. Similarly, the institutional landlord, such as the Church of England or a large property agency, is not in the same league as the individual who lets out a few homes. Once more the aim of such subdivision is to introduce some elements of free market renting, even if it cannot be applied to private rentals as a whole.

The analysis is that some of the groups command more influence than others do. This is not necessarily related only to numbers; it might be the visibility or the capacity to cause trouble which makes them influential. In this context eviction has an emotional pull difficult to deal with. The sight of people being put out of homes they cannot afford to rent is a distressing one. Few people in politics would want it blamed on them, and business agencies which might otherwise go into property rentals to individuals do not do so because of the damage which evictions might do to their reputation and standing.

One answer might be found in short-term leases, where the owner is guaranteed to receive vacant possession after they expire. New leases can then be negotiated. The short-term lease does not lead to the same images of a family being evicted from its lifelong home, with the rapacity of a greedy landlord to blame. Variants of some of these ideas have been tried, and more being evaluated. The idea which underlies them is very different from that which sought to introduce a full free market, ride the storm to push the idea through, and assure the legislators that the fuss would die down eventually. It seeks instead to circumvent the hostility of the groups involved by ensuring that the policies are such as will not place them under threat.

The changes in policy style which the micropolitical approach has brought are evident when it comes to the methods used with those parts of state industries which make losses. When mounting losses turn the attention of government towards individual factories or plants which account for a disproportionate share of the deficit, the threat of closure provokes a predictable response. The workforce demonstrates volubly, perhaps threatening strike action. In extreme cases it might occupy the threatened plant. The elected representatives of the area put pressure on the government, which feels by this time much opposition and few supporters. As always, those with the benefit fight hardest.

Governments in the past have often retreated under fire, withdrawing the threatened closure, taking less political damage by continuing the subsidy than by going through with the policy of ending it. More recently there has been a change in approach. Now the effort is made to secure the acquiescence of the workforce. The union leaders and shop stewards still resist, but by making very generous redundancy offers, or providing relocation grants, the government makes the proposal more acceptable to the workers.

In place of the subsidized job is offered a cash sum sufficient to enable some to start up in business; for older workers it might provide the basis for an early retirement, using a combination of state benefits and capital to live off. The threat to the benefit of the job in one location is balanced sometimes by the offer of an alternative job in another. Every effort is made to minimize the number of actual job losses, the reckoning being that this is the most sensitive area of the political market, the one where trade-offs have to be made.

The combination of generous redundancy terms, relocation offers sometimes combined with retraining, and the offer of alternative jobs elsewhere in the company, all defuse the resistance which is encountered. The result is that the closure of some parts of loss-making activities is now possible. The exercise might cost more in the short term than forcing through simple closure, but when it has been achieved successfully there is a long-term saving not available where closure is thwarted by the potential losers.

The reform of the laws governing the trade union movement and its activities provide a classic case illustrating the difference of approach which separates the two styles. It had been appreciated by previous governments, both Labour and Conservative, that laws which might have been intended to protect trade unions had given them too many powers and immunities. Fears that this power would destroy the economy and society if left unchecked led Harold Wilson when Labour Prime Minister, and Edward Heath when Conservative Prime Minister, to attempt legal reforms to bring them within the law. Both failed. The Labour proposal had to be withdrawn ignominiously, and the Conservative law was rendered inoperable by mass resistance, and was immediately repealed by the next government.

The Thatcher administration brought in a series of labour reforms which transformed the climate of industrial relations and trade union activities in Britain. It apparently succeeded in achieving what its predecessors had failed to bring about. In fact what it did do was to achieve something different.

The two attempts which failed both tried, for the most part, to take away the powers enjoyed by trade unions and their members. A feature of both of them was to have been new curbs on activities and new restrictions, both backed by the sanction of law. Certain classes of industrial action, previously permitted, were now to be made illegal. Union leaders and members who defied the new law were to face heavy fines, failure to pay which could lead to them being imprisoned. In each case the reform was to be brought about by a major Act of Parliament.

The Wilson proposal was withdrawn in cabinet, after it became apparent that hostility from unions, their cabinet supporters and union-sponsored MPs would be too great. The Heath proposal became law but was defied successfully, with the government backing down from major confrontation by not implementing it. The two proposed reforms both united the trade union movement against them. The union leaders urged resistance, and the members rallied behind them to defend what they perceived to be their rights. The unions in Britain had increasingly enjoyed the advantage of legal protection and immunity unique in law. Things could be done in the course of industrial disputes which would be regarded outside them as illegal, even criminal. Naturally enough, the threatened group defended its benefit, and did so successfully.

The Thatcher reforms were very different. In the first place they came in a series of Acts of Parliament. The first one, introduced by James Prior, the Employment Secretary, was believed by many to be all there would be. Indeed, even he may have believed it until Conservative backbench opinion forced a further one. Each measure seemed very limited, perhaps calculated to fall short of anything which would arouse a major outcry. Each seemed relatively mild; it was the cumulative effect which added up to real reform. Thus, with no individual Act to focus all of the resistance, the notion was accepted that there would be a continuing series of reforms until sufficient had been achieved.

The second major point of difference is that most of the Thatcher reforms did not take away the power of the unions. In the place of giving government powers over the unions, the reforms for the most part gave the members power over their leaders. Rather than taking away the powers, most of the measures redistributed them so that the members had to be consulted. Ordinary members, long used to seeing militant leadership take action, and later seek backing at works meetings by the intimidatory show of hands vote, now found that the new laws brought in their opinion much earlier by secret ballot. They acquired the right to elect their leaders in a similar fashion. In other words, the very forces that worked previously for the militants were now used to give power to the ordinary members.

Yet another central difference is that the most significant of the Thatcher reforms were features of civil rather than criminal law. That is, if certain provisions were not complied with, those engaged in the activity were not subject to criminal prosecution, but to civil action. If the premises of firms other than those in the dispute were picketed, the firms so abused could sue in civil courts, seeking injunctions and perhaps damages. If strikes were called without a ballot of members, the action was excluded from the legal immunities which applied to trade disputes.

These were three crucial differences: the reforms came little by little, they devolved power down from the leaders to the members, and none of the major reforms exposed union leaders or members to criminal prosecution. In these three significant differences lie the reasons for the success of the Thatcher reforms, as opposed to the failure of the previous attempts.

It is not the case that the Thatcher reforms succeeded because they faced a union movement weakened by unemployment. No way has been suggested in which this alleged effect might have worked. If industrial action had led to workers being dismissed, or replaced by unemployed persons, there might be a case for the idea; but it was just as unthinkable then as earlier that any firm would have been allowed to get away with such tactics.

The Thatcher reforms succeeded because they took account of the interest groups affected, and took pains to avoid the very kind of direct confrontation which had defeated the earlier proposals. It was difficult for the militant leaders to rally their members in opposition because each measure was relatively mild. Each one was a small increment on the previous ones, not quite enough to generate outraged hostility. Furthermore, the members were hardly likely to rally against measures which gave them more powers. The union leaders might object to being obliged to submit to a ballot by the members, but the membership was not likely to take the same attitude. The powers were not generally taken away by government, they were devolved downwards from the leaders to the members. Finally, there was no confrontation with criminal law, no spectre of union leaders or militants being led off as martyrs to prison cells. There were none of the opportunities by which union leaders might have evoked the familiar loyalties of their members in mass defiance of the new laws.

The reforms succeeded where others had failed because they were the products of a new style of politics, of a new approach to the formulation of policy. They took account of the realities of the forces which operate in political life, instead of treating it as an empty slate waiting to be written upon. The previous attempts had committed the fundamental mistake of macro-politics: they had looked at the prevailing situation and at the desired situation, and had taken no account of the ground in between. The new method picked out a careful pathway across that ground; it is one of its main characteristics that it does so.

The methods of dealing with the closure of loss-making operations in the state sector, and of introducing reforms into the field of labour relations both played a part in the 1984–85 strike in the coal mining industry. A strike by the miners' union had defeated the Heath government, after plunging the country into power cuts and a three-day work week. The strike which took place under the Thatcher government was a failure. The differences are revealing.

The second strike, although led by the president of the National Union of Mineworkers, was only a strike by part of that union. If it had taken place a few months later than it did, the new law would have required a ballot, and the union had twice voted down strike action in pithead ballots. Because it was called without a ballot, sections of the union, particularly the Nottinghamshire miners, felt justified in not joining it. The new laws which covered the picketing of secondary firms made it more difficult for the other unions to be forced to help. Firms were able to go to court for injunctions, and the miners' union was found guilty of contempt of court for disobeying them. Its funds were seized for non payment of fines, not to be released until the leaders undertook to comply.

The new climate of industrial relations which the reforms brought in made it difficult at every turn, even for the union with the reputation as the strongest and the most militant. Even the fight itself was blurred as to the central issues. It was claimed by the leaders as a battle to save jobs, and to prevent pit closures by the Coal Board. Yet the proposals guaranteed that not a single miner would be forced out of a job. All men displaced from pits due for closure were promised jobs in other pits, with generous relocation grants. The most generous voluntary redundancy payment in British history was offered to miners who chose to retire. As there were no forced job losses, and huge cash sums for miners who chose to quit instead of taking a job at another pit, there was some confusion as to the issue at stake. It boiled down to a fight over the future size of the industry, a factor of interest to the union, but hardly a crucial issue for the present workers.

The strike was a failure, unlike its predecessor, and resulted in the break-up of the miners' union. A major factor which enabled the strike to be defeated was the new approach to job losses, and the new way in which labour reforms had been brought in. Whereas the government of Edward Heath had used the head-on confrontation approach on both issues and had lost, the government in power a decade later used policies which assuaged the interest groups and offered trade-offs to compensate them for any benefits threatened by the changes.

The experience of the trade unions under the Thatcher government brings out a very important point about micropolitics. It is that the leaders of interest groups and minorities do not necessarily represent the views of their members. This can be true even when they are democratically elected by a fair ballot. When political activity is confrontational, with groups fighting to secure their advantage, it is in their interest to select leaders who are good at this type of activity. They will often tend to choose leaders who are more militant and more aggressive than the membership as a whole; that is why they are good leaders. Society will find its groups strident, demanding and ready to use force at the start of a dispute. This is a reflection of the type of leaders chosen in such a climate; the trade union leadership has provided a good illustration of this effect.

When policy is formulated to take account of political markets it becomes less confrontational. Benefits are not taken away without anything being offered in return; instead they are traded. There is less need for aggressive leadership. Indeed, the members of an interest group may often perceive a clear conflict between their own benefit and that of their leaders. The latter may have risen to prominence by their ability to fight, and may seek to justify their position by fighting, but their members may gain more by trading benefits than by militant action.

A repeated pattern under the Thatcher administration has seen the management make an offer which was rejected out of hand by union leaders. When the required ballot to decide on industrial action has been conducted, the members of the union have rebuffed their leaders by voting against a strike. The experience with the trade unions illustrates the general point that leaders of minorities and interest groups do not necessarily represent them. This means that policies must be tailored to the members, rather than to the leaders. Militant leaders always howl for more benefit and rarely admit that any offer is more than a pittance; that is their job. Their members, on the other hand, might be quite happy to trade what is offered. In practice this can produce situations in which the leaders of minority groups can be hurling angry rhetoric and abuse, while the minorities themselves are quietly accepting the status quo of the new political market. The events are more important than the words which accompany them.

11 Privatization

The word as well as the idea of privatization were comparatively latecomers to the Thatcher administration. The 1979 manifesto on which the election was fought had made reference to the sale of the aerospace and shipbuilding industries, as well as the National Freight Corporation, but with no indication that this was to be more than the 'denationalization' long advocated as a goal of Conservative policy, but rarely achieved. The 1976 publication by the Conservative Party, *The Right Approach*, had stated that 'in some cases it may also be appropriate to sell back to private enterprise assets or activities where willing buyers can be found.' The key word is 'back', indicating an intent to undo some of what years of nationalization had done, even if only a small amount.

Privatization as achieved in practice has been vastly different from the token sales of a small brewery and a travel agency which took place in the 1970–74 administration, or even the return of parts of the steel industry to the private sector in the 1951–55 administration. Both of these were cases of denationalization, a term which implies the undoing of something done previously. The word privatization has gained currency since the 1979 government took office because of a general recognition that it is something new. It does not revert to previous

169

circumstances, but achieves a new state of affairs instead.

In no cases since 1979 have parts of the state sector been handed back to previous owners. In every case of privatization they have found their way into new hands in the private sector, new hands which have in many cases differed a great deal from those of the previous owners. The policy of privatization is a new one, owing much to the type of policy analysis which took place during the period when the Conservatives were out of office.

Although it is commonly thought of as no more than the sale of state assets, it is in reality a more complex series of policies designed to have performed in the private sector activities which have hitherto been done in the state sector of the economy. There is no simple formula or recipe for doing this. On the contrary, a great variety of different techniques has been developed, each of which has been designed to deal with a particular state operation or activity.

A considerable degree of the expertise which is now possessed in methods of privatization has been learned in practice. Government has learned in office which methods work and which do not. It has learned how to handle the various interest groups involved, and to secure support, or at least acquiescence, from powerful groups which could have thwarted the attempt. While the general outlines of this approach were understood in theory by the policy research organizations which started out from the public choice critique of conventional politics, the details were filled in gradually by experience.

This learning process is illustrated vividly by the contrast seen in the failure to sell the gas showrooms in 1981–82, and the huge success gained with the privatization of British Gas in 1986. The differences in technique show the increased sophistication of the approach used five years later. The first venture had involved an attempt to separate the profitable gas showrooms from the rest of the industry, and sell it to private buyers. It seemed reasonable on the face of it, since the showrooms were not an integral part of the production and sale of gas, but merely high street stores from which gas appliances were sold and maintained.

It incurred the immediate wrath of the industry's management. Sir Dennis Rookes, chairman of the state industry, led a determined lobby to keep his empire in one piece, with the support of the entire management team. The workforce threatened strike action, rather than see the gas showrooms taken out of the industry and sold off to private business. Scare stories were spread about the 'cowboys' who would come into the market for quick profits, with insufficient regard for safety. The general public showed concern at the prospect of losing its gas showrooms and having dangerous appliances fitted. Legislators felt the mounting pressure of the opposition, and the government sensed the support of backbenchers wilting under the campaign. The proposal was withdrawn, having managed to alienate the bureaucracy and management, the workers, the public gas users and the legislators.

The contrast between this débâcle and the 1986 public flotation of British Gas could hardly be more marked. The privatization of 1986 enjoyed the support of all major groups involved, and was a major success for the government. The difference was to be found in the realm of policy: much had been learned during the five years which separated the two attempts.

The management had objected strongly to the break-up which the first proposal had involved. The second version kept the industry in one piece, and secured the support of the management. Even the dour Sir Dennis made public relations appearances to promote the privatization, albeit without actually smiling. The

support of an industry's privatization by its management board is an important element in success. The
board has the capacity to do a great deal of damage, and
to lower expectation about future performance, and
hence the price obtained by the sale. It also has effective
lobby power in public debate, especially among those
who are opposed to the private sector. The earlier
attempt to break off and sell the gas showrooms had
seen a vociferous and effective lobby conducted against
it in Parliament. Keeping the industry intact offered a
trade-off. The board liked the power and authority as
heads of a major public enterprise, but liked even more
the prospect of becoming the directors of a powerful,
profitable and private corporation.

The workforce, which had threatened strike action
and staged a token stoppage when the first proposal
was made, supported the second one. Of the share
issue, a substantial number was set aside for the gas
workers. Everyone received a small free issue, and then
had the right to reserve a larger number without having
to ballot for them. With expectation about the sale and
the subsequent value running high, over 90 per cent of
the workforce bought shares in the new company. In
this way they achieved two important objectives: they
became part-owners of the company, with a personal
stake in its future performance; and in addition they
made a substantial capital gain on the sale, a gain which
totalled several thousand pounds in some cases.
Potential buyers are attracted to a company whose own
workers buy shares in it; it is a sign that they will work
with the company in future, rather than hold an
antagonistic relationship with it.

The general gas using public, put in fear the first time
by ideas about unqualified personnel and perhaps
dangerous corner cutting in the private sector, took to
the sale of British Gas in a big way. Gas users received a
preferential share allocation if they chose to apply,

obtaining favourable treatment in any ballot for shares which an oversubscribed issue might necessitate. They were offered the alternative of vouchers toward gas bills, or a bonus share allocation, if they held on to their shares.

To encourage the maximum participation by the general public, the shares were offered on easy terms, with only 50 pence required to secure each share, and additional payments coming in later years. Finally, there was a complete media blitz of advertising for the public flotation, with sums counted in hundreds of millions going to pay for the promotion of the sale. The success was measured by the very large participation by first-time share-buyers, most of whom chose to hold on to the shares despite an initial premium of over 30 per cent.

The government and its supporters gained because the other groups did. A policy success reflected on them. In more detail, they now had more share-owners than ever before, over five million owners of British Gas shares to oppose subsequent nationalization by a hostile government, and the fruits of an advertising campaign which had advertised privatization and capitalism as well as gas shares. It was, as some observers remarked, 'the most expensive party political broadcast in history'.

There was an added bonus to government, in that the £5 billion of revenue it received from the sale became available for it to use in its current budget to relieve the pressure on spending, or to reduce taxation. Although this practice has been criticized, and still is, there are arguments to support it. There is no capital account in Britain, nor proper depreciation of it. Funds used to purchase from the private sector have to come from current spending; by the same token, funds obtained from sales can go there. A view of privatization as the squandering of 'precious national assets', is inaccurate.

They are no less national assets by being in the private sector; in fact privatization improves them.

The difference between the two privatization attempts can now be summarized. The first alienated the interest groups and failed, whereas the second offered them all trade-offs and succeeded. The lessons of the years which separated the two had been learned by experience. Policy required more than good intentions to make it a success. It needed in addition the technical accomplishment to let it satisfy the various groups involved in public enterprises, and to offer them trade-offs for their benefits which they would willingly accept.

Many of the lessons which were applied to the public flotation of British Gas were tried out on the sale two years earlier in 1984 of Telecom, the former public sector telephone and telecommunications industry. In no sense was this denationalization, since it had been in the public sector virtually from its inception, and had been part of the post office for most of that time. Telecom was the first major utility, as opposed to a state industry, to be privatized, and thus broke new ground.

Telecom was, when it was privatized, the largest company ever to be floated on the stock market, just as British Gas was to be two years later. At a valuation in excess of £3 billion, it doubled the rate at which British state sector industries were being sold into private hands. The pattern of making trade-offs to interest groups, familiar now since the sale of British Gas, was carried through with remorseless precision in the case of Telecom.

The management were allowed to take it complete into the private sector. Advocates of pure free market policies fought a rearguard action to have Telecom split up into competing companies, or at least broken into regional companies whose performance could then be compared. It did not seem to occur to them that while this might be the ideal solution, it was not one which was possible. A fight to privatize Telecom in pieces was a fight for a policy that would fail. Telecom's management supported the privatization of the industry in the way it was proposed.

The workforce was instructed by the union leadership to oppose the move, and a campaign was mounted. Its logo showed a telephone cord being cut by shears, presumably the fate which awaited the service under capitalism. Against this, the management offered shares set aside for the Telecom workers, making them part-owners of the new firm, and giving them potential for capital gains if the value went up. In the event, some 96 per cent of the workforce took up their offered shares. Thus the labour force, which might have opposed the move, became part of the team.

The general public was allowed to buy the shares in instalments, with only 50 pence per share required as initial payment. People who became shareholders were offered the choice of a bonus share issue, or of reductions on their telephone bills. At flotation time, some two million people bought the shares, after a heavy oversubscription, and two-thirds of buyers chose to retain them, even though there was an immediate premium of nearly 100 per cent. Advertising on a very heavy scale was pioneered for the Telecom sale, and did bring the required response from the public.

Telecom was thus a test bed for the techniques to privatize a big public utility. Every single possible objection by any group was anticipated and dealt with wherever it was appropriate. Concern was raised that this vital strategic utility might pass into the hands of foreigners, so one golden share was built into the sale, to be retained by the British government, and to confer voting control in the event of attempted foreign takeover. It was argued that a private Telecom would not find it profitable to operate and maintain the rural pay telephones, so a requirement to keep a set number was built into the law which privatized Telecom. It became a legal obligation upon the new company, and was a known liability, albeit a small one, to potential buyers.

Considerable doubt was raised about the effective monopoly which Telecom enjoyed, and fears were raised that it would abuse its position. The monopoly enjoyed in the public sector and the abuse of it were not raised in comparison. Two methods were used, in addition to the building in of preconditions into the act of Parliament. One of them used 'peripheral competition', under which Telecom, although not faced by a competitor of anything like its size and power, did have to meet smaller competitors in each of its markets. Thus it faced the Mercury link for business telecommunications. It faced Racal/Vodaphone for cellular radio. It faced competitors for the supply of equipment, for transmission of computer data, and for most of its activity. Each of them was small, but together they meant that Telecom risked losing its customers in many of its markets.

Also used was the device of an agency to oversee the industry and promote competition. Rather than follow the US path of regulatory agencies setting rules which limited entry, OFTEL was specifically charged with promoting competition. When Mercury applied to extend its services to private customers, OFTEL agreed, this falling within its brief.

The combination used to limit the abuse of monopoly power mixes legislative preconditions, peripheral competition and an agency to promote competition. It was tailor-made for Telecom, and would not necessarily be applied in the same form to other industries. There is a strong empirical streak in it, and a determination to use experience as a learning process. Fortunately, Parliament can always come back in the future if it does not get it right at the first attempt. Discontent with the standard of service achieved by Telecom after privatization became pronouned in 1987, and led to proposals for change from OFTEL. Following criticism by both shareholders and customers, the chairman resigned in September 1987, and there was talk of new controls perhaps being needed if Telecom failed to perform better. The events illustrated the point that Parliament can always return to the task if it fails to get it right the first time. If the sale of Telecom had had to wait until a perfect system was devised, it would be waiting still.

There were charges over the Telecom sale that the government had sold it too cheaply. After all, a premium of 100 per cent made it look as though it could have fetched double. This is almost certainly incorrect. It was important to make the first utility flotation a success, and to have the shares taken up. It was also important to involve the general public, and to attract as many of them as possible as share buyers. This would spread the base of ownership and make nationalization by a subsequent government harder to do. All of this meant that a premium on the sale price was required. The offer price was difficult because no one knew what it might be worth. Many of the nationalized industries, including Telecom, had for years used accounts which would have brought laughter, if not criminal prosecution in the private sector.

It should be noted that the government did not try to ascertain the correct price for itself. It used financial experts from the City of London to do that, if it was wrong, part of the blame lay at their door. But it did not have to be right the first time. By selling just over 50 per cent of the company, the government retained the option of disposing of its residual shares at higher prices later on. It is usually the case that firms become more profitable and more efficient in the private sector, so the tactic of starting with just over 50 per cent and unloading the rest in later tranches gives the government more for its later sales. This is the case with Telecom, as it has been with other sales.

A notable feature of the Telecom sale was the heavy involvement of private expertise. Over the privatization programme, a fact to emerge early on was that the process can itself be privatized. As more and more has been done, greater use has been made of firms from the City. They have supplied analysts, merchant banking, and the promotional skills required. Government has not bothered to learn how to sell companies; it has bought in the services of those who already know. These firms have themselves developed into an interest group which gains from privatization, and have instigated new proposals for it, both in Britain and abroad.

A small but important gain comes from the use of private firms to steer through the privatization package. It is that government and Parliament are thereby able to keep some distance back from the process. Once it is in the hands of the experts, it becomes their responsibility. This is not simply an excuse for government to pass the blame elsewhere if things go wrong; by appointing the firms concerned government takes overall responsibility. What the use of private expertise does do is to keep legislators away from the fine details. It would not be desirable to have Parliament set the flotation date, the issue price and the number of shares. Nor would it be helpful if individual legislators felt pressure from their electors to seek special advantages for them when the details were being determined.

A look at the record on the pricing of public flotations shows how fraught with difficulties is the whole field. At the sale of Amersham International, a small radionics firm which was one of the early public flotations, there was a big premium on the issue price. Lengthy charges followed from opponents of privatization that the government had sold a national asset off too cheaply, to the gain of its monied friends in the City of London. This charge is raised whenever there is a premium.

The tactic of securing wide participation in the sale by ordinary members of the public blunts the charge, but does not eliminate it. To be accused of selling national assets too cheaply, to the gain of ordinary members of the public, is easier to take than a charge involving 'monied friends in the City', but there is still a mistake implied. When the share price is set too high, and not enough applications come in, the shares open at a discount. This is also called a failure by opponents. Too much demand is failure and too little demand is failure. Only a narrow band apparently counts as success. It should be noted that when the demand is low and the shares open at a discount, the government and the public still get their money. The practice of underwriting with merchant banks and financial institutions means that there is a guarantee in advance that the shares will be sold. The sale is only called a failure in the sense that it fails to attract popular interest from investors.

Even the sale of BP shares still in government hands, interrupted as it was by the sudden fall in share values on 19 October 1987, brought in the money. The underwriters, accused for years of 'easy pickings', found themselves caught by a commitment to pick up part-paid unsold shares at 120p when the market had taken them down to 70–80p level. The outcome was that they paid. Panic was calmed by Chancellor Lawson's offer of a buyback base price of 70p per share, but in the event only 2 per cent of the issue was returned. The government argued, correctly, that risks such as this were why underwriters earned money. Sometimes the price would be wrong.

In fact, the record of pricing has been quite good, especially in the light of the novelty of the activity. Lack of proper accounts and lack of experience in selling off parts of the state made the selection of a price difficult. Despite this, there have been few real mistakes. The policy has been that it is a good thing to have the shares open at a premium, to encourage future investment and to gain political support from those who benefited from it. Of all of the privatizations by public share issue, only those related to oil opened at a discount. Given international concern about the future of the industry, its vulnerability to overseas events, and the wild fluctuations in the price of crude, this is understandable.

In other cases not only has there been a premium on the first day of trading, but there has been a consistent pattern of the shares of privatized companies out-performing the stock market average. Both of these are desirable objectives in the early stages of the priva-tization drive. They bring major satisfaction to several of the interest groups involved, including the new ones. Management and workforce are obvious beneficiaries from a rise in the value of the shares they hold, and a rise in the profitability of their company. It is important that they make more gains from the new arrangement than they enjoyed under the old. This will provide an incentive for the employees of other state companies to embrace privatization when it is proposed.

The new class of shareholders, many of whom are firsttime buyers or small shareholders, should see visible capital gains. By being owners of part of the nation's business, they acquire a stake in seeing a climate favourable to economic enterprise. If they see themselves becoming personally better off as a result of policies which favour free enterprise, they will be more inclined to back it themselves. Not only that, but the larger the wealth they hold in shares of former state corporations, the harder will it be for a future govern-ment to plan for its confiscation. Already those who oppose privatization and want to reverse it have stopped talk of taking away the shares of the small

investor. They now talk of bringing the firm back into
the state sector while leaving the shares in private
hands. It remains to be seen whether the firms would
perform as well under government management as
they do with private directors, and, more importantly,
how voters with shares would estimate that outcome at
the time of an election. Given a choice in 1987, they
rejected the option.

There is a clear difference in attitude to privatization
between those who advocate full free market solutions
and those who start from the analysis of the public
choice school and devise policies to work within the
political markets. The former group constantly criticize
government for its failure to create a pure free market
situation, and regard measures to trade benefits with
interest groups as a sign of weakness and lack of
commitment. They show no sign of understanding that
it is these trade-offs which make the exercise possible in
the first place. Nor do they see that in the absence of
such measures the reform would not emerge successfully through the political process.

Some supporters of market economics seem to
suppose that the only purpose of privatization is to
expose state enterprises to all of the competitive
pressures of the marketplace. Unless there is a
completely free competitive situation at the end of it,
they call it failure. This is a misconception: the purpose
of privatization is not principally to make state industry
competitive, it is to make it private. While competition
is certainly desirable and is to be sought wherever
possible, there are still advantages to be gained even
when the competition secured is imperfect.

Public choice analysis leads to the conclusion that
state sector activities lie within the political domain.
Instead of commercial and competitive pressures, they
face political pressures. Because their operations fall
within the ambit of direct legislative input, they are

subjected to the pressures which impinge upon the legislators. Public sector operations lie within a political, not an economic market.

A few everyday examples illustrate the effects of this. If funds are sought for expansion or capital investment by state firms, this counts as government borrowing and is part of the public sector borrowing requirement. It must fit into targets set for the PSBR, and must thus compete with other government priorities instead of standing on its own. If government is squeezing total borrowing, the cash will not be there, however worthy the need. A private sector firm, by contrast, attracts investment on the basis of its ability to use it to good advantage and make a good return to those providing it. The public sector cannot be funded on a commercial basis.

Decisions made in public sector firms are subject to political involvement, even down to the fine details. The decision to build a new factory in the private sector is made on a commercial basis depending on such factors as costs and proximity to markets. The public sector firm faces political inputs on a similar decision, with elected representatives attempting to secure the factory for their district by political pressure. The convolutions required in the event of closure of a plant in a public sector operation have already been referred to. The point is that a state firm is a political football, to be kicked around by the interest groups and those who apply political pressure on their behalf. It does not make commercial decisions any more than it raises finance on a commercial basis.

To these factors can be added the fact that public operations are often characterized by state monopolies with all that follows in terms of producer capture, over-manning and unresponsiveness to consumer needs. If privatization can wipe this entire state clean for a fresh start in the private sector, then it makes obvious gains.

If it can wipe part of the slate clean, then it is still worth doing. If, by wiping part of the slate clean, it exposes an operation to pressures which will ultimately wipe the rest of it, it is even more worth doing.

Some observers see a public monopoly as harmful because it is a monopoly. The point is that a public monopoly is subject to twin evils: the fact that it is public, and that it is a monopoly. Of the two, the fact that it is public constitutes the greater evil. It is a greater source of distortion and misallocation. If there are occasions on which a monopoly is privatized as a monopoly, at least it can be said that a private monopoly is better than a public one. A private monopoly is more vulnerable to technological innovation. It is further from the political domain than are the state monopolies, and it lacks the political clout which they wield. Whereas private monopolies are eroded over time, public ones are sustained by new laws brought in to protect them from new threats.

It was not possible to make Telecom properly competitive within the private sector. Micropolitical analysis suggests that if this had been attempted, the privatization itself would not have gone through. Telecom is, however, subject to more commercial pressure than it was, and faces much more competition than ever it did in the state sector. These are both important gains achieved by a workable solution, and not ones to be discarded in favour of more perfectly competitive solutions which would not work.

Time is an element in this. As new technologies develop, Telecom will not have the power of law to exclude them as it did before. It is even conceivable that legislative action might eventually be contemplated to produce a more competitive situation. In that event, privatized companies will find that they are without the friends in high places that their status in the public sector gave them. As private enterprise firms, they will be expected to survive competitive pressures without legislative assistance.

At the minimum, privatization exposes state firms to commercial pressures. At its best it turns them into viable and competitive entities, capable of making their way successfully and of holding their own in the open market. Many cases of privatization lie in the area between these two; what is important is that events must be set in train which will lead progressively towards the second scenario. If the climate cannot be made fully competitive at the outset, then the policy has to be structured so that it becomes more so in the future, instead of being allowed to slip back.

It has been the case in several industries that preparation for privatization has itself brought about major reform, in advance of the actual move. The knowledge that a state operation is to be sold, like the knowledge that a man is to be hanged in a fortnight, concentrates the mind wonderfully. Efficiency is improved, economies are made. By the time the firm reaches the target date, it becomes a much more saleable commodity than it was before the process started. This policy of preparation has seen firms which were grossly overmanned and producer-oriented within the public sector become lean, efficient and profitable by the time they reached the market place.

British Airways provides a classic example. When the decision was first made in 1983 it was making huge losses, sustained by state subsidies. It was overmanned, and with a great deal of slack in its operations. By the time of its sale in February 1987, it was both popular and profitable. Its workforce had slimmed down from 59,000 to 39,000. It cared visibly about customers, and took care to ascertain and respond to their needs. It was regularly voted to be the best international airline by important groups of air passengers. A complete new look accompanied a new approach. The company was

turned from an ailing and flabby giant into a healthy
and very competitive company. When the public
flotation finally came, British Airways was a good
commercial investment. It was not life within the
private sector which did this, but rather the preparation
for that life.

How was it possible to do this, given its status as part
of the state sector, subject to all the pressures there? The
answer is that it was possible because of the techniques
used and the prize at the end. Employees were not
fired; they were offered generous terms for voluntary
redundancy. The index-linked pensions were not
cancelled; they were bought out for cash sums. It took
money at the front end to turn British Airways around,
but this was more than made up by the new profitability
and the valuation this put on the sale. Morale in the
company was sufficiently high that when impending
lawsuits repeatedly delayed the date of sale, the
employees threatened strike action if it were not hurried
forward and completed.

The workers were, as so often in other companies,
taken aboard as partners on the privatization. It is
doubtful to say the least if any of these reforms could
have taken place in a public sector operation without
the prospect of privatization at the end of the day.
Without the need to be competitive and profitable
within the private sector, the interests of the involved
groups would have lain elsewhere, and management
could not have succeeded in its drive for efficiency.

The lesson drawn from the experience of British
Airways is that a loss-making operation can still be sold.
It could, of course, be sold anyway, in that loss-makers
are bought and sold every day on the stock market.
What the British Airways experience proved is that a
loss-making concern can be turned around and sold off
as a viable operation. The preparation for privatization
can itself be a sufficient incentive to turn a loss-maker

into a profitable and competitive outfit.

The market holds it to be a general truth that once a reputation for quality is gone, it can never easily be recovered. Whether it was easy or not, British Airways did recover very rapidly from a very low reputation for quality of service. In a very few years it rose from a very low rank in the ranking of quality to contest the top spot itself. It was not an isolated case. Jaguar cars had lost their former reputation for quality after a sojourn in the state sector. They lost out in America because they were regarded correctly as unreliable. Quality control had given way to public sector practices in which political goals won out over any market considerations. After privatization, Jaguar regained their former reputation for high quality and reliability at an unbelievable speed. The shares which their workers took out at the time rose in consequence by 2,000 per cent, in which circumstance lies no small part of the story.

12 What About the Workers?

An important element in the success of privatization has been the support of the workforce. The offer made to them must be such as to equal at least the perceived benefit they already receive. It may be, of course that their current benefit will be discounted. If the future of the state sector operation is in doubt, the work force might not attach much value to the job security which state sector employment normally carries. They might, in a situation such as this, accept privatization of the operation even where an ostensible reduction of their benefit was involved. The definite job in the private sector is worth more than the possibility of continued employment with the state.

In circumstances such as these, a workforce has accepted the sale of a state-owned enterprise even where this has meant a drop in manning levels. The perceived alternative was complete closure of the operation. A major factor in the success of moves such as this has been the treatment offered to displaced workers. If no forced redundancies are involved, then the potential group of those who might be unwillingly displaced has zero members. This effectively limits opposition to those such as union activists who do have an interest in total numbers.

The offer made to miners whose pits were scheduled

for closure is a good indication of how benefits are traded. Relocation to other pits was offered, complete with a moving allowance. Retraining was made available. Terms for voluntary redundancy were totally unprecedented in the amount offered. If the closure plan went ahead, a miner stood to lose the job in the place he lived; but the certainty of a job in another pit and help in moving seemed a reasonable alternative, given the impossibility of keeping all of the pits open.

The usual way of securing the support of the workforce for the move to the private sector has been by share allocation. A block of shares is set aside for the workers in the industry to take up if they wish. Sometimes, as in the case of British Gas, a number of shares are offered free. Sometimes the workers can purchase a higher number than are available to the general public. This was the case with both British Gas and Telecom. Sometimes those who work for the company are allowed to buy shares out of their wage packets on extended credit, usually interest-free. This happened with the Jaguar car company, and has been done in some of the shipyard sales.

The aim of management is to maximize worker participation in the sale of the company. This secures their support for the move, and neutralizes what could present serious opposition to it. It does more than that, though. When workers have a direct stake in the firm, they identify its future with their own. It shakes away the old attitude of 'us and them', and has workers identifying with the company, instead of seeing it as adversary. This makes for better industrial relations and less disputes. It also makes for a higher share price, other things being equal, as potential buyers weigh up the company's likely performance in the future. There is a further bonus to government, in that a society which has ordinary workers owning shares in their companies is likely to oppose state takeovers and all of the trappings of centralism which other political parties might propose. There is a built in bias towards private property and capitalism if its benefits are visible and widespread, and if ordinary working people see them selves as part of that system, and see the advantages they derive from it.

Not all privatization takes place by public flotation, however. A small but significant fraction is achieved by private sale. Here, as in cases where private contractors are brought in, it is very important to ensure that the workers are taken into account in the transfer. It must be done in such a way that the benefits they had as state sector employees are traded for alternative benefits which are no less acceptable. Sometimes the closure of the state operation has been announced first, with the private sale coming in the form of a rescue package which can keep open the activity. Sometimes the private buyer is able to offer a visibly better future by integrating the operation into a wider base, by putting in the expertise in management and marketing needed to make a go of it, or by supplying the investment needed to modernize and re-equip. Some of the warship yards and Channel ferries serve as examples of these techniques.

At the other end of the scale are the cases in which no outside buyer at all is involved, but in which privatiz- ation takes place instead by a buyout involving the management, the workforce, or both. These cases show how carefully constructed policies can be used to transform both the industrial climate and the commercial viability of state enterprises. The exercise redirects the source of benefit to the two groups, management and workers, and thus redirects the trades they make in the political market. Whatever their interests as state employees, they become vastly dif- ferent as owners, worker or management, of their own enterprise. Their whole priorities shift, and they demand very different types of outcome from the political process. Some of these buyouts feature among privatization's biggest successes.

One of the first management–worker buyouts was of the National Freight Corporation, which handles the transport of goods by road in Britain. The buyout came at the instigation of management, an initiative repeated many times subsequently in other industries. Very often it is management's idea, and the management team which makes an offer. In the case of National Freight, although most of the shares were taken up by management with bank support, great efforts were made to involve the workforce. They were successful in setting a classic precedent.

The workers of National Freight, including drivers and loaders, checkers and sorters, bought into the new company. Some mortgaged their homes to buy shares. Others pooled their life savings. They estimated that the new company would be profitable, and were prepared to back it. Several of them were interviewed and made television appearances talking about how it felt to own their own company. It was made a condition of the buyout that the shares could not be resold until after two years.

The company was an immediate success. It proved highly profitable in the private sector, and marketed its services in a way which implied that it knew and cared about what customers wanted. The share-owning workers saw the value of their shares increase first four-fold, then eight-fold, then ten-fold. then 54-fold. All of the worker and management owners made several thousand per cent capital gain on their initial investment.

At one stage National Freight Corporation had to shed some of its workforce. It did so quietly, if sadly, on a commercial basis. What would have generated a storm in a public sector company, and been the pretext for strikes and perhaps factory occupations, was taken in its stride. The company remains profitable. It hired a concert hall for its first annual shareholders meeting, having no idea how many of the many thousands who worked for the company and owned its shares would appear. Several thousand did, and its annual shareholder meetings are still reckoned to provide one of the most knowledgeable company audiences in Britain, since they all work for the company as well.

If National Freight was a model, there have been many copies of it. Management buyouts have been more numerous, but ones which involve a significant worker input make more news. Neither of the two types of buyout receives anything like the publicity attached to a public flotation; they represent some of the lesser-known successes of privatization.

There are direct management buyouts, such as those of Leyland Bus and of the Unipart subsidiary of Leyland. Many of the sections of the former National Bus Company are going to management buyouts. Even in cases where management alone makes the running, efforts are made to bring in the workers in some way with a collective stake. In many cases finance has been provided by Unity Trust who invest on behalf of the trade unions. While not the same as share ownership by individual employees, it does provide for a stake in the company on a collective basis, and thus neutralizes some of the political opposition they might stage.

In cases where workers are a significant part of the consortium, novel methods are used to maximize their possible holding. Those who suppose privatization to be no more than the selling-off of state assets to the private sector should study the extraordinary and creative techniques used to achieve full worker participation in these deals. Workers are allowed to buy on credit, paying for the shares by monthly payment from wage packets. Sometimes shares are locked in a fund for the workers, and released a few at a time as they are paid for. Sometimes local banks are brought in on the deal, with special terms for worker-buyers being part of their contribution. In many examples, bearing in mind that much of the workforce is unsophisticated financially, programmes are conducted to educate them in the operations of the stock market, the role of investment, and the importance of profits. Observers might suggest that this is a major social good in itself, and comes not before time.

All of this shows how very much privatization is a political, and not just an economic, activity. Privatization has its effect at a level which includes political markets as well as economic ones. Involvement of the workforce in share purchase is one method of altering the patterns of political trade. It is notable that when the sale of a state company has involved a special allocation set aside for employees, the take up rate has every time exceeded 90 per cent of employees.

The buyout of the Vickers shipyard by the Vickers Shipbuilding Engineering Ltd Employee Consortium in 1986 saw many of the tried and tested techniques used alongside some new ones. It serves to illustrate the extraordinary lengths to which the policies will go to promote the desired ends. In this case novel credit terms combined with an intensive education programme to enable most of the shipyard workers to participate. This was a group without substantial savings or financial knowledge, so everything had to be aimed at making participation easy. In addition to the workforce, the management, the banks and other investors, a novel feature of the Vickers sale was that favourable rates for shares were offered not just to workers, but to members of the local community in Barrow and Birkenhead where the two yards concerned were located.

The most dramatic feature of the Vickers privatization is that the sale was made to the second highest bidder.

The top bid was that of Trafalgar House, a giant conglomerate. The consortium of management, employees and community participants was successful, even though its offer was less. With so much involvement, it was thought to stand a better chance of making a go of it. There may well have been some commentators criticizing the fact that this was a political, rather than a purely economic, decision. It does show, however, what privatization is about.

The management–worker buyout has been very fruitful as a method of privatizing fairly small entities: small, this is, compared with giants such as Telecom and British Gas. When the outfit is small enough for a real sense of community to be possible, there is a potential candidate for a buyout. Management will be likely to know both the potential and the problems, and to have observed over many years the performance within the state sector. They are in a position to know what improvements could be made by changes in operating methods, and by changes in the attitude of the work force. This is why it is crucial to involve them, no matter how creative the accounting has to be to achieve it.

It is significant that a large number of buyouts have been on the small scale. The first group included some of the British Rail hotels which were sold early in the exercise; and the last group includes many of the bus companies making up the National Bus network. The wheels of policy have certainly turned when it is a Conservative government actively involved in the establishment of small co-operatives. Yet the management–worker buyout has been one of the most successful of the privatization techniques.

There is an obvious question concerning the role and position of the unions as the ostensible representatives of the workforce. The privatization programme has shown that while the unions could be regarded as representing the interests of the members on such things as pay and conditions within the existing structure, this did not apply when the structure itself was under discussion. In some, if not most, cases of privatization there has been a fairly clear distinction between the interests of the union leadership and those of its members.

Union leaders have had a vested interest in the public sector as such. State sector union membership has been highest in both blue-collar and white-collar jobs, with the latter being very much higher than in private industry. Unions in the public sector have usually been able to establish cosy working relationships with their equally public sector management and administration. Each had to take more account of each other than of consumers or the general public. Pension arrangements far in excess of private sector schemes and closed shops characterized some of the public sector benefits which unions had been able to accrue.

Unions have usually opposed privatization, recognizing that they would find life much less easy in the private market. The notable exceptions have been cases in which government or management made absolutely clear its intention to close down a plant or activity, and where privatization appeared as an agent of rescue. The union response has been to oppose privatization except where the only alternative was immediate closure. The question arises as to why that response has been so ineffective, given the enormous powers the unions were perceived to have in 1979.

An immediate possible answer is that those enormous powers were derived in part from the perception of them. While government and trade union leaders met at Downing Street twice a week to discuss matters of state, union power seemed institutionalized. When a new prime minister ceased to consult them on non-labour matters, the power evaporated because it was never a real power in the first place. A second possibility is that the union leaders' power was so eroded by legislative action by the new government that it could not be used successfully against privatization. The first alternative may have merit, but timing does not permit the second explanation, in that unions resisted in vain long before the new measures began to bite into the power of their leaders.

The most plausible account is that the policies which implemented the privatization programme were carefully designed to circumvent union opposition, and succeeded in doing so. An examination of the tactics used by union leaders shows the difficulties which they found themselves up against.

Some of them conducted expensive public relations campaigns. This was the case for the unions opposing the use of contractors for local government services, who spent over £1 million in one year, and for the Post Office Engineering Union (later to be called the National Telecommunications Union), which spent £1.5 million on a one and a half year campaign. In each case this involved the message being put to their own members and to the general public by means of information packs, leaflets, stickers and video films shown at meetings. Active members were given the line to take for media appearances, trained in presentation, and media coverage was arranged for them. Special attention was devoted to marginal constituencies, and to groups such as the old, the disabled and the isolated, who might have been worried about the telephone service which they depended upon.

This made little impact, since one of the tactics used by the government was a vast advertising campaign to promote the flotations. Even a £1 million public relations drive is swallowed up like a minnow by the campaigns around it costed in hundreds of millions of pounds. Those highly professional and slick campaigns might have been designed to sell the shares, but they also sold privatization. Part of their message was a reassurance about the future of the service.

On a practical level, the policy specifically undermined one by one every possible source of objection. If rural dwellers were concerned, then there would be a requirement to maintain the pay telephones in country areas. If consumers were worried about the level of charges, these would be tied to the rate of inflation for several years. If foreign takeover was a threat, the golden share would deal with it. The ground of opposition on which the unions might stand was chipped away, square inch by square inch.

A more promising initial tactic of the unions was to secure a united front with management. If both management and unions of an industry opposed privatization, it would be difficult to achieve. They gained some success, with Lord Kearton of BNOC, the British National Oil Corporation, opposing the sale of oil and gas holdings, and Robert Atkinson of British Shipbuilders opposing the sale of the warship yards. There were a few others from the Nationalized Industries' Chairman's Group, but the government undercut this in two ways. First, as vacancies occurred, it put supporters of privatization onto the management boards. Secondly, it secured its own united front with management by taking them in as partners on the privatization.

Industrial action itself has rarely been used. There were token strikes in the gas industry to oppose the showroom sale, in the Channel ferry services to oppose the sale of Sealink, and in the Royal Ordnance factories. A year before Telecom was brought to market, there was union action against Mercury, the competitor in business communication which would be licensed after the sale. It was stopped by legal action after failing to have the required impact to influence the decision to privatize.

This kind of industrial action has not been effective, and has been limited to small-scale action by militants partly because the union leaders could not necessarily count on the backing of their members for more widespread or long-term action. It was the opposition of management which stopped the sale of the gas show rooms; that same management put through the 1986 British Gas sale.

The failure of industrial action to influence events shows to some extent the position in which union leaders were placed by government policy. The detailed proposals for privatization which were finally presented did not give public expression to the view that public sector workers were overpaid, pampered and powerful. Instead they sought to secure the interests of those workers in the new arrangement. They had the effect of dividing the interest of the members from that of the union leaders. Those leaders thus found uncertainty in the ranks behind them; they could not claim the automatic loyalty which direct confrontation produced. In the case of the National Freight Corporation, for example, it was clearly to the advantage of their members to support privatization and to participate in it.

The policy of management and government has been to achieve this effect in as many cases as possible. Not only have attractive offers been made to involve the workers, but education campaigns and promotions have sought to persuade them to participate. When the employees have weighed up the advantages offered on the one side against the likely future in the state sector on the other, the overwhelming choice has been to disregard any opposition from union leaders, and to take part in the process of change. It says much for the standing of nationalized industries that the workers have in several cases been enthusiastic for privatization, taking a visible pride and excitement in the new venture.

Meanwhile the union leaders, whose first response was to pass motions at annual conferences calling for nationalization without compensation, and pledging a campaign within the Labour Party to reverse all that has been done, now come to terms by accepting that much of what has happened is irreversible. The new interest groups, drawn from the employees as well as the general public, are already too powerful to take on.

A sign of the times has been the speed with which some unions, so reputedly slow to change their position on other issues, have met the challenge by shifting their stance on privatization. Of the four unions involved in the National Freight Corporation, three eventually backed the consortium of management and workers which took the operation into the private sector. The National Union of Railwaymen became a shareholder in Gleneagles Hotels, one of the companies running some of the hotels formerly owned by the state through British Rail. Other unions did not fail to note the popularity among their own members for the employee allocation of shares in British Aerospace, Amersham International and Cable and Wireless. The government certainly did not fail to note it; it used the observed support of union members in these early examples of privatization to establish the precedent for a policy approach which led to widespread employee backing for the sales of Telecom and British Gas.

It remains to be seen if workers gain from privatization in their role as employees. That they gain as shareholders is beyond doubt as a general case. Part of the micropolitical strategy has been to give the workers a new role as shareholders with the intention of showing them visible gains in that role to balance against any misgivings they might hold about the effect on the other role.

The early results are positive on that other role, despite the dire forecasts of union leaders, but the timespan has been short for a final assessment to be made. Wages have not declined on a comparative basis. Indeed, as companies have taken advantage of their private sector freedom to expand markets and increase their profitability, workers have gained from wage increases as well as from the capital growth of their shares.

Industrial relations have not deteriorated. It is a striking fact that most of the large labour disputes since the advent of the 1979 government have taken place in the public sector. The firms which have been privatized have not been characterized by any huge increase in industrial action. There have been disputes in newly privatized companies, including Jaguar and Telecom. They tend to be brief, and calculated not to damage the company's viability. In general, there are less disputes in the private sector, and the new firms fall into that pattern.

Union leaders have expressed concern over job losses after moving to the private sector. Associated British Ports, for example, use contractors now for some services they used to perform by direct labour. Cable and Wireless shed jobs, so did British Aerospace. On the other hand Amersham International and Britoil took on more workers. The effect of privatization on job levels seems to vary from company to company, with market position being the factor most responsible. The job losses in British Aerospace and Cable and Wireless were attributed to the competitive position, perhaps indicating that job levels in privatized industries are exposed to market forces and determined accordingly.

One possible effect relates to a phenomenon of the public sector, where union power often results in a lower differential between the skilled and unskilled than exists in private industry. Unions in state industries, in other words, bid up the pay of the more numerous unskilled at the expense of the smaller numbers who have professional or other qualifications and skills. One would expect that in the private sector this would be corrected. Firms have to increase their reward for top personnel and skilled workers, or risk losing them to rivals who outbid them. Therefore, once they are in the private sector, firms initially have to make awards which give more to the highly qualified. This has happened just as predicted. After the distribution which characterizes the private sector has been reached, however, one would expect pay settlements to respond to the market.

Looking over the range of benefits which accrue to workers, the conclusion is that policies can be carefully constructed which bring them immediately perceived benefits in their capacity as shareholders of the firm, without loss of their perceived longer-term benefits as employees. Indeed, their future prospects from the standpoint of opportunities for advancement can be improved in addition. Given this, and with evidence of it available in profusion from the numerous examples of privatization so far, it is hardly surprising that employees of state firms have perceived their potential gains from privatization and have cooperated with it more often than not. The policy details have secured what they were designed to achieve.

PART IV
SPECIAL TECHNIQUES

13 Routes in Depth

Privatization is one of the techniques which derive from the type of analysis which recognizes political markets and seeks to work with them. More accurately, it is a range of techniques. One fact which emerged very early is that no two cases are the same. Every single activity in the public sector has unique characteristics which distinguish it from all other ones. This means that all of them present unique problems. The techniques which work on one area cannot simply be applied to others without a regard for the differences between them.

It is true that there are broad principles, and that a variety of methods derived from those principles has been employed. It still leaves the detail of individual cases to be attended to. No one can know in advance which methods will apply; each case has to be studied before possible solutions can be attempted. The sale of British Gas was not exactly the same as that of Telecom, though there were obvious similarities. One difference was that 100 per cent of British Gas was offered for sale, whereas only 51 per cent of Telecom was released at the first flotation.

Micropolitics demands a study of each individual case, including those involving privatization. The analysis should focus on the various interest groups

who derive and trade advantages within the public
sector status quo. After the analysis comes the policy
formulation. This is a creative exercise, requiring
solutions to be proposed to the problems posed by the
public sector situation, and for a policy to be woven
which circumvents them. Sometimes a method of
dealing with one group's benefit will create problems
for another; so care must be taken that the proposed
policy has no internal contradictions. Rarely does the
finished policy show the simple elegant lines of a clear
ideology. It is far more likely to be bristling with *ad hoc*
clauses tacked on to cope with special interests.

If the exercise of dismantling the public sector can be
compared with any other activity, it is like that of
dismantling an unexploded bomb. The first task is to
remove the cover-plate and to examine the wiring.
When all the connections have been traced and a
picture of their role has been formed, the calculation has
to be made concerning how they should be disconnected
and in which order. The analogy is not a very good one,
except perhaps that if it is done wrongly it can blow up
in the face of whoever attempts it.

A glance at the different techniques used in privatization shows the enormous range of policy which
micropolitics can give rise to. Even on the very limited
range in which a public enterprise is sold, there has
already been used in practice a large variety of different
ways of selling. Sometimes all of it is sold in one piece,
sometimes sections are separated off. It may be 100 per
cent sold, or only 51 per cent. The buyer might be a
private corporation, a worker and management consortium or the investing public. It could be sold for cash
down, or on easy terms. City firms could be called in, or
not; public advertising may or may not be used. The
price of shares could be fixed in advance or determined
by tender. Variations and permutations of all of these
methods have been used so far. The range of them is as
large as the number of examples of privatization,

because each individual case is different, and each case requires a separate policy.

Direct sale to the private sector is one of the devices suggested by micropolitics as a solution to some public sector problems. It must be done in a way which suits the particular industry and the economic circumstances surrounding it. Amersham International was sold straight off by flotation. No large-scale advertising was used, but City professionals were used to pilot the sale to market as they do regularly for private issues. It was sold in a piece, and 100 per cent was offered. The price immediately rose, accompanied by the soon to be familiar charge of 'underselling'.

British Petroleum was a low-key privatization and was, incidentally, the first. Government owned just over 50 per cent since the crisis of 1976 had produced requirements from the International Monetary Fund to make the Labour government sell some equity. The pretext was a 1979 sale, in which the government allowed its share to fall below 50 per cent. Treasury rules made the company now private. It became more profitable, its shares rose in value, and the government was later able to sell further tranches at higher prices. For Cable and Wireless, an initial sale of 49.4 per cent in 1981 was followed by a rights issue in 1983 in which the government, by not exercising its option, allowed its stake to fall to 45 per cent. However, privatization by accident or stealth is not a normal option; the circumstances were, as they always are, unique.

Just over half of British Aerospace was sold, with an employee allocation, as in Amersham, and the first 'golden share' to guard a strategic industry from foreign takeover. The government later sold all its residual holding except this one share.

National Freight Corporation was sold 100 per cent to the management and worker consortium, with assistance from banks. Shareholders were not allowed to resell for five years. Redhead shipyard was closed and then sold to a worker consortium which reopened it. The hotel chain and the Channel ferry and hovercraft services of British Rail were detached and disposed of separately. So were a large number of subsidiaries of other state industries.

The 1981 sale of Cable and Wireless shares was at a set-price; the 1983 tranch was by tender. By contrast the first sale of Britoil in 1982 was by tender, and the subsequent 1985 tranch was at set-price. The Enterprise Oil privatization was under-subscribed; for Jaguar shares they fought in the street to get applications in on time. Customers of Telecom were offered the choice of reduced telephone bills or bonus shares if they bought in; for gas customers the benefit was the certainty of a preferred allocation of shares, as well as the bonus.

Every sale is different not only because every case is different, but also because new twists are constantly being thought up. No 'right way' exists because there might be a variety of ways of doing it successfully. Those who claim that privatization is just 'selling off state assets' should note the huge variation of the techniques used. It suggests that the aim is to achieve rather more than a simple sale. Substantial benefits are targeted at important groups as political trade-offs for losses they might otherwise sustain. In many cases the aim is to make some groups sustain benefits in order to make the process less susceptible to later reversal.

Direct sale, while it involves promotional campaigns and attracts interest by its razzamatazz, is only one highly visible technique. Others have been tried as successfully, if not as spectacularly.

One method seeks to leave the public supply intact, while growing an alternative alongside it in the private sector. Without there being a direct threat to the existing supply, circumstances are created in which people have an effective alternative choice. As more and more of them exercise that choice, the total proportion produced in the public sector declines as a fraction of the total supply.

When this method is used, it is the public itself who determine the rate of privatization. They effectively privatize the service themselves as they elect in increasing numbers to buy the private alternative. The long-distance inter-city bus services in Britain were deregulated in 1981 to the extent that private operators were allowed to compete. Their entry led to spectacular fare reductions, down to one-third of the state monopoly levels in some cases, and to vastly improved services and innovative levels of comfort. The public started using the private services on the first day, reducing the proportion of bus transport performed in the public sector.

This technique has much to commend it for more sensitive areas of service where the public would like a better service without risk to the existing one. Health is an obvious candidate, in that the security provided by the National Health Service is clearly held to be of great value, however much the service could be improved. By leaving the NHS intact, but encouraging the spread of private medicine, the government can create circumstances in which the proportion of private medicine increases as people make the choice to use it.

This has happened since the Chancellor restored the tax-exempt status of employer-provided health insurance schemes for low wage earners. Even though the salary level has to be below £8500 to qualify, and although it is limited to employer-provided schemes, it does provide an incentive, and takes the choice of private medicine down market. The numbers covered by it in Britain have quadrupled since 1979, and include hundreds of thousands of trade unionists for whom it is a negotiated benefit.

The advantage of this approach is that the NHS is still

there for those who need it and wish to make use of it. But as more and more turn to private medicine, they relieve the public sector of a part of its burden, enabling its scarce resources to be turned more accurately toward those who need them. Micropolitics points to the groups who turn to private medicine, identifying them as the articulate middle classes, of high visibility and effective at applying pressure to the system to secure their ends. Once in private medicine, they constitute a major interest group anxious to retain its benefits. The more of them who can be encouraged to make that choice, the stronger does private medicine become, and the stronger the groups who will fight to retain it. Attention is turned, therefore, to other ways of helping private medicine to grow. These might involve extending the modest tax concessions, or perhaps making charitable donations easier to make on a tax exempt basis.

The technique is to grow the private secta alongside the state supply as an alternative which does not threaten it, but which offers the public a choice. Government policy and generally rising standards can move that choice down-market until it lies within the range of most people. Gradually, and as a result of free choices made by individuals, the state system will slowly turn to provide what people think it should concentrate upon.

This method of growing a private alternative supply alongside a state provision left in place is one of a range of micropolitical strategies covered by the general name of 'micro-incrementalism'. They represent an attractive variation in which people themselves make the changes by their own decisions. The policy research team produces proposals whose effect is to create circumstances under which people find choice worthwhile. They find it advantageous to choose the private alternative to the state supply. But the choices are made gradually by individuals, and over months and years they cumulatively produce the new reality. The most secure revolutions are ones which people make for themselves over time; these are the ones we call evolution.

Policies which encourage exit from the state supply come into the class called 'micro-incrementalist'. At the heart of the strategy to promote choice must lie a policy which makes the alternative more attractive. It might make it cheaper, it might make it better, it might make it easier. In the background is the central fact that people have already paid for the state supply. If other things were equal, only the very rich could have choice, by being able to afford to pay twice over. The policy can make sure that other things are not equal.

It can take the choice down-market by a variety of strategies designed to increase access to the alternative, and therefore to encourage exit from the state. It can make the payment tax-exempt; it can make it a valid business expense; it can repeal a monopoly; it can remove some of the barriers to private supply and remove some of the burdens from it. None of these is in any sense a 'clean' solution. Conventional free market politics would probably advocate biting the bullet and undertaking to end the state service. Such a policy would fail because it would not deal with the fears and anxieties of consumers any more than it dealt with the benefits enjoyed by the state sector groups. By taking the issue head on, it would meet all the enemies head on, and all of them together.

It is basic to the strategy of micropolitics that not all of the enemies are met together. On the contrary, considerable ingenuity and effort goes into turning some of them into friends, and into using alliance with some groups to outweigh the opposition of other ones. A further innovative tactic used to achieve this is that involving the subdivision of classes. It is possible to look at problems in terms of the broad classes of activity or status of those involved. Thus we might talk about the difficulties which face 'landlords', 'tenants', or 'businesses', and look for solutions which cover the whole of the class.

This approach has two drawbacks. In the first place it ventures towards the holistic approach, dealing with the class as a whole. Secondly, any proposals which emerge are likely to generate opposition in large groups, as they bring benefits and penalties to the broad classes or to those whose interests they oppose. Thus, measures which bring aid or relief to 'landlords' are likely to incur the hostility of 'tenants'. Those which help 'businesses' can bring down the wrath of 'employees' or maybe of 'consumers'.

Micropolitics recognizes the merits of subdividing these classes into smaller ones, in order to treat them separately. It achieves a reduction in the size of the opposition by reducing the size of the groups dealt with. More importantly, it identifies the parts of those classes with which the problem or its solution resides, and deals only with them. Whereas macro-analysis sees the large groups and operates at that level of detail, micro-analysis goes onto a much finer scale, looking at the sub-sections of those groups to identify where the problem lies, and how it might be solved.

To give an example, there may be a problem caused by the lack of private rental property, and its causes may lie in the operation of rent control and total security of tenure. It is possible in theory to solve the problem by dealing with the whole class of private rentals, but in practice the opposition of all of the tenants and their supporting groups could thwart it. Analysis on the smaller scale recognizes that it is a shortage of new rentals which causes much of the problem, and is therefore prepared to consider subdivision of the class in order to deal separately with 'new landlords'. It might show that the problem could be solved if people owning one or two extra homes could be tempted to let them, and might propose a subdivision of 'small landlords' with their own different rules and exemptions.

Similarly there is a problem for business, in that the levies and burdens which fall upon it are a disincentive to expansion and job creation. Much effort that would otherwise go into enterprise is being diverted to compliance with regulation, and the jobs are not being produced in sufficient numbers. Analysis at the macro-level recognizes this, and proposes reduction of taxes and regulations. This would be excellent, if it could be done, but involves major confrontation with large and powerful groups. It is unlikely to succeed, given prevailing political markets. Micro-analysis sees that the burden falls more severely on small businesses who have neither the staff nor the resources to cope with it as the large ones can. Moreover, the new jobs in an economy are overwhelmingly generated by small businesses. The micro-solution suggests that a new subdivision of 'small businesses' be recognized and treated separately. They feel the problem more heavily, and are the source of its solution. It might propose special circumstances to deal with firms which employ less than twenty persons. In doing so it will not incur the wholesale hostility which a total restructure of the laws governing business as such would have evoked.

Dealing with subdivisions of classes means two things: that the groups in opposition will be similarly subdivided, and that it will be possible to focus more accurately on the source of the problem and the means of its solution. Micropolitics is thus characterized by its readiness to create and to recognize novel classification of sections of larger groups, and to contemplate special treatment for them. This is by no means as remarkable as it sounds. To the micro-analyst it is obvious that the corner shop with two employees faces very different circumstances to the department store with 20000. If the application of rules designed for large stores causes excessive problems for the small ones, it seems reasonable to recognize their differences and to treat them accordingly. There is clearly something wrong if the laws designed to protect employees in factories cause the small businessman with one assistant to devote his time to checking temperatures and the size of toilet seats instead of making more sales and generating more jobs.

Two questions arise in response to this attitude. The first is about the boundaries which are created. If subdivisions are given special treatment, there is a disincentive on the boundary which deters people from moving into another class. If small landlords receive special treatment, it might be against their interest to become large ones. If firms employing less than twenty people receive special treatment, they will be deterred from employing the twenty-first. This is correct, but trivial. Subdivision of classes does involve boundaries, but what it does is to move them, breaking one big hurdle into more smaller ones. There is a big gulf for a business to jump when it takes on its first employee. A subdivision which creates 'small' businesses reduces that gulf but interposes a smaller one later. Instead of incurring all of the levies and burdens at once, the subdivision phases them in for the firm as it grows in size.

That said, policy which derives from this kind of micro-analysis directs considerable ingenuity to lessening the impact that might be caused by 'boundary effects'. It constantly seeks innovative proposals to diminish the hurdles which are interposed between the divisions. One hope is, of course, that the experience of deregulation and the lifting of burdens will bring such benefits as to make further action easier to accomplish. That is, although the initial actions are limited to specific subdivisions in order to limit opposition by tackling the problem only where it is most acute, the hope is that a successful result will leave other sub-sections clamouring for similar treatment, and that the practical results will diminish the opposition to extending it.

The other objection is that it is not fair to single out specific sections for favourable treatment. If it is right to deregulate and lift burdens, it should be done for everyone. This may be true, but the question is one of whether it is possible to do it for everyone. If the answer is no, and that opposition from the interest groups will prevent it, it then comes down to whether it is better to do it for some than for none at all. The micro-analyst suggests that it is indeed better to do it for some, the more so if most of the problem can be solved by doing so. There is always the added bonus possibility that doing it for some now will make it easier to do it for others later.

It should be pointed out, in fairness, that there is a school of thought which works at the macro-level and suggests that special treatment for subdivisions makes it less likely that the policy can be applied generally. By solving most of the problem through selective targeting, the argument runs, the pressure which might lead to a general solution is weakened. By leaving things as bad as possible, the pressures are left in place which will one day demand a solution for the whole class of activity. The logic of this position is that improvement should be avoided because it hinders the pursuit of the perfect. This is apocalyptic politics, taking no steps until the great day dawns when they can be taken all at once. It bears little relation to the real world, in which improvement is made by degrees, and in which problems which are left unsolved continue to become worse indefinitely. 'There is', as Adam Smith pointed out, 'a lot of ruin in a nation'.

There is a similar tactic to the subdivision of classes; rather than separating off some groups for different treatment by status it does it by geographical area. The policy is that of the small-scale experiment. Given the dire warnings which are uttered when deregulation or the easing of controls and burdens is raised, and the forceful opposition which is engendered, the proposal is made that the ideas should be tested in a limited area to observe the effects. If the predicted mishaps and disasters occur, then there is no need to experience them in society at large; they can be confined to the test area. By the same token, if benefits yielded vastly outweigh any adverse effects, the measures can be put into effect on the larger scale.

This is the type of thinking which produces proposals for such innovations as enterprise zones and freeports. The deregulated climate might accelerate business activity, leading to the creation of wealth and jobs, as its proponents claim. On the other hand, without the guiding hand of regulation, there is a measure of uncertainty as to what might happen. The idea of the special zone is that it enables a test to be made. After results have been observed, the argument about consequences no longer need be conducted at the theoretical level; there will be practical experience to judge from.

Furthermore, the experiments can be established through the political process because they offer special advantage to selected areas. Those who stand to receive such benefits fight harder, as always, than those who must confer them. Thus the areas which stand to be designated for experiment form an effective lobby in support of the policy. The proposal for freeports in Britain was followed by applications from 46 localities seeking the status, all of whom supported the proposal in general in the hope that they might be among those who benefited in particular. Locally elected representatives of all parties backed the applications of their own area, showing once more the strength of interest over ideology.

The argument that the whole country should be given the status of a freeport or an enterprise zone is not relevant. The point is that it is not going to be. A chance is stood by the small-scale experiments, but not for the sweeping macro-scale proposal. The small experimental areas, if they succeed, could leave others clamouring to be treated in the same way, setting up a lobby for deregulation.

There are, however, more serious objections. The first is that the experiments are not valid on the small scale because they operate on a differential effect. That is, they attract business growth to them because of the benefits they offer within their perimeters, and thus deprive other areas of that growth. This is true to some extent, and the task is to find out how much. It is certainly true that enterprise zones have attracted growth which might otherwise have taken place else-where. By offering a holiday from local rates and easier planning laws, together with other incentives, it is more advantageous for some types of business to expand there than at their present location. Two examples are the hypermarkets which have tended to locate there, and the printing plants, already planned, which have opted to move to enterprise zones.

The tendency is less strong for freeports because of the emphasis on using them promoting overseas trade. The freeports aim at jobs which would otherwise be done abroad. In both enterprise zones and freeports, however, the experiment must be backed by analysis of how many of the new jobs were simply 'moved' from elsewhere because of the differential effect. Experience in Britain suggests that a high proportion, perhaps roughly half, of the new jobs in the enterprise zones are not really new, but that this does not apply to the very small number of jobs being created in some of the freeports. This, while qualifying the results, does leave a net gain of jobs created by the climate of lower burdens and regulations. This does suggest that more jobs can be created by deregulation on a wider scale.

A more serious objection is made on the basis of micro analysis itself. It suggests that insufficient account has been taken of the bureaucracy as an interest group. While the experiments might attract the support of the localities and their representatives without being large enough to provoke widespread opposition, not enough has been offered in trade to the bureaucracy supposed to administer the experiments. The result will be that when detailed proposals are formulated in the Civil Service, they will be such as to absorb the experiment within the conventional framework, instead of letting it strike out onto new ground.

Critics point out that this has happened to a large extent with both enterprise zones and freeports. Enterprise zones were meant to be areas free of regulation and restriction; instead the Civil Service has made them into extensions of regional policy, turning them into islands of subsidy rather than zones of enterprise. The freeports have fared even worse, being hamstrung at every turn by Treasury officials determined to subsume them under the existing regulatory framework and allow no special rules to apply there.

If this allegation is sustained, and it must be said that there is considerable evidence to support it, then it will to a great extent invalidate the experiments. It will not invalidate the principle of geographical experiment on the small scale, however. What it will do is to send proponents of it back to the drawing-board to formulate policies which can overcome or circumvent bureaucratic opposition in the same way that they are constructed to outflank opposition from other groups.

The principle behind both limited geographical experiments and the subdivision of classes is that it is easier to move on the small scale than on the large scale. Action in limited areas or on limited groups deals with minorities, and it is fundamental to micropolitics that minorities have more power than majorities. They are able to identify their benefit more immediately, and to isolate its value. What is conceded in general by the public at large in order to sustain the benefit in particular is always of lower value and less worth fighting for. Whatever benefits accrue from selective treatment, be it deregulation or lowering of the burdens, are thus easier to secure for experimental groups.

It is hoped, of course, that these beachheads, once secured, can be extended. The criticism that the selection of an appropriate boundary is an arbitrary choice can be turned into a virtue. It is true that it is arbitrary. What counts as a 'small' firm might be one with less than twenty employees. It might just as well be ten, or twenty-five, or even fifty. The original selection of a boundary, arbitrary though it may be, is based on two criteria. First it is chosen on the basis of its ability to solve the problem.

If a significant proportion of new jobs are created by firms with less than twenty workers, and if there is a measurable jump before the next group makes a sizeable contribution, then there is a good case for fixing the initial boundary at twenty. If studies show that 80 per cent of all private rentals are likely to come from landlords owning less than five properties, there is a *prima facie* case for fixing the class of small landlords so that it consists of those who fit into that category. In other words, the first selection is empirically based on the contribution to the solution which will be made by the group chosen.

The second basis of choice of group size is the likelihood of the size of the opposition to it. If there would be a great deal more hostility to giving special

exemptions for firms of less than thirty employees than
to firms of less than twenty, prudence suggests choice
of the lower figure. A similar criterion applies to the
selection of category to qualify as 'small' landlords.
Neither of these two is in any sense 'fair'. On the
contrary, the assumption is that the whole system is
unfair. Any decrease at all in unfairness is therefore an
improvement. The determination of the maximum
which can be achieved at each attempt is an empirical
one, derived from the two criteria referred to.

The fact that the boundaries are arbitrary, however,
can be turned to advantage. Once the categories have
been selected and the benefits of selective treatment
have been reaped, and seen to derive from the reform,
there is little reason not to move them. The success of
the process itself creates a demand from the next group
to be included. In this way it might be possible to
proceed by extending boundaries to a more general
qualification for the special treatment than would have
been possible initially. If the boundaries are indeed
arbitrary, they can be moved.

The same empirical streak which runs through the
selection of the boundaries for groups which are to be
subjected to different treatment permeates all of the
techniques considered in this section. Just as the
selection of group size is determined by its likely
contribution to the problem and the desire to keep the
number of opponents down to manageable levels, so
the choice of geographical test areas, the number of
them and their size, are determined by similar factors.

If exit from state supply is to be encouraged so that
private alternatives can grow, the estimate has to be
made concerning the level of incentive which will prove
sufficient. Tax concessions normally involve loss of
revenue, so the calculation has to be made as to the
degree of savings which can be achieved if state services
no longer have to cater for certain numbers. Again, the

calculation is empirical. The estimate must be made of what will be saved if 10 per cent, for example, opt for private medicine, versus the cost of whatever concessions are needed to encourage those 10 per cent to opt out of state provision.

Many of the calculations will involve not so much empirical study as guesswork backed by market research. There is no accurate way to determine how many people will choose a private alternative, given a particular inducement, short of actually offering it. The estimate may be based on surveys of intent, but no one can tell if the intentions will translate into action. Nonetheless, to secure the acquiescence of a government attempting a regimen of fiscal responsibility, it may be necessary to propose reforms which are at least fiscally neutral. The incentives must be set in such circumstances so that savings made possible outweigh the revenue forgone. And this is a matter of practical calculation.

If anyone had supposed that the understandings brought by the public choice school would enable a clear and coherent system of policy formulation to be built upon their base, they must now be having second thoughts. They need not. The system is clear and coherent, but the policies it produces are not. The basis is one of computation of advantage, and of the construction of policies which offer acceptable trade offs for it.

The benefits and advantages enjoyed by interest groups stick out like protein groups on the surface of foreign bodies entering the bloodstream. The policy to cope with those interest groups must, like the antibodies which cope with invaders, be constructed to match them and neutralize them. Each one may look unwieldy and appear to be put together on an *ad hoc* basis; but the unity lies in the method of construction and the principles by which it is performed.

14 The Role of Choice

When it comes to the supply of services rather than goods, the public sector is geared for the production of a standardized output. It is marked by uniformity rather than by variety. This is to be expected, given its structure and status. The decisions as to which services are to be provided, and in what degree, are largely political decisions. The determination is affected in part by what can be afforded, which itself is determined by what expenditure the political leaders think the public will support.

This is not the same as what people would willingly spend if the decision was their own. It can be influenced by the economic state of the nation, which in turn may be the outcome partly of international events. Political leaders may be wrong; they may underestimate what people would spend themselves, or they may put too high a figure on it, reflecting their own scale of values instead of the general one.

There is the tendency to overproduce quantity, if not quality, in the public sector; hence come such sights as the large numbers of empty bus seats being transported around for much of the day. Adding the effects of producer capture, overmanning and under-capitalization, there is very little room for consumer input except diffusely, through the political process. The system is one in which producers find it convenient to offer a uniform service designed for the great majority of people, though not necessarily what they would have designed for themselves.

One feature which derives from the political market is that state services will normally opt to provide a little service for the many, rather than a lot of service for the few. In the state health service, for example, roughly nine of every ten ambulance journeys are rated as non-emergency cases. This means that people who could use public transport or their own are being given ambulance rides. There is no charge at point of use, and it provides a modest service to a great number of people. On the other hand, the ambulance service lacks many emergency facilities necessary to give life-saving help. Its vehicles are not well equipped to cope with acute heart problems or trauma cases. Other countries with different methods of finance and different markets at the political level do feature well equipped vehicles, but do not devote as many resources to giving free taxi-rides.

Because the public sector is bidding for votes instead of money, its services count heads. A service to the many picks up support even if it is a small one. A major service to the few has rather less value in the political market place. When people choose how much to spend on services, and which ones to buy, they do not necessarily choose the same distribution pattern. Their real concern, and hence the real money, might be saved for the services which really matter to them.

Where there are alternatives to the state sector, even though not within range of most people's means, it is interesting to see what the private competition offers that people think worth paying for. In the case of health it is overwhelmingly the desire to have their case dealt with when they, the patients, want it, rather than when it is convenient to the producers to treat them. Choice of

the time of treatment is ranked very high among those
who buy private medicine. Secondly, the individual
attention is cited. Instead of feeling that they are
processed like sausages in some vast machine, patients
when they are also customers buy a more personal
treatment. Thirdly are ranked the little comforts such as
greater privacy, hospitals run to serve the patients, and
the greater dignity which private medicine manages to
accord to its clients.

In education it is the failure of the state system to
achieve what parents want which apparently motivates
them to seek a fee-paying alternative. The individual
attention which each child is alleged to receive in the
private sector is cited as the reason why parents pay
twice, rejecting the state education they have already
paid for through taxation. Children are felt to be left
more to their own devices in the state system. Whether
they gain a worthwhile education from it is thought to
be a matter of luck. If they live in the area of a good
school or come under the influence of a good teacher,
they might do well. Otherwise they take their chances.
The private alternatives are thought to leave less to
chance, but to take the effort required in each case to
bring out the best in the child. If it is true, one can see
why people are prepared to pay for it.

A further factor which influences the parents who
choose private schools is the fact that such schools
provide the type of education which parents value,
rather than that which professional educators esteem.
There is no producer control in the private sector, so no
imposition of producer values. Parents do not feel their
children are the subjects of social experiment in private
education, they feel instead that they are taught the
fundamental skills which parents want them to acquire.

It is a perfectly legitimate view that state services
provide a standardized output because most people
want and need roughly similar things. Anyone with

extraordinary or special needs can seek the private alternative; meanwhile the majority will be satisfied with the state product. It is a legitimate view but not necessarily a correct one, and it is certainly a difficult one to test. If people can have any colour they want as long as it is black, it is hard to find out whether they have preferences for other colours.

Such evidence as there is suggests that they do. First, in the private sector people express choices in all kinds of services and products. There seems no limit to the degree to which each product or service can be customized for the individual buyer, except the capacity of the producer to accommodate it. Secondly, where public services have been opened up to competition and choice, there has always been a profusion of alternatives made available for consumer choice. And consumers have exercised those choices. While the telephone service was a monopoly, to have a telephone meant to pay a quarterly rental on a bakelite hand set with a rotary dial, looking like the 1930s without the art deco.

When the prospect of privatization was raised, with the entry of some competition, the choices proliferated. One could easily have asserted that most people would be satisfied with a basic black standard telephone. In fact people preferred push button sets, cordless telephones, multi coloured-ones, and ones shaped like Mickey Mouse. All of the evidence, limited as it is, points one way. When people are given the chance to make choices, variety proliferates as they do so.

One of the central tasks of micropolitics is the 'individuation' of state services. That is, the problem is one of transforming a standardized, producer-oriented public sector product into the range of individual alternatives which people would choose to fit their own requirements. The service is 'individuated' by being broken down from a basic identical output into the proliferation of varieties which are geared to meeting

the preferences of individual consumers. It means
introducing both variation and choice. It means redirecting the forces which determine production so that
they either bypass the political process completely and
come from the economic pressure of consumers, or they
take place still in a political market, but one changed so
as to reward the satisfaction of individual preferences.
This is no small task.

A feature of public sector supply, especially when it
exercises a near monopoly for most people, is that it
becomes difficult after a time to conceive of life without
it. The prospect of a Britain without universal state
health or education is, for most people, unthinkable.
This is not because it would be calamitous, it is simply
because it is unknown. Never having seen alternatives
to it, many people cannot even think that any might be
possible. To them it is a question of how the state service
might be improved or made to respond more to their
needs. The idea of replacing it has no place to rest
within their imagination.

Hardly less difficult to deal with is the fact that long
use of a public monopoly supply has made people
accustomed to its merits, even while they are aware of
some of its shortcomings. The merits give it a perceived
value which they do not wish to see placed in jeopardy.
The presence of a National Health Service means that
no one will be denied treatment on account of poverty,
and means that no illness need prove financially
ruinous, no matter how catastrophic it might be from
the medical points of view.

Universal state education has brought every child the
right to a schooling regardless of the means of the
parents. Children denied their chance because their
parents could not afford continued schooling feature
now only in stories from the bad old days. The
combination of tax-funded state provision and state
compulsion to the age of sixteen means that the basic

education is assured with little financial impact on parents.

These values cannot be treated lightly. They are genuinely held, as those who would dismiss them soon find. People really do value the security which the free health service brings. They feel the benefit of a free school place for their child. There is no point in telling them that these services are not free, that they do pay through taxes, or that they could afford them in the private sector. That is not how they perceive it. Most people look at the amount of money they have left after necessary expenditure and conclude that they would have none left for private services if they had to pay for them. Complex taxation sums are abstract to them because most people actually think that their services are provided by 'the government', and that the money to fund them comes mostly from sources other than themselves.

That they are wrong is not relevant; they believe it to be true. The real situation is very different. Not only do they themselves pay for state services, they pay expensively. The public sector is top heavy on administration, inefficient in its use of personnel, and poor in its application of capital and technology. The chances are more likely than not that the standardized service most people receive from the state costs them more personally than would a private sector equivalent with variety responsive to their individual needs and requirements. The reality to be dealt with, however, is that people do not perceive it that way. Herein lie the ways in which political markets operate.

The micropolitician has to accept these attitudes as facts. While it might be possible to change them in the long term, they colour the present reality, and cannot be ignored. It is theoretically possible that the attitudes could be changed, and that a long-term programme of public education could persuade people to abandon them and set sail happily into the uncharted waters of the free market. No one knows if such a project would succeed, or how long it might take. We do know, however, about the force of an interest compared with that of an idea.

In yet another inversion of conventional thinking, micropolitical analysis suggests that it will be easier to change the attitudes after the policies have changed, rather than before. It recognizes that the advantages of choice and variety are difficult things to teach at a theoretical level. People are much more likely to see the practical benefits when they are present, than to imagine them when they are not. One of the aims of this type of thinking is therefore to secure elements of choice and variety in a system dominated by uniform state supply. If they can be introduced in a way which poses no threat to the security so valued in the public sector provision, there will be no mass hostility from consumers of the service.

On the contrary, there will be support from those who do wish to exercise their new choices, without opposition from those whose state provision is left intact for them to use as before. As more and more people make use of the choices, and draw the benefits of a more varied and responsive service, then the advantages of them will be perceived more readily in practice than could have been managed in theory. Having experienced for themselves the benefits which choices bring in some areas, people are more likely to be disposed to accept them in others.

Thus the individuation of standardized state services is achieved not by a sweeping conversion to free market ideals, but by steady progress to introduce gaps in the uniformity here and there, and opportunities for people to give expression to their preferences. All of this has to be done without putting at risk the inherent security which people value so much about the state supply.

It may be argued that this piecemeal progress simply puts off the day of reckoning when the state system must be tackled head on, complete with the security people have come to depend on. At that time, it could be claimed, people will have to be cut loose from its protection and set adrift to float on their own devices. This is erroneous for two reasons. In the first place if such a day were to come, people would fear it far less if many of them had already grown used to making their own choices, and if some had acted to secure their own service independently of the state. Secondly, the demise of the state system, if it comes about, could be with more of a whimper than a bang. If the numbers who decide to make alternative provision grow sufficiently large, the state supply could end up as a tiny proportion, irrelevant to the lives of most people.

In many ways this is the most attractive fate which could befall a public sector service: to proceed from a near universal service offering a standardized output, to one in which individuals make choices and generate variety in response, and to finish up as a mixed system in which the public element is sufficiently small to be inconsequential. The upper tier of the state pensions scheme in Britain seems to be headed for such a fate. The provision that people may opt to leave the state earnings-related pension scheme (SERPS) is accompanied by tax advantages for those who do so. The choice to leave can only be exercised by people who select an alternative private scheme; but the tax concessions make such schemes more attractive for most people. The result has been that over half have already left the state scheme, and have instead chosen from the various private schemes one tailored more closely to their individual requirements. The state scheme is gradually being individuated by the choices of individuals.

Moreover, the numbers in private schemes strengthen

the power of the interest group which supports them, and diminish the strength of the group supporting the state scheme. The result has been to make it possible to alter the balance even more. The government has trod carefully, making sure that no disgruntled group whose advantage seems threatened will oppose them. The changes proposed will not apply to benefits already promised, and will not affect anyone who reaches retirement age before the end of the century. But the effect will be to accelerate slightly the rate of exit from the state scheme, bringing closer not the day of reckoning, but the day when it fades to insignificance.

The approach to state pensions illustrates an important technique which can be used in the process of individuating the state services. It is that of blocking future entry, while guaranteeing the benefit of those who are already in. By cutting off inflow to the state scheme, government sets in motion a long-term process of change. It may take more than a generation before the last of those within the state scheme finally work their way through, but the alternative supply is growing all of this time, and forms an effective interest group long before the final demise of the state supply.

Restrictions on entry will typically be imposed to prevent new workers joining the state scheme. Instead, they will be invited to enter into one of the private alternatives offered. If it is something like a state pension, it will be the insurance industry and the private pension schemes which take up the slack. The age of maturity, or leaving school, or starting the first job, are reasonable cut-off points to choose for requiring new provision. Birth is not usually a suitable point because children do not make decisions for themselves.

The advantage on entry restriction is that it does not affect any person currently dependent upon the state scheme. For them, and perhaps for the rest of their life, the state supply will be kept available. Without new entrants, however, the proportion using it will diminish over time. Even though the state supply might be guaranteed, thereby deflecting possible opposition from current consumers, accompanying measures will be put into effect to make the alternatives more attractive, and to encourage those still entitled to it to make provision elsewhere by their own choices.

In addition to various methods of lowering the price of private alternatives, including tax exemptions and rebates, the rate of exit from the state system can also be accelerated by cash offers to those who forgo their right to future benefits. The offer by British Airways to its employees while they were still in the state sector was of cash to those who switched from high benefit index-linked pensions to conventional ones. It was high enough to persuade them to make the change. The same principle could be used to promote more rapid exit from other state schemes to which viable alternatives existed.

Cases involving pensions and insurance would prove too costly if government had to redeem immediately all of the benefits people had been promised from the system. Only a slow rate of exit could be afforded if the redemption cash had to be provided for each person wanting to go private. The solution here would be to offer a bond from the government, redeemable on retirement, for each person leaving the state scheme to take into the private sector. The move to make pensions portable is part of an overall strategy aimed at individuation. If the pensions rights become the property of the individual, to be disposed at will, then schemes can be offered tailor-made to the needs of that individual, instead of to the convenience of the producers of the service.

Useful though the various methods of encouraging exit might be, and advantageous though it is to have policies which close off further entry into state schemes, they are only part of the task. The huge section of the population who see no valid alternatives to staying in the state sector, even if they are incorrect to see it this way, constitute a major group still dependent on services dominated by producer needs and still having access only to basic standardized output. The task must include ways of introducing mechanisms into the state system itself to foster the growth of variety and choice. Individuation need not be confined to the private sector if creative policy engineering can devise ways of opening up the state products to individual needs.

This means a realignment of the forces which have impact upon the output. They tend in the public sector to derive from producers, leaving no effective forces impinging on it from consumers. How, then, to change it? One group of methods is based on re-routing the funding of public services.

The typical method of funding state sector activities has finance for them raised by government, paid to the Treasury, allocated to the ministry responsible, and passed on to the administering agencies. These might be local education authorities, the British Rail Board, the regional health committees, the University Grants Committee, or the Post Office. In some of them, such as railway travel or electricity supply, part of their funding comes from user charges, but for most people there is no alternative supply of rail travel or electricity.

The method of funding keeps the service producer-oriented. Since finance comes from the administering body, it is used to pay for whatever that body specifies. That body can go through the motions of consulting public requirements, but it need bow no lower than it wishes in that direction. The convenience of being able to offer standard services far outweighs the advantages of offering the public the range and variety of individually tailored services they might prefer. There is, moreover, no comeback. Denied alternative choices of service, the public has to take the standard product.

If they pay partly through user charges, they have the limited option of curbing their consumption or turning instead to a technological competitor. There may be no choice of railways or electric companies, but they can at least turn to road transport or opt to use more gas. If they pay entirely through taxation, as in education or most health services, they do not even have this choice unless they are rich enough to pay twice over.

In order to bring some variety and individual choice to standard state services, the funding must be re-routed to give effective power to consumers. It does not have to get into their hands either physically, as in tax rebates, or by token, as in voucher schemes. All that is required is that the allocation of funding has to result from consumer choices. This is just as well, given the entrenched and bitter opposition to voucher schemes, and to public apprehension about their unknown effects. Tax rebates are contentious, too, with opposition from the Treasury itself to the potential revenue loss, and from those who advocate fiscal neutrality instead of attempts to influence behaviour through tax policy.

The discussion of state education, and the comparison drawn there between micropolitical strategy and more conventional proposals, shows how funding can be directed according to consumer choices. In the case of education, the switch to direct funding of schools on a *per capita* basis, combined with open entry to allow parents a free choice of schools, suffices to give effect to consumer preferences. The parent chooses the school and the money follows the child.

It is an important corollary that there must be provision which allows for variety in order to make that choice effective. There is little point in introducing choice into the state sector, and in devising arrangements which direct funding in the direction of that choice if there is nothing to choose between. The third element in the education proposal was for schools to be given independence under their governing boards. Without the ability of schools to pursue different educational objectives and to follow different approaches to education, the choices made by parents would be meaningless. Open entry to the school of their choice, and a system to direct funds according to the choices made, would be valueless without the variety which admits their preferences into the system. The basis of the proposal was its three parts put together: open entry to give choice, independence to permit variety, and *per capita* funding to direct resources to what parents chose.

It is important, therefore, that redirection of funding should be accompanied by measures designed to introduce variety into the state system. If its uniformity is to be broken up, there must be alternative options available within it, and a means of ensuring that the satisfaction of consumer needs controls the allocation of funds.

The technique thus has several elements. In the first place it must take away the total discretion of the administration board. This has to be replaced by a system which allocates funds on the basis of some formula whose key element is demand by consumers. Secondly, it must decentralize authority to such an extent that local centres are able to make independent decisions over their own operation, and to modify it as they see fit. While it might be advisable to retain the reassuring rein of minimal standards, it should be a loose one. In the case of education, for example, any overall requirement should be confined to core curriculum only, and be measured by achievement of it rather than by input toward it. Thirdly, it must ensure that choices are permitted between the varieties available, instead of people being allocated to the nearest service point for administrative convenience.

The elements of this technique could be applied to several state monopoly services. Its aim is to break up the standardized output into a variety of alternatives which respond to consumer choice. At the heart of it lies a decentralization of power which will be opposed by some of the producer groups, and which needs to be structured in such a way that it attracts the support of consumer groups in large numbers, and at least some of the producers. The term 'consumer groups' does not refer to any organized pressure group allegedly representing consumer interests, but to numbers of individual consumers. Experience shows that the 'consumer' pressure groups are producer satellites or represent ideological lobbyists.

Such a technique would be a viable way of changing the standard nature of university education in Britain. The present funding is from taxation to the University Grants Committee to the courses and the institutions which find favour with them. If the funding were to be redirected, it would be via the students. The present system gives them little input, except as recipients of what is on offer. That offer exhibits a surprising uniformity considering the variety of individuals and individual needs in higher study.

Without changing the total level of funding which goes to higher education in Britain, and without changing the source of it in taxation revenue, it would be possible to individuate the public sector standardized product of university education by directing the funds to follow student choices. If the funding bypassed the UGC, and were allocated according to the institutions selected by students, universities would have an interest in satisfying demand. No doubt a fluttering of hearts would occur at the top tables; long experience of feeding at the public trough makes producers think of the public they are supposed to serve as an unfortunate but necessary nuisance.

The process might involve students receiving fee

certificates to hand in, or might simply have enrolment in various departments determine the size of grant for each university. Either way, the redirection would make the choice of students effective. Universities which attracted them would flourish, others would decline, unless of course they were able to change. Some producers would perhaps claim that students know nothing about education, just as some warn of parental 'interference' in schools. Instead of the huge enrolments in easy courses of zero educational value which might be predicted, however, the overseas examples suggest that students might choose courses more related to intended careers.

From the point of view of political strategy, the redirection of funds has the advantage of preserving the most valued elements of a state service, even while individuating its previously uniform output. The free school place is still there, and the university course paid out of public funds. Opposition is not aroused from those who simply wish to preserve the security which that brings. While it might be argued that there should not be free school places or publicly funded degree courses, this range of proposals is designed to improve their responsiveness to consumer wishes if they do remain. The technique which acts by redirecting funds shows that even if their hold on the political market is strong enough to resist market alternatives, it is still possible to introduce some market elements by carefully contrived policies.

What is being done, of course, is the introduction of competition within the state sector. As well as the various expedients to promote competitors outside it, and to take the ability to choose them down-market towards ever more people, it is possible to generate competition internally. By decentralizing power to local centres and redirecting the funding mechanism, a situation can be created which makes it in the interest of producers to satisfy the demands of consumers instead of those of the administration board.

Private markets are characterized by the proximity of funding and consumers. If the consumers are attracted, the funds come along with them, so producers compete to bring in customers by offering what they want. The devices to achieve some individuation within uniform state services are techniques to achieve a linkage of funding and consumers similar to that of the private sector. Once such a linkage is achieved, some of the forces which it drives in the private sector will operate within the state system. It will not be a perfect copy, nor even a close one, but it will contain variety, competition and choice, will direct funds to where the demand is strongest, and will tend to bring more satisfaction of individual needs than is achieved by the normal model of public service operation. It will be an internal market.

The promotion of competition within the state sector as well as outside of it is a technique which works if the system is altered so that its pressures sustain it. There is no point in trying to have elements of the public sector compete against each other if no consequences follow from it. If there are no rewards for those who compete successfully, and no penalties on those who fail to do so, then nothing is achieved. What makes it work is the policy to redirect funds towards successful competitors at the expense of unsuccessful ones, and the independence of decision action which is devolved down to local centres such as individual schools and universities.

Unless the plan is conceived as a whole, with its interlocking parts reinforcing each other, it becomes no more than another one of the futile attempts to graft private sector characteristics on to public sector operations. The desirable features of private businesses are not accidental, they are a concomitant of the pressures and forces which drive the private sector. The attempt to make the public sector more efficient, more

cost-sensitive, or more responsive to consumers, needs
to be accompanied by forces to drive it. Unless those
forces are somehow set in motion, the desire becomes
no more than wishful thinking, and has, at best, only a
limited and short-term result.

The thinking behind individuation is that these forces
can be set in motion within the state service. It takes a
great deal more ingenuity to make such attempts both
workable and acceptable, but it can be done. This
means that as well as the alternatives which give scope
for variety and choice in the private sector which
parallels the public operation, the state service itself can
be made to break into varied offerings which compete
against other sections.

As a final example, the National Health Service is
generally regarded as the most sensitive area in which
to attempt reform. A widely held attitude esteems the
security it brings, and opposes any move which might
jeopardize it. Yet the NHS is typical of its class. It offers
a standardized service, and is characterized by its lack
of attention to consumer requirements. Its long waiting-
lists bear witness to its inability to match supply to
demand. It might also be noted that the NHS is
notoriously unable to exercise any control over its costs.
Indeed, for many areas it has no idea what they are. It
presents a difficult case for the exponent of micropolitics to work on.

There are solutions, however, which can improve it.
There is the rapid growth, already noted, of private
medical facilities which are mushrooming alongside it.
Measures to encourage that growth and to accelerate it
are already in operation and more could soon be put
into effect. None of this need bring major hostility from
interest groups, since no significant ones are threatened.
Even the general public which depends on the NHS
does not oppose the spread of private medicine. One of
its effects will be after all to relieve the burden of
demand on the state system.

The question arises as to whether a scheme can be devised which, like those suggested for schools and universities, might re-route the funding within the system so as to give effect to consumer preferences. If this can be achieved, it will gradually succeed in individuating what has hitherto been a uniform, unresponsive output. The answer is that such a scheme can indeed be devised. The state may be large, but so is human creativity. Armed with a valid method to direct it, there are few problems so big that they cannot be brought down by it.

The first step might be to augment the total funding which finds its way into health, not by increasing its allocation from the taxpayer, but by encouraging people who can afford it to add their own resources. Other advanced countries manage to achieve a higher level of spending on health as a fraction of GDP because people spend more personally, and perceive benefits to themselves and their families.

Tax incentives can provide the means of encouragement, reducing the cost of private insurance to large numbers who cannot quite afford it at present. This has the advantage of simultaneously increasing the total spending on health, even while it reduces the demand on the National Health Service. The NHS would be in a far worse position without the 9 per cent already in private medicine or the 400,000 items of elective surgery performed privately.

The obvious avenue for improvement in the NHS is its lack of any intermediate facilities between general practitioners and hospitals. It is overwhelmingly a two-tier system. If the doctors' prescriptions do not cure the patients, they are sent on to hospitals. The private sector and health systems overseas have a range of facilities between the two, featuring such things as group diagnostic facilities and out-patient clinics. Since much of the treatment which is given expensively in hospitals could be performed more efficiently outside them, and since such treatment would be more local and more consumer-friendly than large-scale institutions can provide, there is an opening for possible reform if the interest groups can be assuaged.

One answer might be a reorganization of the NHS to include health maintenance organizations. These HMOs work in other countries to provide total health cover, and include doctors, clinics, specialists, diagnostic facilities and hospitals. All work within the HMO to provide whatever health care is appropriate. They will usually receive a fee on behalf of each patient, making it in their interest to keep their customers healthy in cost-effective ways. They have the range of intermediate facilities so absent from the NHS, and have to attract and keep patients who have the choice of going to other HMOs instead.

The principle could be introduced into the NHS. In place of the Regional and District Health Authorities there could be created independent Health Management Units (HMUs). General Practitioners would sign up with one, taking their patients in with them. An individual patient could always change HMU by changing doctor. The doctors would then be paid by their HMU for work done, with fees for each consultation and each item of treatment.

When patients were sent for treatment by hospitals or specialists their HMU would select an appropriate course of treatment. They would have an incentive to choose a cost-effective supply from the alternatives available. Each hospital would have to know the cost of all of its activities, and to perform them efficiently. Otherwise HMUs would not make use of them.

The system which these changes produced would induce competitive pressures into the system, bringing the benefits of efficiencies and innovative techniques. It would enable management at various levels to be more flexible and to take independent decisions. The doctors and their patients would have a choice between HMUs, and the HMUs would choose between the services of different hospitals for their patients.

The HMUs could be financed by an annual allocation for each patient, and would have to provide health care for that sum, up to standards determined nationally. If a patient left one HMU and joined another one, their annual allocation would move with them. This would mean that the money would follow the choices made, as it would follow the child within an internal market in education.

There could be refinements to make this system work. HMUs would not be able to refuse patients, except for a limit on their total size. Even then they would have to establish waiting lists. The annual allocation could vary with the category of patient, or even the geographical area of residence, to reflect the different health care costs.

This does not incur the odium which would greet an attempt to replace the NHS. Instead it promises to improve it. Patients see their doctors as before, and it is still free at the point of consumption. They receive hospital and specialist services and these are still free. The change is that an internal market has been created in which there are variations and choices, in which there are incentives for efficiency and competition, and in which the resources of the state are redirected as a result of those decisions. It could be done, and has the advantage that each of the elements which would make it is worth doing individually.

The effect would be to set in motion a train of events which would gradually individuate the service to conform to the various needs and preferences of consumers. It would still be a public sector supply, and still a National Health Service, but pressures and forces within it would now be working to produce different results. HMUs which satisfied consumers would receive more funds, and others would be encouraged to do the same. Cost-effective HMUs would be able to offer greater rewards to their participants than inefficient ones, so talent would find new opportunities.

The example of the National Health Service indicates the range of problems to which these principles can be applied. Once political markets have creative solutions applied to redirect their forces, major reforms can be achieved. The NHS is almost the limiting case; if the methods work there, they can perhaps work anywhere.

15 More Technical Devices

Two other methods deserve special attention. One of them attempts to introduce pressures into the public sector to make it respond in some degree to consumer demand. In the absence of the ability to shop elsewhere, the consumer normally has no choice but to take what is offered. This being so, there is no incentive to make that offering correspond to what consumers actually want. The producers have more capacity to make trouble than consumers do, so their needs count for more.

There are cases where it may be impossible to apply an intricate solution which involves redirecting the funding of the public service and promoting variety within it. Even in such difficult areas, there are devices which can introduce some pressures to assist consumers. One of them involves establishing a right to the service offered, with provision for consumers who fail to receive it to seek satisfaction elsewhere. For example, it is often a feature of public operations that they produce what those involved in production find convenient, and keep consumers waiting for what they want. Delays and waiting-lists are common features of public supply, in everything from health to housing.

Having to wait for service is one of the least popular features of public services. Even consumers who value the service and the security which they feel through the public funding of it, do not like the delays. All things being equal, they would rather have the public supply serve them now rather than later. If no other provision is made, this can prove useful material to those who wish to increase public spending. They can point to the delays, attribute them to shortage of funds, and use popular hostility to them to fuel the campaign for an increased allocation. Since the profession and the producers will support it, backing from lobbyists and consumers as well can create powerful pressures in the political market. Even though they might know that additional funds would not cut waiting-lists significantly, government might have to vote them.

An alternative is to reject the notion that if the public sector fails it needs more money, and turn to the private sector to help out. If the public supply involves lengthy delays, there is some justification at least for turning elsewhere. The establishment of a right to the service can be interpreted as meaning that if the public sector cannot itself deliver it, then the consumer can get it from somewhere else at public expense. It is important to stress the last three words. Anyone has the option of avoiding the queues and delays by buying a private service instead. This is not what is meant by a right to the service. What it does mean is that if someone has paid through taxation for a service, they have the right to get it, even if it means using public funds to buy privately.

In practice this means that after a period deemed to be as much as can be tolerated, people acquire the right to receive service from elsewhere at public expense. To give specific examples, when tenants require repair work done to state-owned houses, there are often lengthy delays even for urgent work such as the repair of roofs and windows. Local housing departments may use the delays as a justification for increased funding, which would be unlikely to cut significantly into the delays, even if granted. A more imaginative alternative sets a time limit for the public sector to respond, and permits the tenant after its expiry to hire private contractors from outside, and bill the public service for the work done.

There are obvious protective clauses to be built in in practice. The cost of work done by private contractors must not exceed what the state would have spent on the job, and there must be clear evidence that the public service concerned knew about the repair needed, yet failed to carry it out within a set time limit. The cost of private contractors is highly unlikely to exceed the cost of in house labour, to judge by almost every comparative survey which has been done.

The introduction of the notion of a right to the service, a right which can be exercised elsewhere if the state fails to deliver, puts pressure on the state to deliver the service itself. If the tenant who fails to receive his repair job in an adequate time can go elsewhere and send the bill, there is a strong incentive for the state to make sure the necessary work is done on time. If it fails to do so, a part of its service will be automatically privatized, and it will lose part of its funding to a competitor from the private sector. Naturally, it will act to prevent this if it can. Thus the right to service, when introduced, puts into the system the pressure from consumers which the ordinary market cannot do with public monopolies.

A right to service is something calculated to be popular with the consumers of state services. On the face of it, it does nothing to threaten the public supply. It simply permits those who fail to receive service within a reasonable time to have the state buy it from outside. The general public can see the right to service as an important guarantor; they recognize straight away the value which it gives them, and support it accordingly.

The producers of public sector services do not, of course, like the idea of their customers being able to buy services from other producers and send in the bill. However, this is a rare case in which the force of one pressure group is sufficient to outweigh the force of another. There are more dissatisfied consumers, or ones who perceive they might be, than there are producers upset at having to concede them new rights. The basic integrity of the public supply is not threatened. Indeed, if it does its job none of it is threatened. Consumers who acquire the means to jump over delays and waiting lists count for more than do producers who are happy with things as they stand.

What happens in practice is that producers take good care to make sure that very few cases actually get to the point where private contractors are called in. What they do is to beef up the service and streamline it so that it responds more effectively and more rapidly. They monitor applications for repairs, and keep careful tabs on how long consumers are kept waiting. As the cut-off date approaches, they go in to begin the necessary work. All of these are things which a good private business does anyway, forced by the pressures of the market. If it should fail to do this, a bad reputation will spread, and customers will melt away. The notion of a right to service simply substitutes alternative pressures in the public service to make up for the absence of the normal ones.

The principle, moreover, can be extended right through the public sector. In a surprising personal opinion given during the last strike of water engineers in Britain, the former Master of the Rolls, Lord Denning, expressed the view that there already was a right to service in common law, and that the public could have work done privately and send in the bill if the state failed in its obligations. This was never tested in court, and may or may not be true. Whether or not the right exists in common law, it can certainly be supplied by statute wherever the public service is felt to merit its introduction.

Waiting-lists and delays for hospital treatment or other medical needs are not among the popular features of the National Health Service. They are frequently cited by producers and the lobbyists who support them as reasons calling for increased funds. But they might just as well be used to vindicate a right to treatment like the right to have state houses repaired. If the public service takes taxpayer funds, they have a valid claim on its output.

A right to treatment in the Health Service might involve the NHS in the obligation to provide treatment within, perhaps, six months. If it failed to do so, it would be required to purchase treatment for the patient from the private sector. This means that there would be an automatic upper limit of six months on the waiting lists. The introduction of such a measure would be very popular indeed among patients or potential ones, even among those who were enthusiastic about the NHS. It would be popular with some doctors, nurses and specialists, but would not go down very well with area health administrators. They constitute a small group, albeit with some capacity to cause trouble.

In practice, once again, there would be an immediate change in the attitude to waiting lists. Administrators would monitor them and make much more efficient use of surplus facilities in some areas to cope with shortages in others. No doubt sophisticated measures would allocate patients to available treatment centres whenever vacancies arose. As the cut-off time approached, massive efforts would be made to treat patients in time. The effect would not be to have large numbers having private sector treatment paid for by the state. It would be to have more efficient use of state resources, and greater awareness of waiting times.

A further practical consequence of no little significance is that it would be very popular with government, and would increase the popularity of the government by immediately taking away criticism brought on by waiting lists for hospital treatment. If patients did actually reach the point of being treated in the private sector, they would hardly complain. Nor would government find its costs excessive. They would certainly be less than the extra funds it would take to upgrade the NHS to that level without the additional pressure.

The notion of a right to service is a good application of the micropolitical approach. The state service is left in this case as it is. It has the first chance to provide the service. Only if it fails to do so within a reasonable time is the alternative activated, and then the benefit goes directly to the consumers. The device introduces a very limited partnership into the public services. It allows the state sector to do what it can, and then brings in the private sector to do whatever it cannot do. If the NHS cannot treat patients within six months, only then is private medicine brought in to fill the gap. If the housing authority is unable to repair roofs and windows within a reasonable time, only then are private contractors called upon to do the work.

The device is carefully calculated to offer consumers what they want from the state service: responsiveness to their needs. Long delays until producers get round to providing a service are ended by the threat of private service and, where necessary, the reality of it. It thus introduces pressures into public services on behalf of consumers, even where it is inappropriate to open up opportunities for variety and choice, or impossible to do so. The pressure is supplied by the mere threat of an alternative after the expiry of a deadline. In putting pressure on state producers by this technique, government takes pressure off itself which the delays and waiting lists were imposing. Instead of being forced politically to increase funding for the state service, government uses the private sector to force the state service to improve. All of which makes the device a powerful tool.

The other method meriting special attention seeks to deal with the problem of capital depletion in the public sector. The basic difficulty is that capital spending has few supporters compared with current spending. Expenditure on the current side pays for services, which pleases consumers, and pays for salaries, which pleases producers. Pleased consumers and pleased producers lead to pleased governments. All of this creates a powerful tug on the current side. If not enough money goes on current spending, the producers can interrupt the service, and irritated consumers can put pressure on government.

The capital side has no such protectors. Its main beneficiaries are future consumers, who have little to trade in today's marketplace. Capital investment keep up the supply of equipment and premises, and makes sure that the service is up to date with its technology and does not have to rely on used and worn out stock. It is because the pull is very much stronger on the current side that the problem of capital depletion occurs. It is always easier to raid the capital side of the account to meet strong demands on the current side. Thus, over the years, the typical public sector service exhibits a decline in the proportion of funds allocated to capital, and a steep decline in the capital used per employee.

Not surprisingly, the public sector services are notorious for their under-capitalization. They have to stretch old and worn-out equipment far longer than would be tolerated in their private sector equivalents. The public has to make do with patched-up stock and over-extended premises. Victorian hospitals, antiquated schools, overcrowded prisons, shabby railcars; all are products of a system which feels an unbalanced pressure on the current side and is unable to keep up its capital stock.

Usually there is pressure from producers for increased spending. Just as this is advocated to relieve waiting-lists, so it is put forward as the answer to capital depletion. More spending is put forward as an answer for all public sector problems. Depletion of capital does ultimately put pressure on government for what is called 'reinvestment,' but is really increased funding. Pressure from producers and consumers alike eventually mounts to the point where government feels compelled to act.

Unfortunately, increased funding is not a valid answer to capital depletion. With the pressures still in place pulling expenditure toward the current side, new funds feel those forces just as much as the old funds did. The influx of new money makes it harder for administrators to resist demands by the workforce, and harder to cut back on unnecessary or wasteful services. The money is there to fund them. The effect is to pull much of the new funds to the current side, intended though it was for capital replacement.

The problem is that chronic shortage of capital means that poorer services will be offered from the public sector, and the means of improvement will erroneously appear to be increased expenditure of taxpayers' money. This is not a good situation for those who think that services should respond to demand, offer variety and choice, and be funded according to consumer prefer-ences. It locks most public services into a self-defeating spiral of decreasing quality.

The method involves a technique for introducing private capital into the public sector in a way which increases the investment in capital items, without funding a further upward twist in current spending. It seeks to bring in private capital on an investment basis. Private capital is available, provided that circumstances are suitable. In years when public capital has been squeezed to its lowest ever proportion of total spending, the private markets have been awash with capital for stock purchases, new issues, and shares in privatized companies. The cash is there; the problem is how to entice it into the public sector.

Straightforward government borrowing is not appropriate. It makes funds available for spending at government's discretion, which means no difference in practice from increased funds raised from taxation. Government borrowing has to be financed and eventually repaid. As a source of revenue it is not subject to restraints to limit its use any more than is taxation revenue. When government borrows more, public spending increases and the pressure to hold down the costs of each department diminishes. Part of the reason for the squeeze on funds is a desire to limit total borrowing.

For technical reasons there are difficulties involved in direct capital investment by the private sector. Instead of lending the government money, the idea has been put forward that private cash should go directly into public projects. Government would then pay to use the capital plant, be it buildings or equipment, thus giving the private investors a return on their capital. Private investment might build a bridge, for example, with government approval, and then receive its return as the government paid it to use the bridge. This could cover capital items as diverse as sewage plants and museums. The advantage is that government gets its capital investment now, without having to put cash up front, while the private investors receive a return on their money.

Effectively this is a lease-back arrangement. Private capital is used for necessary public works, and government pays to lease them from their owners. The public has the use of them, although they are privately owned, and government pays for the use rather than the construction. Much needed bypass roads, bridges and tunnels could be built under this system, without the necessity of a huge capital outlay from the public sector. The proposal has many advantages and one fundamental flaw.

The principal merit of the proposal is that it switches capital expenditure by government over to the current side. Recognizing that the public sector causes an inevitable depletion of capital, this method supplies that capital from outside, and funds it out of current spending. Instead of paying out capital to build the required roads and bridges, the government pays only to use them. Capital comes from the private sector, which has it to spare, instead of from a government hard-pressed to keep down spending. The payment for it is a current operating expense, and secures the service of the sewage plant or museum for public use.

Unfortunately, the proposal falls foul of Treasury rules. It has been tried successfully in several American states, but cannot be applied in Britain in the form described. The problem is that if the payment from the government is guaranteed, the Treasury rules treat the investment as government borrowing, and count it as part of the total. Even though the investment comes from private sources, it must be accounted for as a portion of total borrowing by government. The official view is that without the element of risk, it is not a genuine investment but a loan. If the private investors had simply lent government the money in return for set annual payments, the effect would be the same.

While this rule would appear to exclude the proposal altogether, what it does is to require an amended version incorporating some element of risk. The micropolitician, if private capital is to be brought to the rescue of an under-capitalized public sector, now has to devise schemes which involve the risk factor that comes in ordinary private investments. This is less straight-forward, but does overcome the objections that private capital is nothing more than a thinly disguised loan.

There is a risk factor in that no one can know for sure just how much use will be made of new capital stock. The government might receive advice on the likely usage of a new road, or the number of vehicles per hour anticipated for a bridge or tunnel, but the figures are only estimates. Similar calculations about the use of museums or other public capital projects can all involve elements of guesswork. This provides the loophole through which risk can enter to sanctify the scheme according to Treasury rules. What is involved is hard bargaining between a government anxious to gain access to capital funds, and investors equally anxious to secure a good return on their money.

A figure must be agreed for the break-even usage of a bridge, for example, and for the rate per vehicle to be paid by government to the investors. If more vehicles make use of it than that figure, the investors will gain, but if it turns out to be less, they will lose. This has the advantage of incorporating a genuine risk element to prevent the capital sum having to be included in total government borrowing. It has another important advantage as well. Because the financial calculations devolve on actual usage of the facility, there is a strong incentive for only those schemes to be financed for which private investors anticipate heavy usage.

There is a degree of contrivance about the notion of expected use and the concept of a rate of return which fluctuates depending on whether the actual use is higher or lower than expected. This is because the rules themselves are rather arbitrary. The definition of genuine risk is found in the realm of rule making, rather than reality. The same is true of ownership. When government holding moves from 50.1 per cent to 49.9 per cent, a company suddenly enters the private sector as if by magic. The point is that rules and definitions involve arbitrary boundaries. Just as these can work against some proposals because of rigid interpretation, so they can work in favour of others which are tailor-made to fit around the rules.

The likelihood is that private capital will need to be attracted to public investments. There are many ways of using money to make a return in private investment, and any public schemes will need to be at least comparable in terms of risk and rate of return if they are to attract funds. This means that if agreements are made between government and potential investors, they will need to err on the side of the investors. That is, in calculations concerning the likely use of any public facilities built with private funds, potential investors will need to feel that there is a reasonable chance of the target figure being exceeded.

Fortunately there is a margin which makes this possible. Public operations in general make less effective use of money than their private sector equivalents. This is because they are subject to political forces which distort their spending patterns. They tend to be over-manned, as well as under-capitalized, and this applies to their maintenance and operation of capital items as well as to the provision of services. Other things being equal, one would expect private firms to spend less on maintaining and operating capital items than the equivalent work would cost in the public sector. This provides a means for private investment to seek out profits from its application, even while giving the public sector good value for money.

A scheme involving the public use of private funds will normally be for the construction of a capital item, for the operation of it over a number of years and its maintenance during that period. The public sector rarely builds with its own in-house constructor and labour force; more commonly it invites tenders from private contractors. If a project is undertaken with private capital, the actual construction will proceed similarly, though perhaps with some opportunities for savings through innovative techniques and less rigid application of bureaucratic rules. The real saving is made possible by the private performance of maintenance work and operation. These are quite often done by direct labour from the public sector.

Private investment agreements will usually be able to present a total package which is attractive to government in that it costs less than government itself would have to spend to attain the same results. The package is similarly attractive to investors because it offers a long-term agreement reasonably certain to pay them a good return with low risk. Anyone who supposes this to be only a theoretical point should examine such schemes operating in the United States. It is becoming quite usual for private firms to tender for the construction and operation of a state prison according to public specifications, and to do so in a way which not only provides the building, but gives the state a substantial saving in the cost per day of keeping prisoners.

In Britain it would be possible to provide a risk element which would seem high enough to Treasury officials looking at the cost the package would impose if done by government, and low enough to private investors looking at the lower costs achievable in the private sector. In this way the need for a risk element can be met without unduly deterring potential investors. The point could be made that this complicated process is not devoted to producing real risks, but to the production of what can be passed off as risks in order to avoid having genuine private investment counted as part of government borrowing.

It should also be pointed out that while the return to investors is measured in financial terms, government also makes a political return. The calculations may be about costs and possible density of usage, but if the project goes ahead with private funding, the government ends up with capital projects for which it does not have to put up public funds. It gets its bypass road, its bridge, tunnel, prison, museum or sewage plant without having to increase taxation or public borrowing to pay for it. It also gets the gratitude of those who use these facilities.

Of course, government will have to pay for the use of them, but this is more acceptable than public capital spending in several respects. Government would have to pay to use its own facilities in the sense of operating them and maintaining them; and its payment to the investors covers those costs as well. Moreover, government is used to current account spending. It is quite able to allocate sums over a number of years to pay for the provision of certain services. What it finds it difficult to do is to make adequate provision for capital replacement and acquisition without having the funds pulled over to the current side.

There is also the fact that the payments have to be made over a number of years, perhaps a large number. Governments are not very good at spending money now in order to secure future provision. A property of political markets is that present voters have a great deal to trade in them, future voters have little. This is why in areas such as pensions the rewards come now, the payments later. The use of private capital to build public facilities fits in with government's usual pattern of giving the present a premium and the future a discount. The capital projects are built now, but the money is paid for over the years, much of it by future taxpayers who do not have much clout in today's marketplace. So today's electors get their facilities and tomorrow's electors do some of the paying. From the point of view of today's government, this is by no means a bad arrangement.

This is not a flattering view of government; it simply recognizes the pressures which fall upon it. In the normal course of events government has to cut back on capital spending because the need to achieve political gain pulls it to spend more on the current side. The new proposal is skilfully crafted to counterbalance the tendency by an opposite force. It creates circumstances in which government derives advantage from capital spending now, with an immediate political gain, even though the investment comes from the private sector.

Each of these two methods supplies the means of correcting to a limited extent an inherent defect of the public sector. The idea of a right to service forces the public sector into an attention to consumer needs it would not make without it. The idea of using private capital for public projects enables capital spending to bring gains to government it would otherwise lack. Both methods illustrate a common style of approach. The analysis of the way in which the public sector operates identifies the shortcoming, and the policy is tailor-made to correct that particular shortcoming, or at least to mitigate its impact.

There is no fixed list of such methods, no set range of techniques which covers the whole field. A facet of this approach is that it is limited only by what creativity can produce. A great variety of techniques might be proposed to cope with each of the various shortcomings of the public sector. Once the political market is understood, devices can be introduced to redirect the forces that operate within it. This is all that micropolitics seeks to do.

PART V
SUMMATION

16 Range, Limits and Origins

Micropolitics has so far been examined as a technique. Attention has been focused on how its mechanisms and devices start from the analysis of public choice theory, and move from that critical examination to a creative counterpart. The analysis tells us why certain policies fail because they do not take account of political markets. The new policies produced by micropolitics try to overcome the objections which caused other policies to fail. They do take account of the political markets, and are designed to work with them rather than to override them.

The assumption has been throughout that micropolitics will bring more market forces into the economy. The pressures which dominate the public sector operations are those which give prime place to political rather than to economic factors. Public choice analysis shows why this is so, and how it comes about that situations are produced by the public which are not to their advantage. Consumer wants and needs which would be effective in the private sector are squeezed out because the political system governing the state sector denies them sufficient power. Micropolitics has been treated as something which can redress this fault. Its products cited and examined have been those which act to neutralize the political forces, or to set opposite ones against them, or to redirect them to serve similar ends to those achieved in private markets.

It is appropriate to ask, however, whether micro-politics must of necessity serve such ends, or whether its techniques might not be applied with equal success in the opposite direction. If it is a technique, value-free, and nothing more, it could in principle be applied to serve other ends. It might be possible by devising new policies working with interest groups to achieve more centralism, less consumer input and market forces, and a larger public sector than before.

There would be little point. The conventional approach has proved quite sufficient to achieve all of these things. In democratic societies the political system acts to subvert the market process and has no need of the extraordinary measures here described. The findings of the public choice school show how people lose a little at a time the freedom to choose their own goods and services as the political provision of these items is made instead. Interest groups bid and trade in the political market to greater effect than individuals can wield, even if they add up to a majority. The advantages gained by groups in political markets exceed in their impact the gains which individuals can make in economic ones.

In the absence of the extraordinary techniques examined herein, the democratic process itself will replace economic markets by political ones. This is one of the central implications of public choice analysis. It describes a process, and in doing so implies a trend. More and more of the provision is taken out of economic markets and supplied through political ones. This process removes power from the periphery and concentrates it at the centre where it can be used. It may be that socialists and other centralists will try to achieve their goal of a planned society in easy stages, rather than by overnight change. What Fabianism does is to introduce the unacceptable at an acceptable pace.

The first conclusion is thus that micropolitics is irrelevant to the centralist design; conventional macro-politics is sufficiently adequate for the task. In a struggle on the macro-scale, those who advocate free markets will lose to those who advocate a range of collective provision. The reason is that the ideas behind free markets are perceived to run counter to the interest of groups involved in the process. In a version of the prisoners dilemma, it is in the interest of each group to sustain its own advantage and have others give up theirs. So everyone defends his benefit.

Micropolitics was conceived as a means of reversing the tendency towards political markets at the expense of economic ones. It offers techniques and instruments by which that process can be set to work in the other direction. The basis which underlies all of its technical devices is the alteration of circumstances such that individuals and groups will perceive greater advantage in the extension of free market characteristics. Some-times this will involve the movement of numbers of them to seek an alternative supply from the private market; sometimes it will involve putting market elements to work within the public sector. At the bottom line of all of its creative policies lies the preference of both the interest groups and of the individuals who comprise them.

Micropolitics introduces marginal utility into politics. It seeks to influence decisions on the margin, at the point where people form a view that one choice gives them more benefit than another. It promotes and encourages those choices. It tries to extend the range over which they can operate, and to coordinate circum-stances to make some outcomes visibly preferable to others. The motor which drives it is choice. If people cannot make choices they are not able to opt for the alternatives made more attractive by the micropolitical strategies. It therefore seeks to extend choice at every possible opportunity. With each success it breaks open yet another part of the public sector to the impact of preferences.

It feeds, furthermore, on its own successes. As the choices of individuals accumulate into a new reality, people perceive the direct benefits which those choices brought about. The advantage gained by each choice also advertises the advantage of choice itself. The more that people gain by exercising choice, the more likely it is that they will accept the introduction of choices elsewhere. If choices in transport have given them both improved services and lower prices, they will be more ready to accept them in other areas.

Micropolitics, if used to open up the public sector to individual choices, can be self-accelerating. If use of its techniques were attempted for the opposite purpose, it would ultimately be self-negating. Even if some early success were achieved, victory would involve a limitation of the choices which had made it possible. It would mean that part of an economic market ruled by individual preferences had been swallowed into the public sector and was now ruled by interest group pressures instead. The result would be one in which choice had diminished, and there would be less scope for new micropolitical strategies to take the process further.

Not only is micropolitics unnecessary to achieve centralist ends, it is inappropriate. For free market ends each success makes new policies easier. With centralist objectives the reverse would be true instead; each success would make subsequent ones harder to achieve. Even if it were possible to apply this approach to swell the size of the public sector, it would be a misapplication of effort. Micropolitics has been devised for the specific task of setting the growth of the public sector into reverse, and has the values of that task built into it. It works through the operation of mechanisms such as choice, opportunity and enterprise, all of which are incompatible with public sector economics.

For centralists to take up micropolitics in an attempt to augment the size of the state sector would be for them to enter a contest in which they were handicapped. If they can exploit the desires of interest groups to gain benefits at the general expense, and a political system which encourages them to trade such benefits for support, they have no need to take up battle with armaments which are unsuited to their purpose. The instruments designed for other purposes would prove unwieldy in their hands.

Micropolitics moves down to the micro-scale because it recognizes that it can win on the level at which motivated individuals make decisions. It can create circumstances under which the marginal utility of specific courses of action is enhanced for individuals who can choose them. As they exercise the choice in that direction, they constitute an interest group to set against those which already operate on the macro-scale. Micropolitics thus produces a set of techniques whose application results in the transformation of public sector supply into private economic markets. If it can take the state operation itself into the private sector it will. If it cannot do so easily, it will resort to alternatives. These include the replacement of a standardized state supply by private alternatives, or the introduction of free market features such as variety and choice into the state system itself.

The range of micropolitics is the whole of the public sector of the economy. Within its ambit come all of the state industries and utilities, state services, transfer programmes including welfare policies and the regulatory activity of government. It produces tactical devices in all of these areas aimed at the strategic objective of a society which has its choices made by individuals for themselves instead of by powerful groups on their behalf, and which is oriented to meeting the needs of consumers rather than those of producers.

Although there is an *ad hoc* look to the devices which emerge as the products of this type of thinking, it is only a surface look.

At a deeper level there is a unity of analysis and purpose. The approach does not seek individual tactical victories on a case-by-case basis. The methods are all designed to work in the world of interest group pressures, and all to give individual preferences primacy in the political process. The public sector presents many aspects, all different, and all sustained by different groups and different forces. To the micropolitician these aspects are like a series of locked doors; the objective is to open them up in order to let in consumer choices and responsiveness to individual need; and the instruments are the keys which each of the micropolitical techniques constitute. No two keys are identical, but information learned about the opening of one door can be used to help unlock others.

It is precisely this range of techniques which explains the vast difference in achievement between the administrations espousing conservative ideas in the early 1970s and those which came along a decade later. The Nixon and Heath governments did not manage to gain many successes for economic markets and individual choices, despite a climate of ideas which had helped to elect them on that kind of programme. The Reagan and Thatcher governments enjoyed more success because of the micropolitical techniques available to them, and the strategic thinking which lay behind them.

Like many scientific theories, it originated from the perceived inadequacies of the prevailing model. It was the experience of the failures under President Nixon and Prime Minister Heath which led some analysts to the conclusion that it was not enough to win the battle of ideas, or to elect people committed to them. It was important to have policies which could succeed and which could work. The insight came about because the public choice theories began to gain prominence at a time when the failures of the two administrations were becoming apparent. Some of those who had worked to win the battle of ideas, and to elect those prepared to support programmes based on them, saw in public choice analysis the explanation for failure. Some of them also came to understand that it might be possible to derive policies which could overcome the objections encountered by conventional ones.

The result was the concentration of some groups in the 1970s not on the battle for ideas, but on policy engineering. Instead of simply waving free market flags and shouting the traditional battle cries, attention on both sides of the Atlantic turned instead to the technical and mechanical details of policies which could circumvent the public choice objections. A new awareness of the power and role of interest groups led to the formulation of policies designed to prevent them from thwarting the introduction of market elements into the state sector. In some cases this involved a rejection of the conventional market alternative on the grounds that it took insufficient account of the forces at work in political markets. In other cases it took the form of working for partial market solutions on the grounds that these would not only succeed, but would establish a base on which more market elements could be constructed later.

Over the course of the 1970s, the broad principles behind the new style were developed, and many of the policy options which it was able to generate were researched and polished. The new policies caused some puzzlement, not only by their originality of approach but also by the limited nature of their objectives. Instead of seeking the immediate replacement of the public sector by private alternatives, they appeared to look for more modest progress. The introduction of alternative choices here and there was accepted. If an operation as a whole could not be taken into the private sector, perhaps the production could be. If current beneficiaries were too powerful to oppose, the prevention of new entry into those benefits was sought instead of their abolition. If attempts to terminate the public supply met too much opposition, means were sought instead to encourage exit from it by ever increasing numbers. If the value generally placed on certain aspects of the public services guaranteed their survival, then techniques were developed to incorporate internal competition and choice. Where the state sector proved to be entrenched, means were investigated whereby its funds might be redirected to follow consumer needs.

All of these methods of circumventing the built-in opposition of interest groups seemed to others as unnecessary compromises, and unjust ones. The aim of securing free markets seemed to have taken second place to that of winning a few short-term political victories. Instead of abolishing the advantages which some groups had secured through political markets, the new tacticians seemed intent on exchanging them for others. On this point, if not on the others, the perception was correct.

The new policies were not simply half-hearted or inconsistent versions of the old ones. They were ones specifically designed to function in the reality they faced. Unlike the policies which had ignored that reality or sought to abolish it, the new techniques examined it, exploring where its strengths and weaknesses lay. At its most vulnerable points they proposed to introduce new options calculated to divert the pressures which sustained it in its old form. They sought ultimately the same free markets and individual choices as they had before, but now with a realistic eye as to what could be achieved and when and how.

The successes achieved by the new-style policies allowed for the rise of the attractive but erroneous view that the work of the lonely scholars, their acolytes and their advocates had finally paid off and brought results in its train. That these results had not come in the earlier administrations which attempted them was put down to a wrong climate or wrong personnel. In fact, it was wrong policies. It was the policy engineers, coming in the wake of the pure scientists of political and economic theory, who made the machines which changed events. The ideas had been sufficient to win the intellectual battle, but this was not enough. Men and women with spanners in their hands and grease on their fingers had first to devise the ways in which the ideas of pure theory could be turned into technical devices to alter reality. The idea at the core of micropolitics is that creative ingenuity is needed to apply to the practical world of interest group politics the concepts of free market theory. Their philosophy owes as much to Archimedes as it does to Adam Smith and Friedrich Hayek. With a lever long enough and a place to stand, they can move the world.

None of this should give the impression that the administrations which assumed office in Britain and the United States at the end of the 1970s had only to apply the policies developed by the new approach while they were in opposition. This misses the empirical elements of micropolitics, and fails to admit how much of it was learned in practice. One of its strengths is its flexibility. It draws back when it encounters superior force, and seeks alternate routes to take it around. Several policies were hastily modified on the basis of practical experience. In fact most of the methods which now characterize the micropolitical approach are distilled from the practical experience of what has worked. Although much work was done in the opposition period to develop the style of the approach and the general outlines of some of its methods, the detail has been filled in during office.

The techniques used to dismantle parts of the public sector, and to open up others to variety and competition, to opportunity and choice, have been developed for the most part by the application of them in practice, and their improvement by the trial and error feedback of actual experience. They were not the product only of theory and analysis, but of testing. One reason why the methods have proved so effective is that they are tailor-made for each of the situations to which they are applied, even to the extent of being modified during the process, as a garment will be altered at a fitting.

What was available to those later administrations and was lacking from the earlier ones was an approach, as well as a set of policy proposals. This approach enabled those existing proposals to be modified in action to succeed better, and it enabled new ones to be developed. Many of the actual policies which have been applied successfully have been developed in practice since 1979; they are not taken from the lore of free market ideas which was generally available before.

Micropolitics thus does not come into the class of ideas for which the theory is fully developed by scholars, and then applied to the world. Very few ideas do. While the analysis on whose base it was developed is certainly theoretical, it derives in turn from the close examination of real events. The creative structure built on that base is only theoretical in its outlines. It points to the broad principles of assuaging interest groups and setting up countervailing forces. The detail of how this is done is left to individual cases, for one of the contentions of the approach is that every case is different and requires a different combination of techniques. Many of the ideas of micropolitics have been abstracted from practical application, as exponents have compared successful attempts with unsuccessful ones in order to highlight the essential ingredients.

The policies which have proved successful are not the product of victories in the world of their ideas, nor does their success owe a significant amount to their general acceptability. They emerged in practice from an approach to problems armed only with broad principles and previous solutions. New techniques were in many cases devised on the spot to cope with new situations encountered in practice. As various expedients succeeded and others failed, so have they been added to the body of policy techniques or left out of future consideration.

The relationship between theory and practice in micropolitics is a complex and interactive one. There has been much discussion in scientific method about whether an observation precedes a theory, or vice versa. After Popper, there is widespread support for the view that there must be a background theory in order for any data to register as significant. In other words, a preconceived theory forms the basis for an observation. The observation, in turn, can lead to the proposal of a new theory. The development of policy on the micro-political model is similarly interactive. The broad ideas about interest groups and their benefits suggest avenues of approach, and the practical test of these leads to modifications in the body of technique. Micropolitics has learned as it has gone along. It is not the product of theory applied to practice; overwhelmingly its ideas are the product of interaction between theory and practice.

Many of the successes of micropolitics have preceded the general acceptance of the ideas on which they were based. In several cases the success of the policy has led to the victory of the idea, rather than the other way round. Scholars have noted some of the many achievements, and started to take an interest in the theory behind the policies which produced them. In some cases the successes in practice of actual policies have led to an increase in support for the free market model in general. It has not been the case that a rising tide of support for free markets has made the policy acceptable. Had that been the case, Nixon and Heath could have done it. It has been the other way round; practical success has justified the idea and won converts to it afterwards.

The success of the new policies is typical of the movements which are led by events. Policy engineers developed the tools on the job, with only broad outlines to guide them, together with an analysis of what does not work. The success in practice of those policies has brought about wider support for them, and interest in the theory which unites them.

Privatization, for example, was not the result of pure theory. It was developed by the micropolitical approach as an alternative to denationalization. The latter stressed only the need to 'return' state operations to the private sector, with no indication given of how this might be done. The new alternative concentrates on the detail of application. It seeks to transfer functions to the private sector by using the forces within political markets, not by ignoring them or trying to override them. Privatization uses dozens of micropolitical techniques, treating each portion of the state as a unique entity requiring a novel and distinct solution.

There was no conversion to this concept which made it possible. The word featured not at all in the 1979 Conservative manifesto, and the idea only in limited outline for less than a handful of cases. The techniques were developed in practice, and the success of some led to others being tried. Policies were tested and then modified. New devices were tried out; some were improved, others discarded. Only after many successes did opinion swing to general support of privatization as an idea. It won its converts after its success, not before.

Even the theory underlying privatization came under study late in the day. Several years deep into the Thatcher government, it came to be appreciated that a new phenomenon had appeared. Scholars in universities and colleges became interested in what was being done, and the studies, monographs and theses began to appear. The events came first, and the theory followed in their wake. Policy engineers constructed machines which worked, and their success brought about support for the ideas of the pure scientists who had long preceded them.

The micropolitical approach clearly distinguishes the governments of the early 1970s from those of the 1980s, but it must not be taken for granted that the later ones had access to a complete printout of policy options. What they did have was an understanding by the policy research institutes of why the programmes of the earlier administrations had not been implemented. It was unlikely, given this, that the same policies would be attempted. They also had access to a new approach to policy formulation, together with some detailed policy suggestions.

Governments are not monolithic entities; they are mixtures, even coalitions. The administrations of the 1980s did not take office determined to impose micropolitical solution across the board. In fact they were driven by forces from many directions and wanted to do many things, some of them mutually contradictory. They were set on applying traditional conservative solutions to a much greater extent than any new micropolitical proposals. There were sections of them which wanted neither, but sought to continue the public sector programmes under better management. The formulae of cutting out wastage and limiting government spending were applied with their usual lack of success. It was the success of the few micropolitical stratagems which were tried which led to more from the same stable being run. The policies which did not bring about good results were dropped in favour of more of those which did.

The rise of micropolitical solutions took place while governments were in office trying them out. They were taken up because they achieved success where conventional policies failed. Whenever the nail was hit on the head, government kept on banging it in. The sections of government which supported other types of policy came to be less influential because they achieved less successes. Many of them, indeed, became enthusiastic converts to the new style. If it worked, they could gain results with it as well, and take credit accordingly.

The success in practice preceded the victory in theory and helped to bring it about. As in previous cases, events were determined by men and women of action doing things that worked, and towing theory in their wake. Their predecessors had tried doing things that did not work and had ditched the supporting theory when the failure became apparent. Now it was the policies which did work which turned the attention to theory.

Many observers have not understood the significance of the method which has been used. On conventional free market policies, there are cases in which the Thatcher administration fell far short of what theory required. Some have taken it that nothing of note was accomplished. There are other cases in which progress has been made beyond the expectations; few, for example, expected that the systematic transfer of major utilities to private ownership would prove to be as rapid or as extensive. It seemed inconceivable to many in 1979 that by 1986 the telephone and gas industries would have been sold off.

The shortfall has centred on conventional free market goals of total deregulation and free competition. There are those who voice criticism that the major utilities have not been exposed to full competition, or that the government should not intrude its political goals of wider share ownership into what ought to be a straightforward commercial sale. The criticisms miss the point of micropolitics altogether. They fail utterly to see that pursuit of a full free market solution would have produced no solution at all, or that the support of large interest groups is needed to achieve success impossible for straightforward commercial sales.

Micropolitics can rarely be used for the immediate attainment of holistic goals. Its character is that of a piecemeal approach. It looks at the small scale in fine detail, and generates proposals to solve each section at a time. It is limited in the scale on which it can operate. Nonetheless, it can produce its solutions in a cumulative way. Those who would have preferred immediate and large scale denationalization from the Thatcher government must have been disappointed at the small scale of what was done. British Petroleum and Amersham International and the others made only a very modest start. However, they soon added up as the pace accelerated.

A further limitation on it is that it works by political trading. It does not win converts through ideas, but wins supporters by conferring advantages. It is limited, therefore, by the benefits which can be found to offer. If entrenched advantages are traded instead of attacked, there will be ones which government simply cannot afford to buy. Micropolitics has no answer to these except perhaps to set in motion a long-term chain of events whose result might eventually bring success. It might prevent new entry into those benefits, but at a price of securing them for those already in possession. None of this is very satisfactory to those who want results within the lifetime of one term of office.

Finally, it must be said against it that in many cases it achieves at best only a partial solution. Contracting out local services is not the same as a free choice for the householder. Persuading 20 per cent or even 40 per cent to buy their state-owned houses does not restore a free market in housing. Introducing variety and choice into schools and directing funds toward the popular ones is a shadow of a full free market in education. Most of the policies deriving from micropolitical analysis have settled for less than complete solutions; they have achieved improvements only. People do not often change overnight. They take time to adapt and to accustom themselves to the new.

It takes time for free choices to spread, and for a new reality to emerge from the old. By working with the interest groups in political markets, micropolitics opts for the gradual way. In doing so, it exposes itself to criticism at any stage that things have not gone far enough, and that more is needed. The criticism is justified; the fact that its policies seek to secure support from interest groups and to divert them to the pursuit of more attractive benefits means that micropolitics will usually offer progress which is both slow and incomplete. It turns to the small scale, to the decisions made by individuals and groups, precisely because of the failures of macro-scale free market policies to gain substantial results. The progress may be piecemeal, but it is progress, it is all in one direction, and it is securely made.

17 A Time to Pluck Up that which has been Planted

It took more than a century for the public sector in Britain to grow to its present size. Some of that growth was gradual, some of it was spasmodic. There have been long slow periods of steady accumulation, punctuated by brief spurts of dramatic acceleration of state activity. By 1979 it was a either a dominant force or at least a major factor in industry, communications, energy, auto manufacture, transport, housing, education, health, pensions, local services, and other areas too numerous to list. It built the roads and ran the buses, it owned the railways and ran the trains, it made the aircraft and flew them, it made the ships and ran the docks. The state was the biggest spender, the biggest employer, the biggest service provider, the biggest manufacturer and the biggest insurer.

Government was Britain's major industry, and was one of its few growth areas. Furthermore, this was not confined to Britain. The nation had exported the idea of state control to its former colonies, and had served as an example to other countries. Many of the defects inherent in public sector economics were known of in 1979; indeed, they had been known of for some years. Knowledge of the wrong, however, did not mean

275

knowledge of the remedy. The overmanning, under-capitalization, producer domination and lack of responsiveness to consumers had all been seen in practice. The domestic customers might have no alternative but to take what was given, but overseas customers proved less tolerant. Instead of continuing to support British state workers in the manner to which they had become accustomed, they took their orders elsewhere, preferring the prices, quality and delivery dates that others were able to offer.

The rise of Britain's public sector to the level at which it posed these problems had not been due to any single cause: rather was it the product of many factors. Some of it was ideological, inspired by a desire to have individual aspirations supplanted by consideration of collective need. Some of it was paternalistic, deriving from the view that people could be cared for by the state better than they could look after themselves. Parts of the economy came into the public sector from a belief that large-scale operations could bring economies of scale. Parts entered by default, out of political pressures to keep ailing industries in business. Most of the steady, remorseless growth was a product of a system which encouraged the making of decisions in political markets rather than economic ones. Other things being equal, the rise of the public sector is a tendency inherent in democratic societies. It needs no contrived or convoluted explanations; it is what happens.

The structural defects of the public sector are similarly inherent. It is not an accident of history that state operations are chronically overmanned and under-capitalized. It is a direct result of their status as political entities, and of the forces which work on them. Neither is it accidental that they favour the needs of producers over those of consumers; given the way in which they operate it could not be otherwise. One of the discoveries made by public sector unions as they struggled to campaign against privatization was the very low esteem in the public eye which was enjoyed by the nationalized industries. The defects of the public sector are widely perceived, even if the causes behind them might not be appreciated to the same extent.

There is one other feature of the public sector which is harder to pin down. It is that state operations are seen as in some way out-of-date, relics of a former time which have survived into the present day like living fossils. Part of this might simply be due to their size. The giant nature of state corporations and their slowness to respond conjure up unconscious association with the popular picture of slow-moving dinosaurs. Part of it might derive from their capital depletion. The state sector has to rely on out-of-date equipment and to keep its capital stock in operation for a longer period than the private sector would accept. This gives it an outdated air, with worn-out equipment and yesterday's technology. A labour-intensive operation, lacking streamlined machines and methods and slow to innovate, conjures up intangible images of former times.

Part of that reputation is a consequence of the fact that many of the public sector operations *are* out-of-date. Many of them stem from the age of mass manufacturing and the production-line economy. Economies of scale resulted from a system which specialized in the mass production of standardized interchangeable parts. The fortune of Henry Ford was not the only one to be built on this principle. First developed by Eli Whitney for the mass production of muskets, it is this system which set the pattern for most of our industry. It meant that large numbers of people would work in large factories doing roughly similar things for the whole of their working lives. It also meant that they would have broadly similar requirements for housing, health, education and social services.

It was against this background that the public sector

grew, with its standardized mass production offerings for people with fairly standard lives. For state services people themselves were the interchangeable parts. Scope for variety and individual choices was hardly missed in the age of mass supply. The state catered for the masses, anxious to provide mass education, mass health, mass social security. These were mass-produced services for mass-production people. The exercise might have had justification while the economy was characterized by that pattern but it lost it when the pattern changed.

The point is that this was the industrial model of the previous age. The economy now is no longer represented by the giants of standardization. The new companies are the small, fast-growing ones. They bring new techniques and new technology, and turn over capital far more rapidly than their predecessors. Instead of the heavy investment once locked into fixed plant, firms increasingly turn to subcontractors to perform tasks from the outside. Where cost-reduction once necessitated standard products, the newer technologies permit individual specification. Consumer products are increasingly customized rather than standardized, with the basic product serving only as the nucleus for individual choices to be added about design and finish.

With this development visibly transforming the scene in both the manufacturing and service sectors, the public sector operations seem increasingly out of place, designed for a world which has already passed. People no longer expect to do broadly similar things in the same place for most of their lives. They no longer expect to spend a lifetime in one activity, let alone with one employer. Their needs are becoming more specialized, more varied, and more individual. They need different, more flexible types of education, more varied pension schemes, health care which is more responsive to changing life-styles. It is against this background that

the state sector operations seem increasingly inappropriate and unable to cope with the changing
times.

All of these factors led to a recognition that the public
sector operations were in need of major change. It was
no sudden flash which brought this about, but a steady
accumulation of evidence and experience over the
years. As early as the early 1960s there was a general
popular rejection of nationalization, a rejection which
led Hugh Gaitskell, then Labour Party leader, to
attempt a change in clause four of the Party's constitution, the clause which speaks of the state taking
over 'the means of production, distribution and
exchange'. At the end of that decade electoral victory
went to a Conservative Party which had committed
itself to substantial denationalization.

Popular and expert opinion alike concurred in the
need to reduce the size of the state sector. It was
apparent by now that the taxation it took to finance it
was draining the funds which were needed to promote
enterprise and expansion in the private sector. Britain's
steady decline, hid by inflationary expansion for some
years, had now become evident. The time was right for
a move away from the public sector, and so was the
general opinion. The major problem was that no one
knew how to do it; governments had tried and failed.

The difficulty was that attempts to dismantle the
public sector or to open up any of its locked-in group
benefits brought hostile reaction from those directly
involved. No government seemed ready to face the
wave of unpopularity which would doom it to certain
defeat. Some observers speculated on the need for a
sacrificial government which would come in to do what
was necessary without any hope of re-election afterwards. Others toyed with the idea of a government
which would not need to be re-elected.

From the perspective given by the subsequent decade,

most of the speculation of the time seems fanciful and difficult to justify in the light of events. At the time, however, it indicates the level of desperation being felt at the apparent inability of the political process to produce solutions to the central problem. No answer seemed forthcoming which could prise away the benefits which interest groups had obtained at the general expense. It was onto this political scene that the central ideas of micropolitics were introduced.

The solution seems obvious now that we have seen it working, but it was not so at the time. It presented an alternative to taking on the interest groups and trying to strip away the advantages they had amassed over the years through the political process. It provided instead a means of trading those benefits. Rather than having political leaders try to destroy or override political markets, it suggested instead that they should enter those markets in order to trade. The resentment and hostility which would be encountered by any threat to their benefits would not be produced by an offer perceived by the interest groups to be more attractive.

Micropolitics came on the scene when people were looking for a politically feasible means of bringing public sector operations under control. This had to mean breaking up some of them, transferring others to the private sector, and opening up some of the remainder to consumer preferences. It had to mean decreasing substantially the role which they played in the economy, and the capacity they had for crowding out growth and enterprise. The new techniques brought with them the realization that this could be done without the confrontation and the unpopularity which had been thought to make it impossible. It could be done by a process of exchanging benefits instead of trying to confiscate them.

In place of the systematic hostility as each group was alienated one by one, there appeared instead the prospect of accumulating the gratitude and goodwill of those who enjoyed greater benefits under the new arrangements than they had received under the old. At the very least, political leaders could hope for acquiescence from groups who had exchanged one benefit for another. The great strength of the micro-political approach is that the trade-offs which it offers to public sector interest groups give them what are perceived as gains. This, in turn, creates an advantage for the political leaders who can take credit for it. In place of the call to do tough things which will make them unpopular, a means is presented by which they can combine doing the right things with the reward of popularity.

In place of angry and bitter tenants opposed to attempts to make their state rentals 'economic', government is faced instead by a contented band of new home-owners, people who bought their state homes at heavily discounted prices, and have seen the value of their investment rise accordingly. Where there might have been drawn-out and divisive disputes over denational-izing the National Freight Corporation, instead there are worker-owners who not only take pride in their firm and its profitability, but who have all made substantial capital gains.

If the process is repeated throughout all of the areas in which solutions have been generated by the micro-political approach, the same pattern is repeated. Out go the hostile and embittered crowd whose benefits were attacked by government, and in come the faces of those who took up the attractive offer and gained accordingly. A government attempting most of those changes by the conventional means would have had to face that hostile crowd. Use of the new strategy has produced instead the satisfaction of those who were able to trade their benefit for a better one.

Governments are used to receiving gratuitous advice

on policy. It usually takes the form of hectoring by academics and other experts for not having the courage to do necessary but unpopular things. Sometimes it comes in the form of 'hair shirt' politics, with the implied suggestion that nettles need to be grasped and bullets bit, and that anything easy is not worth doing. Often the promise is held out that if only government will keep its nerve, eventually the wisdom of what they have done will be apparent to all. 'Eventually' in this context seems to mean 'after the next election'.

Micropolitics is certainly different. In place of the apparent insensitivity to political reality of most advice, this style seems to be more political than the politicians. It identifies the interest groups and points out what they perceive to be their advantage, and how they will use the system to defend it. It then suggests ways of securing the cooperation of those groups by making a more attractive offer to each of them. It is even able to warn political leaders in advance of some of the dangers which proposed initiatives will face, and to suggest ways of making their passage easier. If there are small groups too entrenched in the public sector to accept counter-offers, even here the reform is made to generate larger and more effective groups with which to out-weigh them. In terms of political advantage, there are few methods of policy generation which achieve it so systematically.

Politicians prefer to be popular if they can. While many of them are prepared to do what they perceive to be necessary, they are limited by the need to be re-elected, and by the time-frame within which the gains from policy are realized. If they have any kind of choice, a policy option which does not provoke widespread unpopularity is to be preferred to one which does. It is not easy for political leaders to put through policies which bring long-term hostility in their wake. If they were prepared to undertake the sacrifice themselves, their supporters in the legislature probably would not follow. They would pressurize their leaders into a policy change. Even the Thatcher administration, with its many successes, has been marked by the reluctance of some of its parliamentary majority to countenance anything which alienates significant interest groups, be they of church leaders or country squires.

The basis of the micropolitical strategy is working with interest groups, and restructuring circumstances so that it becomes to their advantage to choose the course preferred by the policy-makers. Since they are freely rejecting what they have in favour of what they prefer, they do not oppose the government which made this possible. If anything, their support is attracted, and they acquire a vested interest in the new arrangement making them less likely to support legislators who might try to reverse it. Those who do propose to delete the reform and revert to the old system find themselves in the unenviable position of politicians who are proposing to cancel an existing benefit. The ire of the interest group concerned is at once aroused.

The micropolitical approach thus has two very important advantages over the conventional style of politics. It solves problems and it is attractive to political leaders. Attempts made simply to replace the public sector by free market alternatives face two difficulties: most of the attempts fail, and the government which makes them also makes enemies. The new style has neither of these drawbacks. Because it offers advantages to interest groups it is popular; and because they accept it, it works. The advantages of success and popularity constitute two powerful advocates for the political style which produces them. Government is quick to spot the merits of policies such as these, and each success makes it readier to take up other similar ones.

On the eve of the 1979 election in Britain, the Prime Minister James Callaghan remarked to his colleague

Bernard Donoughue that he sensed a sea-change in British politics. He was right. People at that time knew that something had finally to be done about the way in which interest groups were operating against the general good. It was widely felt that action of some kind must alter the balance away from trade unions and the state sector, and towards greater choices and opportunities for individuals. On a much broader perspective, something needed to be done to break open the closed institutions, to bring variety and flexibility more in accord with the needs of a modern economy and a modern society.

The political style which recognizes and works within political markets was a timely innovation. It enabled a government to start on such a programme of reform without paying the electoral price widely predicted. It gave the means for a successful transformation to contrast with the previous failures. The pursuit of their own advantage, which had occupied groups in the political process was now turned around. Policies were designed with tempting alternative benefits to offer, and the trade-offs have been made. In one area after another, the barriers against market choices have been weakened or lifted. The monopolies which protected the producers in occupations as diverse as the legal profession and bus transport have been raised a little. The ordinary members of trade unions have been given powers to balance and control those of the leaders.

Most significant of all, perhaps, in view of the long term economic changes, has been the gradual breakdown of standardized provision in favour of variety and choice. Little by little the scope for individuals to secure individual treatment is being extended. The producer oriented public services are being opened up to the impact of choices. In a world where people no longer do most of the same things for most of their lives, they are just beginning to gain access to the varied services they will need. Micropolitics, by working on the small scale where people make decisions and give effect to preferences, is able to introduce elements into the public sector which make it alter and adapt itself accordingly.

These techniques are small in detail, but they add up to large results. The Chancellor of the Exchequer was able to tell the Conservative Party conference of 1986 after seven years in power that 20 per cent of state industry had been privatized, that it would be 40 per cent in just over one more year, and that the next Conservative administration would privatize 'most of what was left.' While the state industries were being privatized, over one million state homes had been sold to their tenants, and with new legislation to cover apartments, the target was a further million. Competition and deregulation had permitted new bus companies and airlines to have an impact on both services and prices. Banks and solicitors both faced competition from building societies, and were offering better services as a result. Trade union leaders were much more answerable to their members, and more restrained as a result. New powers promised parents more say in education, and the first of the directly funded schools were about to be set up. Private medicine was spreading, portable pensions were a reality, and over half the population had chosen private alternatives to the state earnings-related pension scheme. Enterprise zones and free ports were in operation, and private contractors were taking over hospital cleaning and catering and local government services in greater numbers every year.

Individually, each item could be criticized as being too modest, but together they added up to a major shift away from the public sector and from state controls. All of the measures pointed in the same direction: towards more market forces, more opportunities for choice, greater variety and more responsiveness to consumers. The impression given overwhelmingly by the changes was that these were only the first steps. The government gave every indication that the programme would continue. If thwarted temporarily, over such items as gas showrooms or liberalizing shopping hours, it would regroup and come back from a different direction. A setback was seen as a delay, not a defeat. The implication was that new methods would be tried until success was gained.

As it learned to trade in political markets, the government grew more confident and tackled bigger enterprises. Its reforms, which had started more modestly, grew in scale as it mastered the basic skills of the new technique. Bigger industries were privatized each year, as the government moved into what it termed 'the heartlands of the public sector'. It began to make inroads into major institutions, and to tackle the core services of health, education and social security.

It has been common for governments to enter office and implement a batch of reforms in the first flush of victory. Usually they then slide into a more settled routine. Those who expected this in 1979 may have sighed with relief at the modest scale of the early measures; their expectations must have been disturbed by the spectacle of reforms which increased in scale and radicalism as the government learned in practice how to work with interest groups and began to press deep into the state sector.

The techniques which made this possible came at a most opportune time for Britain. As its economy has changed, so the institutions which developed with it have become increasingly outmoded. The decline of mass manufacturing on the production line basis has meant that the services and institutions which served that kind of society are unable to meet the changing needs of the new one. With the changeover to subcontracting, to smaller firms, and to the more rapid turnover and replacement of capital, there is a greater need for flexibility. There are no longer the enormous groups who could be given identical services because they led identical lives.

The old rigid categories are breaking down, and with them the standard provision which covered them. Where there were employed and unemployed, now the boundary has been blurred by a range of intermediate positions. More people are employed part-time; more are self-employed; more run their own businesses, more work as subcontractors. Some people work for part of the year, some work for part of their lives. Some 'retire' early into part-time and self-employed contract work. The institutions which were geared to a straight-forward division into employed and unemployed are unable to cope with the proliferation of new categories. New ones have to be created to cater for them, and space must be cleared for them to develop in response to the many different needs.

The mass services of education, health and social security have to recognize that they are dealing less with coherent masses as each year goes by. People now need different training instead of a standard education; and they need the facilities to enable them to undertake retraining at a later stage. People with different life patterns need different kinds of insurance, different sorts of pension scheme.

The regulations which cover the growth and expansion of business have to adapt to the faster pace which characterizes new economic activity. More service industries, more high-technology products, all demand new institutions and new conditions. The power of either employees or producer cartels to keep out change in order to continue their advantages cannot be sustained in the climate of a modern economy; it has to undergo change itself.

The techniques of micropolitics were not devised to assist with this particular transformation. They were developed as a means of overcoming the resistance of interest groups to consumer inputs within their sphere of activity, and to introduce the elements of economic markets into political markets. It happens fortuitously that most of the devices of the new approach allow individuals to make choices between alternatives. In doing so, they help to create the conditions for varied and flexible services to replace the standardized ones which served a more rigid society.

By restructuring the supply to respond to the preferences of the consumers instead of the convenience of producers, the policies enable different needs to be satisfied simultaneously. The old monolithic state supply gradually breaks down into a variety of offerings from which consumers can pick and choose according to the lives they lead and the needs they experience. The breakup of monopolies leads to new and varied forms of service springing up to meet new demands. Privatization forces companies to respond to the multiple and different pressures of consumers. De-regulation enables new types of product and service to be introduced more rapidly in response to demand.

The effect has been to make the new political strategy the means of modernization. The emphasis it places on consumer preferences has enabled it to create the right circumstances in which variety could develop. Had people wanted roughly the same things, it would have led to roughly similar services. It was because they wanted and needed more varied things under the impact of the changes sweeping through the economy that more variety developed. Although the motivation which led to its development was a desire to see the successful introduction of market elements by dealing with the interest groups who usually opposed this, its effect has been to enable society to adjust to major economic changes and to the social changes which they brought in their wake.

In many ways the most encouraging feature of micropolitics as a method of generating policy is that it is a technique rather than a set of specific goals. In other words it is continuous. If it were only a range of specific measures, its use would be ended once they had all been attempted. Because it is a technique, it is constantly generating new policies. Not only does it enable novel attempts to be made to solve intractable problems, it also enables new problems to be faced and solved as they arise. All of the inroads which it has made so far into the public services and their standardized output make only a start. All the achievements so far attained serve as the base line for further progress. The only limitations are the need to make attractive alternative offers in order to encourage groups to trade benefits; and the limits here might be those of ingenuity rather than of resources. As long as there are reserves of human creativity, new suggested solutions can be generated.

The technique has succeeded in a few short years in reversing the seemingly ceaseless move towards more centralism, more provision through a state supply, and more state controls. The rise of the public sector has been taking place for more than a century. It reached its high water mark in 1979, and is now flowing backward. It is not scholarly or popular opinion which has achieved this, but a technical method which was previously absent. Observers who had thought the constant growth of government to be an inherent feature of democratic societies have had to revise their opinions since 1979. The new methods have done more than stem the rising tide of collectivism, they have set the ratchet into reverse. As each reform creates its new benefit group, so it is locked into place by their defence of that advantage. It will be very hard for a government of different complexion to reverse most of what the new technique has achieved; there are too many interests tied into the new arrangements. People enjoy not only the advantages they have gained in material terms, but the advantages conferred by choice itself: the enlargement of the area over which people as individuals can influence their own lives. People enjoy the ability to determine their own priorities and to allocate their own resources. Once they have experienced this freedom, and seen the material benefits it brings in terms of responsive and varied services, it will be difficult to take it away again. So with each new gain for market forces achieved by this strategy, the ratchet clicks into place to retain it. The state which was wound up for over a century is being unwound in a steady and systematic way.

Nor is the effect confined any longer to Britain. It was Britain which pioneered the use of the new techniques, even though they were developed simultaneously in the United States. Britain was first to elect an administration prepared to try them, and has a constitution conducive to their ready use. The United States has a political market more highly developed, and a Congress which lives and trades by exchanging benefits for political support. It is Britain which has achieved more because its concentration of power enables more initiatives to be tried. The successes gained in Britain, however, have served as an example to other countries including the United States. Britain's achievement in reversing the growth of state power and creating ground for private firms to move in and demonstrate superior efficiency has attracted not only attention but emulation.

Over fifty countries have sent delegations to study the way in which this was done in Britain. British experts have found their services much in demand overseas. Of all of the micropolitical techniques, those involving privatization have attracted the most attention, together with those which make use of outside private contractors. The techniques have been copied and adapted to fit local conditions, and have been introduced to some degree in more than 100 countries. The French have embarked upon a huge programme of privatization; other European powers have made more modest beginnings.

The Pacific Basin countries have eagerly embraced the new ideas, and many of them have set in motion measures to bring the public sector activities towards market influences. Singapore, Malaysia and South Korea have all made notable progress with the devices first pioneered in Britain, and show the same readiness to adapt political stratagems as they have previously shown with advanced technologies. The big surprise has been the rapidity with which the ideas have influenced Third World nations. The poor countries have been as eager to gain the benefits as the rich ones, in many cases more so. Bangladesh has used the techniques extensively to place jute and flour mills into the hands of their workers, with the effect of increasing both productivity and output, and taking away the need for subsidy.

The suggestion has been made that the less advanced countries can implement these measures more easily because the public sector is a more recent phenomenon there. Its roots do not go as deep, nor as far back in time. The advantages which it confers to various groups still have to be traded, but they might be more open to new ideas if there is no long history of public sector monopoly. Whatever the cause, Third World nations have been enthusiastic to develop and apply the techniques. Many of them have economies seriously distorted by state controls and public sector activity; they see in the new methods a chance to create the entrepreneurs and the market opportunities they need to set loose the wealth creating process.

Only slightly less surprising has been the adoption of some of the ideas by communist nations. Without conventional democratic constitutions, there are not the active political markets we know in the West. There are, however, groups who enjoy benefits from the state and who are proving unable to generate efficiency and growth under their present economic structure. The new methods offer them the possibility of trading one benefit for another, and in the process setting some market forces to work to provide the motivation for increased output, improved supply, and greater variety. Communist Cuba has followed the British model of selling state houses at discounted prices to tenants, and the People's Republic of China has traded opportunity for security in farming with spectacular effect on output.

The result of all of this activity has been to make the decline of the public sector a phenomenon on the world scale. It is in retreat nearly everywhere, in communist countries as well as in capitalist ones, in dictatorships as well as in democracies, in poor countries as well as in rich ones, in backward countries as well as in advanced ones. Its effects are being felt in every continent and by every race of people. What started in Britain in 1979 has spread with an astonishing rapidity which not even its most enthusiastic supporters predicted for it. It has become one of the most striking movements of economic organization in the twentieth century.

It is, moreover, a technique still at its beginning. The results gained so far represent the early stages. Most of its development has been made by practical application. The use of it constitutes a learning process, and that process has only been operating for a very few years. As micropolitical solutions succeed, they are refined and adapted, and new twists are added to extend their range to other areas. Governments which use them successfully gain both confidence and expertise, and are ready to move on to their application to new problems. As international experience is augmented by the results of different experiments, so nations copy from each other and adapt ideas to local conditions. There will inevitably be setbacks and mistakes, but these, too, form part of the learning process. The methods used to diminish the role and impact of the state in economic life have already shown themselves to be no short-lived expedient. They are a systematic way by which the tide of state power can be turned back, leaving space for consumer preferences, variety and opportunity. It looks as though they will be making their mark for a long time yet.

In the final analysis it is not surprising that these techniques have succeeded. Politicians have long been used to receiving policy advice from outside. Economists have urged changes in fiscal policy. Constitutional lawyers have proposed new laws. Sociologists and social psychologists, penologists and criminologists, have all urged their advice upon governments. Politicians have received directions from every profession but their own. Not surprisingly, they have found much of that advice inappropriate, unsuitable, or plainly impractical. Their experience of their own field has told them that.

Micropolitics concerns itself with the generation of policies designed for the practical world. It starts out by looking at the political markets which operate, and examines the political problems they cause. Its solutions are designed within the context of the practical. It urges politicians not to resist or to oppose political markets in ways which spell failure and defeat. Instead it teaches them to enter those markets in order to trade. Rather than opposing the self interest of the groups involved, it urges them to bid for it with more attractive offers. It represents one of the few methods of policy generation to emerge looking at the world from the point of view of the profession.

There is a very old proverb in which the wind and the sun make a wager about which of them can remove a man's cloak. As the wind blows more furiously, the man wraps his cloak ever more tightly about him, until the wind gives up, exhausted. Then the sun comes out and the man takes his cloak off. After years of being advised to behave like the wind and expend much effort with only failure at the end of it, micropolitics has come along telling them to behave like the sun and succeed. It is hardly surprising that it has made an impact already, and highly probable that more is yet to come.

Index